PLANNING AND DEVELOPMENT
IN IRAN

PLANNING AND DEVELOPMENT
IN IRAN

by George B. Baldwin

The Johns Hopkins Press
Baltimore

For

Harriet, Alan, and Sally

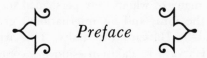

Preface

The book is a case study with three main purposes:

1. To explain economic planning in a developing country in simple operational terms so that those who attempt this task will better understand how to go about it.

2. To show how difficult and futile it is to make and execute a development plan unless the political and cultural environment is congenial.

3. To make clear that economic development and economic planning do not necessarily depend on each other. Iran is a country where economic development is succeeding but where economic planning, as the process is usually understood, has largely failed. The planning has not been a *total* failure; this fact leaves the historical verdict ambiguous and makes it difficult to decide whether the attempt to plan should or should not be abandoned. So far, the attempt continues.

This account is based on intimate participation in the planning process from 1958 to 1961. This was a watershed period. After the political and economic upheaval surrounding the nationalization of the oil industry (a movement that began in 1951 and was resolved in 1954) Iran entered a period of relative stability, prosperity, and optimism. To a number of influential people in Iran, as well as to others in the World Bank, the U.S. Embassy, the Ford Foundation, and at Harvard University, a major attempt at economic planning seemed worth trying. And so in 1957, for the first time, an Economic Bureau was organized within the national development agency (the Plan Organization). It was staffed by a number of well-trained Iranians, many of whom were persuaded to return to their country to join the unit, and an international group of foreign advisers organized by Harvard University. This arrangement had worked well for Harvard in Pakistan—and has continued to do so for over a decade now. But what worked in Pakistan did not work in Iran. If the reasons for the failure (and we can call it that without blaming anyone or wasting tears) had been as well understood in the mid-1950's as they are today, the people who initially backed this large international effort might not have done so. At minimum, their expectations would have been much more modest. Whether, with only modest expectations, the effort could have been mounted is doubtful.

What I have said, I suppose, is that the attempt to plan in Iran turned out to be a high-risk investment that did not pay off. Luckily, there are powerful forces pushing Iran forward that have nothing to do with planning. Whether with planning the country's future might be richer and better than the one she would reach without it is rather an academic question. No one knows.

I was one of seven original members of the Harvard Advisory Group formed early in 1958 to help organize a staff that could bring to the development effort whatever economics has to contribute to such an enterprise. Members of the HAG worked as advisers in a bureau of 15 to 20 Iranian economists, headed initially by Dr. Khodadad Farmanfarmaian. The Harvard Group was organized and directed by Professor Edward S. Mason of Harvard, assisted by David E. Bell and Gustav F. Papenek of the project's home office in Cambridge. The advisory group's work was financed by a grant from the Ford Foundation to Plan Organization under a contract that ran for more than four years.

There were, at various times, many more than the original seven who served on the advisory team during the three-year period I was a member of it. The following individuals whose terms overlapped mine deserve thanks for innumerable contributions to my thinking: Kenneth A. Hansen, the HAG's vigorous leader during its first two and a half years; John H. Kaufmann, Transport Advisor; Baldur H. Kristjanson, Agriculture Advisor; Jerome F. Fried, Monetary and Fiscal Advisor; R. A. J. Van Lier, Social Affairs Advisor; Kurt Martin, General Economics; J. Price Gittinger, Agriculture Advisor;

Poul Nørregaard Rasmussen, General Economics; Ronald C. Mendelsohn, Social Affairs; Lorne T. Sonley, Agriculture Advisor; Bjørn Olsen, Fiscal and General Economics Advisor; and my successor as Industry Advisor, Gregory B. Votaw. The Group's Administrative Secretary, Miss Margaret J. Betz, knew as much about Iran as any of us and deserves to share in the general thanks. In the years I knew it, the HAG had a corporate life whose vigor no member is likely to forget. We habitually gave even more advice to each other than to the Government of Iran, and in the process we occasionally learned much.

It is more difficult to thank the many Iranian friends and acquaintances who contributed to my knowledge and understanding of their country. Within Plan Organization the following deserve special mention: Dr. Khodadad Farmanfarmaian; Dr. Gholam Reza Moghadam; Dr. Cyrus Samii; Dr. Bahman Abadian; Dr. Mustafa Elm and Messrs. Ahmad Nuban and Siamak Mosadeghi, my three longest associates in the Industry Section of the Economic Bureau; Dr. N. Vagar; Dr. Hosain Mahdavi; Dr. Nosrat Ganjei; Darius Oskoui; Dr. Shapour Rasseq; Dr. Majid Majidian; Homayoun Sahba; Eng. R. Asbaghi; Eshmail Ajami; Dr. Taghi Mortazavi; Jamshid Ashrafi; Sharif Adib Soltani; M. B. Kamali; Eng. N. Motamedi; and F. Ghahreman. Outside Plan Organization I should mention also Eng. Reza Niazamand, Dr. Iraj Ayman, N. Halimi, Eng. Habib Nafici, and the following members of the Farmanfarmaian family: Farouk, Hafez, and Satareh. There are others who deserve to be thanked, but an author with as many debts as mine cannot hope to acknowledge them all.

Others with whom I was less directly associated have also contributed to my thinking. Among these are Wilson W. Harwood, T. Marl Hemphill, Charles E. MacNealy, and Frank S. Skowronski, members of the Governmental Affairs Institute, Inc., another advisory group that worked in PlanOrg at the same time that we did. Of those who worked in the PlanOrg's Technical Bureau I am most indebted to Walter B. Ewing, Sidney P. Wheelock, John Grieg, and Emil Hens. Although the HAG was careful not to let itself become identified with foreign embassies and aid missions, several members of the large U.S. Point Four Mission were inevitably helpful to our work and, indirectly, to the writing of this book. The following deserve particular mention: Maurice F. Williams, Ray Coffman,

Lester C. Shephard, Bruno Schiro, Wilford S. Wright, and Ray Johnson. Others who might not guess my indebtedness to them include Messrs. Mehdi Samii and W. A. van Ravesteijn of the Industrial and Mining Development Bank (plus members of the Bank's staff too numerous to mention); Mr. Alan Read of the British Embassy; Mr. Carl F. Kraenzel and Mr. Nader Afshar of the Near East Foundation; G. Leighton Peace of the United Nations; Messrs. John R. Conger, Harlan J. Riker, and Wendell Ford of George Fry Associates, and, especially, Mr. Howard Bertsch, the Ford Foundation Representative in Iran and a knowledgeable and articulate observer of Iranian life, especially of rural affairs. There are many other names I would mention if I did not limit specific acknowledgments to people with whom I worked fairly closely.

The man responsible for suggesting that the book be written, and who made this possible, is Professor Mason. It was he who arranged that I spend the year 1961–62 as a Research Associate at Harvard's Center for International Affairs, where the book's first draft was completed. Earlier, he had generously advanced research funds that allowed me to employ some research assistants while still in Iran. The extent of my debts to Professor Mason will be understood by everyone who has worked for him or with him. Needless to say, neither he nor anyone else mentioned above has any responsibility for facts or views expressed in the book. Even more does this statement apply to my present employer, the World Bank, which I joined after the first draft was finished. In my work at the Bank I have had nothing whatever to do with Iranian affairs.

I always try to pay off my biggest debts last. I can do so only by giving simple public thanks to a long-suffering wife, who will understand what I am trying to say, and to Alan and Sally, who won't. For all the grumbling authors aim at their typewriters, neglected wives and children have much the worst of things while books are in the making. It may help right matters if they know I know this. Fortunately they, too, loved Iran and would happily do it all again.

GEORGE B. BALDWIN

Washington, D.C.

November, 1966

›

Contents

Tables

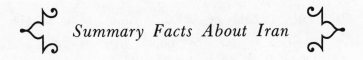

Summary Facts About Iran

Area: 628,000 square miles (about 3 times the size of France, 2.5 times that of Texas); organized into about twenty provinces (i.e., not a federal system)

Balance of Payments:

(in millions of U.S.$)	1963–64	1964–65	1965–66
Merchandise exports	139	153	181
Merchandise imports	508	737	864
Oil Revenues	388	480*	514

Exchange Rate:†

75 rials = $1.00 U.S.
210 rials = £1 U.K.
1 million rials = $13,333
1 billion rials = $13,333,333

Investment and Saving:

	I/GNP (%)	Dom. S./GNP (%)‡
1959–60	18.3	15.5
1960–61	19.0	15.8
1961–62§	16.6	15.5
1962–63§	13.5	14.3
1963–64§	12.6	14.3

* Plus 185 bonus
† Unchanged for past thirteen years
‡ Investment minus net capital inflow (in recent years of high investment Iran has relied on a net inflow of capital from abroad to finance 10 to 15 per cent of its investment activity)
§ Years of recession

National Income Data:

Per Capita GDP: national average just over $200 (average in large cities probably over $400; in rural areas under $140)

Gross Domestic Product: 364 billion rials (1963–64); measure of value produced within the country before allowing for factor payments abroad; the net effect of the latter is a GNP 7 to 8 per cent lower than GDP (GNP measures value of output accruing to normal residents regardless of whether the income was produced within the country or abroad)

GDP: Sectoral Origins

Sector	1959–60*	%†	1963–64*	%†
Agriculture, forestry, fishing, hunting	88.0	30	92.7	25
Mining and quarrying	0.5	–	0.7	–
Industry (excluding oil)	27.0	9	43.3	12
Oil (including exploration)	44.2	15	61.6	17
Construction	12.3	4	14.2	4
Electricity and water	1.1	–	2.9	1
Transport and communication	21.4	7	25.5	7
Banking and insurance	4.2	1	5.5	1
Wholesale and retail trade	43.0	15	54.0	15
Rental value of houses	17.5	6	21.6	6
Government	21.3	7	28.9	8
Other services	13.8	5	16.5	5
Total GDP (factor cost)	294.3	99	364.4	101

* Billions of rials; total for 1965–66 estimated at 450 billion rials
† Figures do not total to 100 per cent because of rounding

Population: about 25 million (1956 census, 18.9 million); growth in early 1960's loosely estimated at 2.5 per cent

Rural (areas of under 5,000 population): 13.0 million
Urban (areas of over 5,000 population): 5.9 million

Population	No. of Areas	Cities of over 100,000 Population*	
		City	Population
over 5,000	186	Tehran	1,512,000†
over 10,000	96	Tabriz	290,000
over 50,000	18	Esfahan	255,000
over 100,000	9	Mashad	242,000
		Abadan	226,000
		Shiraz	171,000
		Kermanshah	125,000
		Ahvaz	120,000
		Rasht	109,000
		Total	3,050,000

Literacy Rate (persons over seven years of age): males, 22 per cent; females, 7 per cent

Price-Level Changes (1959–60 = 100):

Wholesale index, Sept.–Oct., 1966:   107.9
Cost-of-living index, Sept.–Oct., 1966:   114.7

* 1956 census
† 1966 estimate, 2.7 million; this figure implies 6 per cent growth per year over the last decade

PLANNING AND DEVELOPMENT
IN IRAN

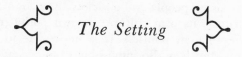

CHAPTER I

The Setting

Introduction

This book is about a paradox. It is the paradox of a country full of the promise of economic development but whose promise is continually being blocked by futilities and frustrations. It is almost as though, in Iran, man seems bent on throwing away what nature has given him, which is considerable. The irony is not quite complete, for Iran is not a country that is standing still. Everywhere there is evidence of progress, of a kind, and much more may be in the making. But the kind of progress Iran can show is almost a progress-in-spite-of-itself. There is certainly much less development than there should have been. And much of the recent growth is hard to trace to the national development effort which forms the subject of this book.

Iran probably has the best natural endowment for economic growth of any country in the Middle East. It has no serious population problem. There is no pressing shortage of arable land. More than half the country has an invigorating, temperate-zone climate. The most noticeable resource shortage is water, but the precipitation that falls on the country's two great mountain ranges, the Alborz and the Zagros, offers many opportunities for expanding the supply. There are several minerals of promise, some already under exploitation. There are still some magnificent forests in the northern provinces of Gorgan, Mazandaran, and Azerbaijan. And then there is the oil, oil that already has the high economic value of an established place in international use. With the oil comes natural gas. There is so much oil and so much gas that no one seriously worries about running out of either for decades to come. Oil itself gives the 22–23 million Iranians as much foreign exchange as the 100 million neighboring Pakistanis earn from all their exports put together.

But Iran is also a people and a society. Any country has its own distinctive history, its own culture, its own polity (to use a word that means more than politics). It is impossible to go into these subjects deeply; but it is also impossible to understand the postwar development effort without saying something about them.

The constitutional monarchy appears familiar enough, until one learns that it works in ways mysterious and unfamiliar. An ambiguous political regime skillfully maintains itself in power despite its apparent rejection by most of the educated younger generation and despite frequent predictions, over several years, of its imminent fall. There is not a little corruption in public life, at all levels. Chronic instability marks the holding of public office. Ministers shuffle on and off the stage in a sort of perpetual musical chairs of personal politics. The central government is burdened with the costs, the inefficiencies, the low salaries, the low morale of a badly inflated bureaucracy. Everything, throughout the country, turns on Tehran. Local government may also be said not to exist. There is no strongly felt social ethic, no ideological yeast at work in society. Public policies, administrative decisions, and national development plans all have to be made with few statistics, with unreliable statistics, and with few other forms of organized information such as good libraries and files, annual reports, public accounts, a reliable press, or professional societies and journals. To anyone working in this milieu it seems next to impossible to get things done, to learn what has already been done or is about to be done, to prevent things done from getting undone, to learn who is doing what and what who is supposed to be doing. Nearly everything the planner weaves by day somehow comes unraveled by night. And eventually one asks oneself how near nothing one can get without having nothing, i.e., before one decides the game of planning is not worth the candle. Iran is certainly not the only country of which one can ask the same question; but it is one of the more interesting ones.

Many things are "right" with Iran, but not the things that lie uppermost in the minds of most Iranians or foreigners. It is easy for the latter to blame all that is "wrong" with Iran on "the Iranians," as if they were somehow of weaker stuff than "Western Man." How long and glorious a history must a nation have to escape such a judgment? The proper perspective is one that looks beyond national behavior to the culture that underlies and explains

4

it. For it is primarily the configuration of a country's cultural and political forces at a given point in history, not the organization and abilities of its planners, that explains the balance between planning and anti-planning. Any mechanistic analysis of planning will founder on this truth.

"Culture" is a woolly word. I use the term to embrace all those subconscious social influences, external to individuals, that lay down the characteristic modes of thought and behavior in a particular society—its folkways, if you wish. The pathways or tracks along which people move by habit and instinct are defined by the "nuclear charges" with which everyone is endowed, in greater or lesser degree, by his culture. Within a culture-bound framework there is still room for elasticity and free will, for escaping electrons. But the prevailing orbits are prescribed by the invisible binding forces of a country's culture.

Admittedly, a cultural perspective does not dig very deep into the many-layered bundle of forces that emanate from a country's national character, its underlying psychological patterns, perhaps even its own distinctive biochemistry. My candle does not shine that deep. I must be content with trying to throw some light on the relationship between an effort to plan economic development and the political and cultural setting in which it occurs. The extent to which a national culture is congenial or hostile to planning surely has as much to do with the results as do the more controllable dial settings of public policy—monetary and fiscal policies, protection for home producers, the encouragement of competition, subsidies and price controls, social security and welfare standards, laws governing foreign investment, and similar legalistic factors. These classical areas of government policy are exceedingly important for Iran's development, as for any country's. But the sum of the choices made on each of these issues does not exhaust the subject of economic development in a country trying to accelerate growth through a formal development plan. The success of the latter centers on politics, not policies.

Iran's Legacy as a Buffer State

It is an important fact of Iran's history and politics that the country has long been a diplomatic battleground of Great Power interests. The expansionist ambitions of the Czars in central Asia and the determination of the British to protect their interests in India (which then bordered on Iran) brought Russia and Britain into diplomatic conflict in Iran. Compounding this political tension was a growing rivalry for commercial opportunity and advantage, a rivalry in which private business interests pushed and maneuvered for privileges that today would be unthinkable anywhere in the world.

Almost all the important concessions were granted either to Englishmen or to Russians. The more important and lasting of the British concessions were the telegraph lines (granted in 1864); the sixty-year banking concession given to Baron de Reuter in 1889, establishing the Imperial Bank of Persia with the exclusive right to issue paper money; and the D'Arcy oil concession (1901), covering the southern provinces. It was on this land that the first commercial oil strike was finally made in 1908, after many failures. In addition to these successful concessions (in the sense that something came of them) there were at least two abortive concessions which were so unacceptable at home and abroad that they had to be canceled, at great cost to the government. One, in 1890, involved a cash penalty of £500,000. The sum had to be borrowed from the (British) Imperial Bank of Persia at 6 per cent and was guaranteed by pledge of the customs revenues from the southern ports. This was Persia's first governmental loan—the first of several unproductive and humiliating foreign loans that explain why many Iranians still mistrust loans from foreign powers.

The first successful Russian concession was given in 1874 to an individual who proceeded to develop the successful Caspian fisheries. A successor to this enterprise is still the sole source of Iranian caviar, though ownership is now wholly in the hands of the Iranian Government. In 1881 and again in 1893 Russian companies were given concessions to construct and operate toll highways. In 1890, the year after de Reuter had been granted his banking concession, the Russians demanded and got a similar concession to establish a bank to counter British financial influence. By 1891 the Banque d'Escompte de Perse was in business. For the next three decades it was skillfully used for political purposes to tie the regime and influential Persians to Russia. However, it never acquired the importance of the British Imperial Bank.

The last strong Qajar king, Nasr ed Din, was assassinated in 1896. The last thirty years of this dynasty was presided over by weak and uninspired rulers. "A gloomier decline of a ruling house than that of the Kajar dynasty during the reign of its last three kings could hardly be imagined."[1] Thus the interventions of the British and Russian embassies in Persian affairs, during the first two decades, far from being totally selfish and evil, were often motivated by the necessity of assuring that the country had a government. Between 1906, when a brief flowering of democratic forces imposed a constitution and parliament (the *Majles*) on an unsympathetic Shah, and the end of the World War I, there was no clear direction to Iran's political life. If there was any it was toward progressive chaos. No organized approach to the key question of finance existed, and the government was chronically short of cash. The bureaucracy would go months without being paid. Government checks were often worthless and would be discounted heavily in the bazaar, where the government would buy them back cheaply when it came into a little cash. The most stable source of government revenue (the customs) was almost completely earmarked for servicing the Shah's foreign loans. Corruption and venality constituted the normal relationship between government officials and the public. Few if any records were maintained in government offices. Cabinet changes were frequent, with the same men often rotating among different ministries with no other aim or policy than to remain in office, any office. When serious pressure developed for reforming some branch of the administration, Persians frequently turned to foreigners—to run the customs, to officer and train the army, to run the Ministry of Finance.

The Russian Revolution was important for Persia. Its immediate effect was to persuade the British that they should strengthen their position in the country. To this end they unilaterally canceled a 1907 agreement with the Czars, an agreement which had formally divided Persia into British and Russian zones of influence. In its place they proposed to the Persian Government a treaty so sweeping it would have made Persia something close to a British colony. The 1919 treaty provided that the British would take over "the

[1] William S. Haas, *Iran* (New York, 1946), p. 139.

whole administration and the officering of the army" in return for commercial advantages and the construction of a railway from Tehran to the Gulf. But as one sympathetic observer remarked, "British policy was based on true insight—Iran could not go on as she was, and something radical had to be done."[2] Although British bribery was effective in securing approval of the treaty from the Cabinet and the Shah, the *Majles* blocked its approval late in 1920. Indeed, it was *Majles* resentment over the handling of this treaty by the government that led directly to the bloodless coup of February 1921, a coup that put an obscure cavalry officer, Colonel Reza Khan, in effective control of the government. The Qajar regent fled the country. By 1925 the cavalry colonel who had vaulted into government as Minister of War proclaimed himself Shah.[3]

The post-coup government refused to accept the proposed Anglo-Persian Treaty of 1919. Fortunately, the Soviets had already decided to reverse completely their country's historical role in Persia: in the Treaty of 1921 they "renounced with one gesture all the privileges the Czars had struggled to win. The Persian debt was canceled, the Imperial Bank of Russia (the Banque d'Escompte de Perse) was turned over to the Persian Government, and the Julfa railway was ceded to Iran. At the same time the Russians evacuated the occupied provinces."[4] The Soviet withdrawal helped the British accept the loss of their proposed treaty.

The events of the early 1920's closed an era of foreign domination of Iran's affairs. During Reza Shah's regime, foreign domination was not an important issue: the British quickly decided to give the Shah their support, and Russia was held off by Reza's suspicion of its intentions. Not until the Allied invasion of Iran in 1941 were Iran's fortunes once again subordinated to the struggles of great powers beyond its borders. In the preceding twenty years Reza Shah Pahlavi built a strong, stable government that changed the face of Persia and restored its ancient name. For all its legacies, Iran had become a twentieth-century country. Persia never was.

[2] *Ibid.*, p. 140.

[3] For an excellent summary account of the rise of Reza Shah to power, see Chapter III in *The History of Modern Iran: An Interpretation,* by Joseph M. Upton (Cambridge, Mass., 1960).

[4] Haas, *Iran,* p. 141.

The Reforms of Reza Shah

Historically, Reza Shah played in Iran much the same role that his admired contemporary, Ataturk, played in Turkey. He was, of course, a dictator. He made little pretense of any devotion to democratic processes. In the end, Reza became one of his own victims, a classic case of progressive corruption by absolute power. That power had given him and his associates ample scope for feathering their own nests, a game he played without compunction. Nevertheless Reza built a nation as well as a fortune.

Reza made the establishment of central-government authority his first order of business. To this end he concentrated on building up a modern standing army and on subduing rebellious tribes and semi-independent local chiefs in several of the provinces. Building the army was a hugely expensive undertaking, with the result that, from the outset, Reza was desperately short of money. Fortunately, even before his coup, the *Majles* had requested the U.S. Department of State to recruit another team of financial experts to help lead the country out of the same fiscal chaos to which the Shuster Mission had addressed itself ten years earlier.[5] From the start Reza found himself with a strong group of foreign experts in the Ministry of Finance who shared his interest in getting control over the country's finances. This was the first of two famous financial missions headed by A. C. Millspaugh. Since Millspaugh could do little without force to back up the tax collectors, there was a natural alliance

[5] Morgan Shuster's well-known book, *The Strangling of Persia* (New York, 1912), is a detailed account of his eight months of service in Persia and of the extent to which the country had become the pawn of Russian and British interests. Shuster's sympathies were clearly with the Nationalist movement, which had wrested a constitution and parliament from the Shah in 1906 and whose resentment against undue foreign influence and privilege he fully shared. Translated into Farsi and still read by Iranians, Shuster's book shows the historical roots of many Iranians' continuing hatred for Russia, their suspicion of the British, their mistrust of foreign loans, and their cynicism about their own government.

Although many things Shuster said of Iran fifty years ago can still be said today, there has been much progress since he wrote. Public finance, for all its shortcomings, is now far better managed. Education has reached a far larger proportion of the population. Public security has become the rule rather than the exception. Production, transport, and communications have been altered beyond recognition. And an immensely profitable oil industry provides a relatively easy source of government income and keeps the economy liberally supplied with foreign exchange.

between him and Reza Khan. This lasted until the two fell out over the Shah's increasing demands for military funds; Millspaugh left in 1927.[6]

The strongest opponents of the new regime were not the tribal chiefs and Arab sheikhs but the clergy. Despite individual exceptions, the clergy was undoubtedly one of the most conservative, not to say reactionary, forces in Persian society. This tradition-bound group controlled the basic civil law of the country, the courts, and the educational system. Reza avoided any direct challenge to the clergy, but he steadily and successfully undermined their control over law and education. He did so by reconstituting the old Ministry of Justice, commissioning a French jurist to revise the civil code, ending the age-old clerical monopoly of education, starting a national university, and adding twenty-five teacher-training colleges to the one that had been established in 1918. In 1928 a law was passed that began a regular policy of sending abroad 100 students every year. The number grew rapidly. "No single institution or group of people was more responsible for bringing Western influences into Iran than the students who had been educated in Europe and America."[7] It could hardly be said, however, that Reza left more than the beginnings of a strong educational base for the country's future. His willingness to invest in education was modest: during the period 1922–41 the military got, on the average, 33 per cent of the budget while education averaged 4 per cent and increased at a rate of less than 1 per cent per year.

In the field of medicine and public health the main steps needed to meet minimum needs had been marked out for the country in a 1925 Report of the League of Nations. By 1941 much progress on this agenda had been made, including detailed plans for the Tehran water supply. The war postponed that project fifteen years. The Pasteur Institute (under French guidance), the Razzi Institute (to-

[6] See Millspaugh's book, *The American Task in Persia* (New York, 1925), written in the U.S. in 1925 when he was home recruiting more men to begin a second, larger contract. Millspaugh returned to Iran in 1944 at the invitation of the U.S. Government. His second mission was much less successful and damaged the reputation he had won for himself by his performance in the 1920's. For an account of this second mission, see his book, *Americans in Persia* (Washington, D.C., 1946).

[7] Amin Banani, *The Modernization of Iran, 1921–41* (Stanford, Calif., 1961), p. 101.

day the best animal serum institute in the Middle East), the medical school in Tehran, the hospitals in some of the larger cities—these important institutions were all begun between 1921 and 1941. So, too, were the important charitable organizations, the Red Lion and Sun (the Iranian Red Cross affiliate) and the Organization for the Care of Mothers and Children, which runs several orphanages.

Economic Developments under Reza Shah

The main economic achievement of Reza Shah's regime was the carrying through of a large investment program without resort to foreign loans and without significant help from what has been the financial cornerstone of the postwar development effort, the oil royalties.

Iran is a large country, three times the size of France, with two huge mountain ranges in the north and south that present forbidding topography. It is not surprising that throughout Reza's regime transport received the largest share of resources. In 1924 a comprehensive survey of the country's transport requirements was undertaken and priorities were established. The key project—the fulfillment of a long-standing national ambition—was the construction of the trans-Iranian railway, from the Caspian Sea to the Persian Gulf, a distance of 850 miles than spans the Alborz and Zagros ranges. Approximately two-thirds of the cost of this hugely expensive project came from earmarked proceeds of the special taxes on tea and sugar imposed in 1925. Almost as much attention (though much less money) was devoted to road-building. The initial motive was to increase internal security—good roads made it easier to put down tribal rebellions. But the economic advantage of good roads quickly asserted itself. In 1925 Iran had something like 2,000 miles of roads, most of them built by the Russians and the British in their respective spheres of influence. By 1938 there were over 20,000 miles (none of them paved). In a single decade transport costs fell 40 per cent in money terms, nearly 80 per cent in real terms. Domestic consumption of fuel oil (mostly for vehicles) rose from 11.9 million metric tons to 86.9 million tons. Imports of automotive vehicles and parts increased from 27.4 million rials to 92.3 million.[8]

[8] See Bank Melli Iran, *Bulletin,* No. 25, p. 208.

The year 1930 marked the beginning of a wider approach to economic development. The main objectives were rapid industrialization, the achievement of self-sufficiency in key consumer goods and cement, and the elimination of a chronically unfavorable trade balance. (No serious attack was made on agricultural problems.) To help plan and direct these developments a new ministry, the Ministry of National Economy, was set up. However, nothing like systematic planning was attempted.[9] The prewar investments were made as separate, individual projects, some well-planned, others not.

Although Reza Shah encouraged private industry, there was practically none forthcoming until the late 1930's, when a few entrepreneurs came forward. The state had no alternative but to proceed with direct investments of its own. Ataturk's *étatisme* was also Reza's. Between 1931 and 1941 the following state industries were started: two cotton mills, several cotton gins, a knitting factory, seven beet-sugar refineries, a cement plant, three small chemical plants, several tea factories and rice mills, a silk-weaving mill and a filature plant, a small copper refinery, a fertilizer-mixing plant, a food cannery, a few coal mines, a vegetable oil mill, a plant for making refractory brick—these were the main projects carried through. Begun but not finished (because the war interrupted shipments from Germany) was an integrated steel mill of 60,000 tons capacity. A few of these plants did reasonably well, but many began to decay as soon as they had been finished because of the shortages of technical personnel, managerial inexperience, poor location, and wartime problems with raw materials and replacement parts.

Reza's reign spanned the Great Depression. He successfully prevented this cataclysm from dominating his domestic economic policy. He did so by abandoning a long-standing policy of free trade and by improvising direct controls over foreign exchange and foreign trade. Indeed, the structure of controls he erected to control the balance of payments lasted, with only minor changes, until 1955. Although world demand for Iran's non-oil exports fell sharply, the demand for oil grew. Even at the low level of oil payments then in effect (Iran was getting $10–15 million annually in the mid-1930's compared with $65 million in 1949), a rising oil income helped greatly in managing the balance of payments. Indeed, it was Reza

[9] With the exception of one short-lived period in 1937 when Reza flirted with the idea of general economic planning (see below, Chapter II, p. 25, n. 3).

who began the practice, still followed, of earmarking a high proportion of the oil revenues to finance extraordinary government programs—originally (and briefly) to buy gold for currency backing, then to finance development programs.

The main impact of the Depression fell on government finances. The reduction of taxable imports forced by the need to limit the trade deficit pinched where it hurt, since about 40 per cent of government revenues came from customs receipts. The stagnation of ordinary tax receipts was partly offset by the rising oil revenues; the latter were occasionally diverted from their earmarked purposes to cover current budget needs. But the increase in oil revenue was not sufficient to finance both the ordinary budget and the accelerating development programs. Consequently by the late 1930's Reza —whose financial policies were generally conservative—was relying increasingly on deficit finance.

The building of modern monetary and financial institutions constituted another of Reza's achievements. We have seen that by 1890 the British and Russians had introduced modern banks and paper money. These replaced a centuries-old system of private money-dealers *(sarrafs)* and metallic currency. But foreign banks, for all their help to private traders, were not adequate institutions for a nationalistic ruler bent on a vigorous development program. In 1927 Reza established a national bank (Bank Melli); shortly afterward he forced the British Imperial Bank to surrender its key note-issue privilege. Between 1932, when Bank Melli began to issue its own notes, and 1941 the note supply expanded eightfold.[10] Over

[10] There is something ironic and amusing in the way the note-cover problem was handled during the thirties, and indeed has continued to be handled. It reminds one of the handling of the debt-ceiling problem in the United States. When Bank Melli began to issue banknotes in 1932, the law stipulated that there must be at least as much gold, silver, and foreign exchange convertible into gold among the assets of the bank as there were notes issued. This represented a 100 per cent cover of high quality. The same law required that each increase of the note issue be approved by the *Majles.* The theory behind these legal requirements appears to have been that money would be valuable only if its supply were limited and that the most satisfactory rule for limiting the supply was to require that it bear no less than a one-to-one relation to the precious metals. This theory may have served a useful purpose during the few years when Bank Melli's initial note issue was replacing the Imperial Bank's notes—particularly because BMI suffered its worst crisis in the year before it began to issue notes. In 1934, however, there began a steady erosion of the note-cover requirements which progressively reduced the amount and quality of the cover. It is almost

the same period Bank Melli expanded credit to private (mainly commercial) borrowers 8 to 10 times and to the central government even more. By 1941 government credit was several times larger than private credit; in 1931 the two had been equal. The combination of rapidly expanding bank credit and government budget deficits led to rising price levels that showed up unmistakably after the introduction of a cost-of-living index in 1936. Reza's development program was being partly financed through the forced savings of a moderate inflation. Exactly the same thing was to happen again between 1957 and 1961.

Iranian Society and Politics

The foregoing account of Reza Shah's accomplishments contrasts sharply with the gloomy comments on Iranian politics and government which opened the chapter. It is indeed true that, all things considered, Reza's economic accomplishments read well. He did little, however, that left any lasting imprint on the style of Iranian politics and administration, a style whose influence on economic planning is almost entirely negative. For decades the government of Iran has suffered from a degree of inefficiency, instability, and corruption that raises eyebrows even among those who know how imperfect are men and governments around the world. Over the years, there have been many able and dedicated Iranian leaders who have attempted to reduce these liabilities to reasonable levels. The lack of significant progress over the past two generations shows how deeply rooted these symptoms are in Iranian institutions and folkways. The economic achievements of Reza Shah and the surge

---

not too much to say that, whenever the government had to choose between limiting its expenditures and manipulating the note-cover so that Bank Melli could advance the necessary funds, it chose the latter course. Although the note issue was increased not solely to finance government expenditures, that was certainly the strongest reason, and it arose again and again. This accommodation of the money supply to the government's expenditure program, rather than vice versa, does not seem to have been casual and wanton. But when the chips were down the money supply always went up. Much ingenuity was exercised to preserve the mythology that there was some kind of backing to the note issue which somehow gave it a value independent of what notes would buy. The fact that there was never any flight from notes into silver (until the Allied Occupation) showed the value of the myth.

of development activity after 1955 appear to have had little effect on the country's traditional political style. Reza's ability to score economic gains in the face of such a difficult political system testifies to the importance of his personality—and ruthlessness—in a highly personal political system.

In law, Iran has been a constitutional monarchy since 1906. The brief triumph of modernizing forces at that time, however, did not have time to strike deep roots. Thus, while the political system of Iran looks very similar to many Western European countries, it does not function similarly. The position of the Shah has remained incomparably stronger than in any European monarchy. Indeed the parliament, made up of a 200-man lower house (the *Majles*) and a 50-man senate, has traditionally been little more than a legitimizing agency of the Court. The latter has typically controlled elections and has exercised great power over individuals and groups both in and out of government. Nevertheless, from time to time there are significant shifts in power between the parliament and the Council of Ministers (or Cabinet) on the one hand and the Shah on the other. During Reza Shah's fifteen-year rule he completely dominated parliament but did not abolish it. The vacuum left by his abdication in 1941 was filled by the occupying powers, not by Reza's son and still-ruling successor, Mohammed Reza Pahlavi, who was then only twenty-one. The present Shah did not really begin to exercise strong control over government affairs until after the fall of Mossadegh in August, 1953. For the past dozen years the Shah has asserted stronger and stronger personal control over all aspects of government.

A striking feature of Iranian politics and government is that they are conducted almost exclusively in one city, Tehran. There are fifteen to twenty provinces, but there are no states with their own constitutions, parliaments, fiscal systems, elected officials, or political parties. The ultimate political units are the country's 275 municipalities and 45,000 villages. Most key officials, however, right down to the mayors of provincial towns, are appointed by the Ministry of Interior in Tehran. The municipalities are heavily dependent on the central government for their revenues, which are woefully inadequate to the modern functions many of them are struggling to assume. The villages, where about two-thirds of Iran lives, have traditionally been governed by the landlords who owned them. One aspect of the land reform that began in 1962 is that it involves not only an economic reconstruction of village life but a political and administrative reconstruction as well.

In days gone by, the richest and socially most powerful group in society was the landlords, a large proportion of whom lived in Tehran. This class provided the natural social and political allies of the king and Court. The other great bloc of social power, down to the time of Reza Shah, has already been mentioned, the clergy. This group was politically important because of the influence it held over much of the population. The developments set in motion by Reza Shah have gradually eroded the weight of landlord influence in social and political life. The creation of a new military class, the growth of commerce and industry, the secularization of many legal and educational functions formerly controlled by the clergy, and, especially, the rapid growth of a modern educational system began to dilute the former structure of economic and social power and to create new groups much more actively interested in governmental affairs and much better qualified to have opinions on them than could be found in the simpler, more homogeneous structure of earlier periods.

The present Shah has recognized and shrewdly manipulated the changing power structure without giving away any of his traditional sovereignty. Whatever showdown may be coming has been kept at bay by the Shah's consummate skill in balancing off personalities and preventing the formation of groups. So long as only personalities (and not organized interest groups) exist, then only personalities need be reckoned with.

There is, in fact, an almost complete absence of groups organized to advance their interests in the competitive battle of life—e.g., trade unions, political parties, professional associations, civic organizations, employer associations, trade associations, and the like. The basic individualism and lack of trust that characterize Iranian society have made the formation of such organizations difficult in any event. But equally important has been the government's quiet discouragement of any such organizations. Iran's rulers have traditionally feared the development of independent centers of initiative and the articulation of group interests. To forestall such developments, the government sponsors and thus controls almost all interest groups that are permitted to exist. It does so both through the painful licensing regulations surrounding the formation of organizations and through government appointment or approval of their officers. It is generally assumed that any organization (or government office) that might present a threat to the regime will have among its members paid agents of SAVAK (the security police), who act as informers. But knowledge of their existence does little to inhibit political discussion at the personal level.

The strength of personal influences and relationships and the weakness of impersonal goals, loyalties, and pressures explain much of the instability of Iran's political life. To the disadvantage of instability must be added that of corruption. It apparently exists on a truly grand scale. It is executed with a finesse and unobtrusiveness that testify to the existence of an invisible web of administrative mores that easily survives the periodic attacks against corruption by the Shah, various ministers, and the controlled press. Indictments and arrests are sometimes made, but anybody who is anybody avoids successful prosecution almost as a matter of right. It is easy to make too much of corruption and to betray self-righteousness in making international comparisons. So far as economic planning is concerned, its main impact is not the extra costs; it is the way the hope of graft distorts people's judgments about projects, generates unhealthy pressures and temptations that should not exist, and makes more difficult the handling of decisions openly and on their merits.

In an atmosphere of personal and purchased favors even those who would like to play by different rules are caught in a system that demands of them certain conduct if they wish to get on with their affairs. Take the important area of tax collection, for example. The basic lack of consensus between tax collectors and tax payers forces both sides to adopt "irrational" practices—arbitrary assessments based on subjective guesses of income, concealment of wealth, falsification of financial returns prepared by intimates of the owners in an atmosphere of secrecy, and arbitrary compromises mediated by payoffs to revenue officials.

Under such conditions an attempt to play by different rules can often be suicidal. So bad practices drive out good under a Gresham's Law of administrative behavior. As a result no businessman can get a loan or a license, or make a sale to government, or secure a government contract, or have a telephone installed, or settle a tax bill, or receive payment on a bill presented, or move goods out of

17

customs without either securing the intervention of a friend in high places or purchasing his objective through bribery, or both. The concept of government existing to serve the public with efficiency, courtesy, and without unnecessary inconvenience is weak. Members of the public do not approach officials brandishing rights which they may expect to exercise and have acknowledged. They come as supplicants for favors which they expect to have to buy or to have granted. And one of the ironies of Iranian administration is that it is made worse by the measures taken to protect it. All official transactions are so dominated by detailed regulations designed to prevent improprieties that even the most routine matters become tangled in red tape. As a result, people naturally try to buy their way out.

The state of Iranian politics and government described above appears to have characterized the country since the turn of the century and doubtless much longer. Yet for years now there has been a gathering consensus that the present basis of political power is no longer legitimate, that it now offends too many people's sense of what is fair and right. This consensus is mainly negative, expressing itself in a widespread political alienation of the younger generation, in a pervasive cynicism about government, and in demonstrations (mainly by students) against the regime. The political mood, therefore, is that of an expectant society, a society in waiting. Everyone, including the Shah, feels he is living on this side of a crisis, a crisis that will surprise nobody. What surprises more is that no crisis comes. The great unanswerable question is whether the historical impasse in which the country finds itself will work itself out slowly, peacefully, and gradually, or suddenly, unpredictably, violently.

The most direct political challenge to the present Shah came from a coalition of political groups called the National Front. This coalition was created by Dr. Mohammed Mossadegh, a distinguished lawyer who became Prime Minister during the period of the oil nationalization crisis (1950–53). It was at the end of this stormy period that the Shah's position reached its lowest point. In the crisis he fled the country briefly until Mossadegh's fall made possible his return.

To many Western observers, Mossadegh was a somewhat bizarre, incomprehensible, and unworkable type of political leader—a demagogue who struck out irresponsibly at the country's most important economic asset and whose political naïveté involved him in relationships with pro-Communist groups to such a degree that a Communist take-over was a reasonable fear in any crisis. This is not the image of Mossadegh held by the younger generation of Iranians, or by many older ones, or even by some foreigners. Many of them regard Mossadegh as a near-charismatic national leader who for all his faults effectively challenged an unfair foreign economic institution vital to the nation's health, who stood for full implementation of the constitution, for honesty in government, and for a much greater measure of intellectual and political freedom than Iran has ever known, before or since.

In the years of his increasingly positive rule since 1953 the Shah has shown a masterful ability not only to survive but also to maintain political control and to create a foreign image of himself as a courageous liberal determined to reform both government and society. Without doubt, the Shah leads most of his countrymen in the art of Persian politics—balancing off contending pressures and personalities by putting people under obligation through favors; silencing potential critics through implicit blackmail, because one knows something unsavory about them; refusing to crystallize issues to the point where definite choices are made, thus disappointing or offending someone; never allowing any individual to become too powerful or too popular; never being so publicly identified with events that it is impossible to shift the blame onto others; and cultivating an ambiguity in political life that softens critics by pretending to espouse their hopes while reassuring vested interests by rarely carrying out promised reforms. The Shah's position as commander of all branches of the security forces (the military, the gendarmerie, the municipal police, and the secret police) is a necessary basis for playing this game successfully. Perhaps the strongest testimony to the Shah's skill is his success so far in retaining effective control over the security forces themselves.

The long-run direction in which Iranian politics should move, and the pace and steps by which they should proceed, are fascinating subjects but go beyond this book. We are concerned not with Iran's political future but with the bearing of traditional politics on the country's attempt to mount a program of economic development.[11]

[11] I have found the postwar literature on the politics of non-Western societies a great help in understanding Iranian political and administrative behavior. (Of the works cited below, the most detailed and helpful analysis of *administrative*

behavior will be found in Riggs' work, although many readers will be put off by his terminology.)

See Gabriel A. Almond and James S. Coleman (eds.), *The Politics of the Developing Areas* (Princeton, N.J., 1960), especially Almond's chapter, "Introduction: A Functional Approach to Comparative Politics." See also the following articles by Fred W. Riggs: "Prismatic Society and Financial Administration," *Administrative Science Quarterly, June*, 1960, pp. 1–46; "An Ecological Approach —the 'Sala' Model," paper presented at the September, 1961, meeting of the American Political Science Association; and his book, *The Ecology of Public Administrative Science Quarterly*, June, 1960, pp. 1–46; "An Ecological Approach Non-Western Political Process," *The Journal of Politics*, XX (1958), pp. 468–86; "Personal Identity and Political Ideology," *Behavioral Science*, VI, No. 3 (July, 1961), pp. 205–21 (reprinted in *Political Decision Makers*, ed. Dwaine Marvick [Glencoe, Ill., 1961]); and his book, *Politics, Personality, and Nation Building: Burma's Search for Identity* (New Haven, 1962). See also Leonard Binder, *Iran: Political Development in a Changing Society* (Los Angeles, 1962). In addition to a theoretical framework, Binder's book contains a wealth of detailed historical and institutional information on the Iranian political system, particularly Chapters IV and V on "Structures of Social Power" and "The Political Functions." Also helpful is the book produced by several members of M.I.T.'s Center for International Studies under the editorship of Max F. Millikan and Donald L. M. Blackmer, *The Emerging Nations: Their Growth and United States Policy* (Boston, 1961).

Pye's article reviews the attempts of political scientists to build links between the individual personality and a society's political behavior. Before turning to Erikson's work, Pye reviews the two main streams of thought concerned with this linkage, one concentrating on the dynamics of personality formation during childhood, the other concentrating on what happens to individuals as they participate in social and cultural situations after childhood. Erikson's work puts him with the first group, though he is concerned with the dynamics of personality throughout life.

Some sociologists doubt that the Erikson-Pye concept of the search for a national "identity" is operationally useful because of the impossibility of saying when a country has or has not found its identity. I would say that a country able to operate its politics on a competitive basis within a context of considerable freedom possesses a widely shared sense of identity. A country unable to do this can be governed only by cliques supported by some mixture of fear and force.

An even more radical attempt to apply modern psychology to an understanding of economic development will be found in the work of Everett E. Hagen. Hagen is more interested in what psychology has to say about the sources of innovational behavior in economic life than about its bearing on political behavior. Like Pye, he draws heavily on Erikson's work, though from many others as well. One comes away from Hagen's rich and suggestive volume with a vague impression that he must surely be speaking directly to the problems of Iran, where nearly every observable social structure is in transition and significant changes in economic behavior are seen. One would need to have a much more complete mastery of Hagen's concepts and a much more intimate knowledge of Iranian life than I possess to attempt to fit mid-century Iran to his model (see Hagen's book, *On the Theory of Social Change: How Economic Growth Begins* [Homewood, Ill., 1962]). The present book, however, is not nearly as concerned with the sources of Iran's economic growth as it is with the country's attempts to manage this growth through economic planning.

20

Iranian politics and an organized development effort are uncongenial bedfellows. This fact was known in advance to the men who organized the postwar development program with which this book is concerned. Consequently they designed a *development* agency (not, originally, a *planning* body) which they hoped could stand outside the traditional negatives of Iranian politics. Events were to prove how difficult it is to insulate any government body from prevailing patterns of political behavior.

CHAPTER II

Postwar Planning: Its Origins and
Organization

There is a difference between economic planning and a development effort centered on a program of public investments. Economic planning is concerned with analysis of where the whole economy ought to go and how it ought to get there; it rarely includes any responsibility for plan execution, which is normally left to the regular ministries. In this sense planning requires a high degree of co-operation and consensus among the various agencies of government, as well as private interests, and reasonable confidence in the executive capacities of government ministries. Where these classic conditions for planning are weak or lacking, a government may establish a special agency to plan and carry out its own development program largely or entirely separate from the rest of the government. The aim is to "get things done."

Iran's postwar development effort has been carried forward by a nearly autonomous agency that does not fit neatly either of these polar characterizations. In the beginning Plan Organization[1] was meant to be more of a planning agency than a go-it-alone executive agency. In its years of greatest influence and success (1955–60) it was much more an executive than a planning agency. The subsequent attempt to develop its role as a planning body and to turn over most of its executive functions to the ministries has succeeded more in the latter than the former aim. In short, the development effort has been presided over by an agency whose aims have shifted with changing pressures and whose limited success has been a disappoint-

---

[1] The full title is correct with or without the article. Either form is sometimes clumsy. I have therefore chosen to use the terms *Plan Organization* and *Plan-Org* interchangeably throughout the text, even though the latter term is not in common use.

ment to many. However, the ambiguities of Plan Organization's role do not reflect faulty design or misguided management. They reflect the political and cultural environment in which it has had to operate. This environment has prevented PlanOrg from ever rising above mediocrity as either a planning or executive agency. This is not to deny its brief spurts of vigor in both directions.

By original intent Plan Organization was to be a rather orthodox planning and co-ordinating body, responsible for supervising the execution of a Seven Year Plan. The latter had been developed in considerable detail before the Plan's administrative arrangements had been established. The Law of the First Seven Year Plan (1949–55) established both the Plan and the machinery of planning. The Plan took the limited form of specific spending targets for six sectors of the economy. Behind these expenditure targets lay suggestions for a great many individual projects thrown up by the engineering surveys out of which the Plan had been built. Originally it was intended that most projects would be carried out by the regular ministries, with PlanOrg acting as an initiating, funding, and supervising agency. But in cases where PlanOrg judged that a project could not be satisfactorily executed by a regular government ministry it was authorized to create a new body or to execute the work itself. In practice, the exception became the rule: under both the First and Second Plans (1949–54 and 1955–62) PlanOrg executed most Plan projects on its own, with a relatively small share of the funds passing through the ministries. Whether this procedure was right or wrong is disputed by knowledgeable Iranians and foreigners alike. Good or bad, the fact of PlanOrg's involvement in executing the Plan forced it to deal with a whole set of operational problems that went way beyond planning. But PlanOrg also remained responsible for planning, a role that was confirmed and strengthened after the establishment of an Economic Bureau in 1958 and its designation in 1959 as the office responsible for preparing the Third Plan. This was to start in September, 1962.

Among the chief planners the subject of PlanOrg's proper role in executing the Third Plan was the key institutional question surrounding the future of the development program. The failure to develop any clear consensus on the planning vs. operational roles of PlanOrg during the Third Plan reflected the planners' differing estimates of the relative competence of the ministries and PlanOrg.

Ironically, nearly all the institutional and administrative problems that preoccupied the planners of 1959–61 had been confronted in almost identical terms by PlanOrg's founding fathers in 1945–49. The latter-day generation of planners did not know this at the time, but it is doubtful if the knowledge would have done them any good.

Origins: 1945–49 and Before

Plan Organization came into being with the enactment of the first Seven Year Plan Law in May, 1949. This Law was the outcome of four years of discussions, negotiations, and preparations started at the close of World War II. Although the then-new World Bank and the American Embassy[2] played important roles in shaping the planning effort, the initiative was entirely Iranian. In no sense have planning and the Plan Organization been alien objectives urged on Iran by outsiders. Perhaps the leading part was played by that remarkable and controversial figure, Mr. Abol Hassan Ebtehaj, for many years Governor of Bank Melli and destined to become Managing Director of Plan Organization during the years of its greatest success following Mossadegh's fall in 1953.

During World War II Iran suffered the demoralizing and disorganizing consequences of a bad inflation. The general price level rose 600–800 per cent over a five-year period. Bad harvests and poor internal transport combined to create food shortages serious enough to produce sporadic rioting. Many of Reza Shah's new industrial plants were forced to close because of shortages of spare parts, raw materials, or managerial talent. Essential imports were in short supply. Unemployment was serious. A new freedom for the press, for political organization, and for trade union activity following Reza Shah's abdication had produced expressions of popular protest unknown in Iran for two decades. And the emergency wartime

[2] The British Embassy, wiser and more cynical about Iranian ways than the Americans, was skeptical of any sort of organized planning effort for Iran and was neutral in the period during which the Plan and Plan Organization were being put together. Some knowledgeable American observers feel the British began to undermine PlanOrg soon after its start because they (like many Iranians) rightly felt that it would interfere with traditional ways of doing business in Iran and that any changes were likely to go against Britain's commercial interest.

mission of Dr. A. C. Millspaugh, recalled to Iran to see if he could manage a program of economic controls, was not proving effective. By late 1944 the Cabinet decided to revoke the special powers given to Dr. Millspaugh and take matters into its own hands. One step taken was the creation of a High Economic Council whose primary duty was to "prepare a general economic plan for the country . . . in conformity with other countries. . . ."[3]

The 1945 High Economic Council came to nothing. As a result, Mr. Ebtehaj, then Governor of Bank Melli, wrote to the Minister of Finance informing him that in view of the urgency of framing a development plan for the country he was establishing a committee within Bank Melli to prepare a draft that would deal with some general aspects of such a plan. He suggested that another committee be appointed within the Ministry of Finance to carry the work forward within the government proper. A series of political shuffles stalled action for a year, but when the strong Qavam government assumed office it approved a decree establishing, within the Ministry of Finance, a "Commission for Drafting Plans for the Development of the Country" (April, 1946). The draft plan produced by this Commission in the summer of 1946 was really the first draft of what became, three years later, the Seven Year Plan Law. During this three-year period of preparation, four foreign influences were to play a major role in shaping the final result—the World Bank, the American Embassy in Tehran, two American consulting firms, and Max Weston Thornburg, a private U.S. citizen.

The summer document of 1946 was presented to the Cabinet as a seven-year plan "for Iran's Reconstruction and Development," a title close to that of the recently established International Bank for Reconstruction and Development. Iran was one of the original

[3] The High Economic Council was patterned on a decree used in 1937 to establish a body called the Trade Council. At the latter's tenth meeting, in the presence of Reza Shah, the Council had stated that its "prime duty [was] to prepare a general economic plan for the country." In October, 1937, the Council approved the formation of a permanent committee charged "with the preparation of a plan for increasing the productive capacity of the Country." But late in 1938, after twenty meetings, it was suddenly adjourned *sine die*. Obviously Reza Shah was not backing "planning" with much conviction. But a seed had been planted. This short-lived attempt at planning was not lost on the man who served as Secretary of the 1937 Trade Council, Mr. Abol Hassan Ebtehaj ("Foundation of the Economic Supreme Council," *Bank Melli Bulletin*, No. 75 [April–May, 1945], pp. 1–12).

IBRD members and Mr. Ebtehaj had attended the Bretton Woods meetings of 1944 when the Bank was organized; he was therefore fully familiar with the Bank's purposes and personalities. He was also hopeful that Iran could finance about $250 million of its Plan for Reconstruction and Development with IBRD loans. But the Bank's response to Iran's informal application was that it would entertain no formal applications except for individual projects whose validity had first been established by competent technical studies. This was the first instance of what has since become (on occasion) a major influence on Iranian planning: the constructive discipline exercised by the necessity of justifying large projects to exacting foreign lenders. (There are other foreign lenders whose influence works in exactly the opposite direction.)

This original 1946 draft was significant in other respects. The conception of the plan was limited: the development effort was to be a program of *government* expenditures. It was not a comprehensive plan concerned with the over-all pattern of saving and investment, public and private. With minor exceptions this same idea underlay both the First and Second Plans. Indeed, the scope narrowed as the Plan matured; the Plan was never intended as an attempt to control all of the government's own investment activities: the Plan *was* what Plan Organization *did,* without regard for the rest of the government. Tehran politics might well have made it impossible to control all government development expenditures even if this had been the aim. As it turned out, the lack of any over-all control later proved troublesome.

The 1946 authors faced up squarely to the limited "absorptive capacity" of government in Iran. The Commission identified as major problems the "unstable loyalty of the Government employees, loosening of discipline, and lack of individual responsibility." "No long-term plan," they wrote, "can therefore be conceived and put into force unless a definite attempt is made towards a fundamental reorganization of the Government Services." These are the words of concerned Iranians speaking to the Cabinet and the Shah. Substantially the same words were addressed to a different Cabinet by the new generation of planners in 1960; there had been no perceptible improvement in the level of public administration during the intervening fifteen years (or at least so the planners believed). In 1946, nobody had yet proposed to by-pass the political-administrative problem by establishing a new, specialized institution outside the regular machinery of government.

The Commission for Drafting Plans recommended that the Cabinet appoint a "Supreme Planning Council" to prepare "a definite plan." The formation of such a Council was promptly approved (in August, 1946). Apart from its duty to study the size of the plan the country might finance from internal and external sources, the Supreme Planning Board was also to draft a statute "of a Committee of Control in the execution of the Plan." The idea of a separate "organization" to administer the plan was still not part of official thinking. Nor was anyone yet talking about using the country's oil royalties as a unique source of financing, one that would link this wasting asset to the creation of more permanent sources of national wealth. But a year later when the Prime Minister addressed the first meeting of the Planning Board the notion of setting up a special fund to finance the plan *was* emphasized. Everyone recognized that unless extraordinary steps were taken to protect the revenues intended for development their money would be used for other purposes. Such had always been the fate of money in Iran—someone was always using it for something else. Mr. Qavam also told the Board that the plan itself should be embodied in a law of the *Majles* "so that no Finance Minister or Prime Minister shall be able, in future, to alter at his will, the terms of the plan." This is the reason Iran chose a "legislative" instead of an "administrative" approach to planning: it was felt that the essential elements had to be tied down in a law so that no politicians or administrators could change them.

The process of planning involves the generation of a list of candidate projects and their subsequent study so that the list can be narrowed down to a list of approved projects formally taken into the plan. This process of nomination, evaluation, and selection continues throughout the life of any plan; but no plan can begin until there is at least some backlog of approved projects. The Iranian planners were having difficulty generating a sufficient number of well-thought-out projects that could give specific content to their general objectives. Consequently, when Mr. Thornburg was in Tehran in the summer of 1946, he suggested to Mr. Ebtehaj and others that they employ an American engineering firm to generate the list of candidate projects any plan would need to have. In

December a contract was signed with Morrison-Knudsen International to conduct a survey of projects and programs that could form the basis of a development plan. The ten American engineers who soon thereafter arrived in Iran completed their field work within four months. By July, 1947, they had completed a report which offered the Iranian Government a choice among three plans of differing sizes (the largest cost $1.4 billion and contained 234 projects; the smallest cost $260,000 and contained 24 projects). The report left it up to Iranian officials to decide how large a program the country could afford and how any plan might be financed. These questions were given definitive answers in an unusually able report prepared by Dr. Mosharef Naficy, a member of the Supreme Planning Board. The Naficy Report provided the basis for the Seven Year Plan Law as finally enacted. The following five points summarize the conception of the development agency at the time the law was passed:

1. The development agency should be independent, insulated from the government's chronic instability and its politics.
2. To assure its independence the agency would be given legal status and financial autonomy. The latter was to be secured by giving the agency its own bank account in Bank Melli.
3. The agency should not be given executive powers. It should not become a government within a government. It should study, advise, plan, guide, co-ordinate, and supervise.
4. Execution of the plan should be a responsibility of the ministries or other regular government bodies, separate from the development agency.
5. The agency's internal organization was sketched only in very broad terms. In addition to a chief executive and supervisory boards, it would have a technical bureau (composed mainly of engineers) and subject divisions (e.g., industry, agriculture, transport). The agency was to be exempt from the government's normal rules and regulations on tendering, salaries, etc.; instead, it was to be given special regulations of its own.

Plan Organization was in fact organized exactly as outlined above, although at one point the Cabinet of the day tried to change the entire conception by sending to the *Majles* a bill that would have reduced the central authority to the kind of interagency "Supervising Board" that had been discussed a year or two earlier.[4] These Cabinet proposals would have meant "decentralization among ministries which have proven in the past not to have been able to carry out plans of even considerably smaller proportions, and a system of powerless supervision over inability, incompetence to act, lack of judgment and of responsibility, with no executive power to impose priority, speed, methods, determination and regularity."[5] What was essential was a central office "where responsibility and authority remain continuously dedicated to the prosecution of the Plan." The twenty-eight-year-old Shah and his twenty-four-year-old brother, Abdol Reza (recently graduated from the Harvard Business School and later appointed liaison officer between the Court and the Plan Organization), also favored the separate-organization approach.

With this close call the concept of an independent authority triumphed. The bill became law on February 15, 1949. The fight over the general nature of the central authority had been resolved in favor of a strong one, but it was still assumed that execution would be through the existing ministries and other agencies of government. The 1949 act does not mention the possibility that Plan Organization might execute projects directly on its own account. But the history of discussions at the time shows that such activities were foreseen in exceptional cases and with the proviso that as soon as PlanOrg-executed projects were completed they would be turned over to the appropriate ministry for operation and maintenance. In actual fact, Plan Organization reversed the intent of the law by carrying out directly the larger part of the Plan, spending only a minority of funds through the ministries. In addition, PlanOrg never developed effective powers of supervision over ministry execution of Plan projects.

[4] The *Majles* Committee charged with studying the bill was persuaded to restore the Planning Board's original concept of an independent authority. Mr. Thornburg, who at this time was recalled to Tehran by the American Embassy for the express purpose of counseling with key *Majles* and government officials during the critical *Majles* hearings, has said that it was pure administrative inexperience which explained why the proposal for an independent authority had been dropped.

[5] Mr. Thornburg's private diary.

Before carrying the story forward into the difficult start-up period and the subsequent disorganization during the Mossadegh years, it would be well to fix in mind PlanOrg's internal organization. At the center was a single executive, the Managing Director, appointed by the Shah for a three-year period upon nomination by the government. The Managing Director was responsible to a full-time seven-man High Council equivalent to the Board of Directors in a large Western corporation. The Act defined the powers of the High Council as follows:

> The High Council shall approve schemes, projects and budgets within the limits of the operational program approved by the Program Commission of the majles. The High Council is also entrusted with the preparation of regulations, approval of contracts and, in general, with the supervision of each and all the duties entrusted to the Planning Organization. (Art. 9)

The High Council was thus an important body, one before which all programs, budgets, and contracts had to be approved.

The six-man Board of Control, on the other hand, was much less important. It was charged mainly with the functions of auditing and financial reporting. Both the High Council and Board of Control consisted of paid, full-time appointees who were not supposed to hold any other employment.

The Managing Director was not a minister and, after his nomination by the ministers, was entirely independent of the Council of Ministers. Plan organization was connected to the government mainly by the obligation to secure approval of its operational program by the Plan Committee of the *Majles*. In practice this has not been used by the *Majles* to exercise detailed control, which has lain where it was supposed to lie, with the High Council.

Only one of the many departmental units created under the Managing Director was explicitly mentioned in the law: the Technical Bureau. The framers of the Plan put great importance on the Technical Bureau; it did in fact play an important role in the life of Plan Organization from the start. To some, this bureau was to "prepare all the schemes with the cooperation of experts from Ministries and Government agencies, for proposal to a high council" (The *Majles* Committee report of 1948). In practice the Bureau's function has been very different: most "schemes" have been prepared initially by independent consulting engineers or equipment suppliers. The role of the Technical Bureau has been to pass judgment on the technical soundness of all projects before they were sent forward to the High Council and to oversee the technical aspects of project execution. In 1948–49 no one foresaw the degree of Plan-Org's reliance on foreign consulting firms that later developed.

As the bill moved forward into the parliamentary stage, its chief promoters had begun looking around for ways of securing the technical services they realized PlanOrg would need as soon as the bill became law. It was the group's unofficial American adviser, Mr. Thornburg, who again suggested that a specific consortium of American engineering firms, originally formed to work in Japan, could be persuaded to interest itself in Iran and might be reconstituted for this purpose. Mr. Thornburg played a key role in reviving this group, known as Overseas Consultants, Incorporated (OCI). He even became the leader of OCI's twelve-man advisory group employed by Plan Organization during the first year of the latter's existence. Originally OCI was hired to conduct a thorough survey of Iranian investment requirements and the adequacy with which the proposed Seven Year Plan would meet them. The five-volume report which OCI submitted in August, 1949, after a little more than six months of work in Iran, was an excellent combination of specific program proposals and general counsel, including proposals for organizing the administration of the development effort and for the financing of the plan. The main significance of the OCI report is that it provided an authoritative basis for programing the financial allocations contained in the law. Since the report was submitted after the bill became law, it cannot be claimed that the allocations of the law were based on the OCI report. Much of the subsequent programing, however, *was* guided by the OCI recommendations.

Plan Organization's Start: The Eighteen Months from Its Establishment to the Assassination of General Razmara

The legal and structural basis of Plan Organization was about as satisfactory as its sponsors could have wished. Yet within a year most of the high hopes had been dashed and people were freely pronouncing Plan Organization a failure. And this despite PlanOrg's success in recruiting a sizable staff of the ablest engineers and administrators in Tehran. Why did PlanOrg get off to such a bad start? Why should its chief foreign architect, Mr. Thornburg, be driven to write, only nine months after PlanOrg's establishment, that the country's development hinged not on a special development agency insulated from unstable politics and a corrupt administration but on a frontal attack against these evils themselves?

PlanOrg's poor start stemmed from inexperience, inordinate pressures, and bad luck. Top management proved incapable of mounting a large-scale program with vigor, and the agency experienced a combination of blighting political pressures and internal dissensions that were much stronger than PlanOrg's structure had led people to expect. Outside events also took an unhelpful turn. PlanOrg was no sooner established than the country began a rapid and alarming political and economic deterioration, the result of bad harvests, mounting Communist activity, and weak political leadership.

The establishment of a new organization of 500–700 employees capable of performing effectively the sequence of tasks involved in starting several million dollars' worth of projects is a difficult task even for experienced executives. A certain amount of risk, confusion, delay, inefficiency, and disappointment would be inevitable anywhere. To minimize these negative forces requires a combination of executive leadership and good administration. The OCI advisory group members were the main source of ideas and "know-how" in the field of administrative procedures. They energetically provided top management with detailed recommendations on all the major areas of administration with which any large operating organization has to be concerned—budgeting, accounting, auditing, personnel, purchasing, project preparation and review, reporting on work in progress, and like matters. By and large, the OCI advisers did not have good luck in getting their recommendations accepted (in the first year, less than a third were acted on and less than a fifth put into practice). The difficulty was not due to straightforward disagreement between PlanOrg's top management and its foreign advisers on how things ought to be done. It was nothing as open and straightforward as differences of judgment and opinion. The difficulties stemmed from the subtler phenomenon of cultural rejection. For example, if attitudes toward the handling of money, the habit of thinking ahead to predict consequences of present actions or inactions, the effect of impersonal procedures on relationships among people (e.g., status relationships, or what it is proper to ask people to do, or implied judgments about motives or ability)— if the customary way these matters are handled in a society does not fit with the modes of behavior required by "modern" administrative practices, then the latter cannot be made to work very well. They simply touch too many exposed nerve ends. Indeed, as the early experience in PlanOrg showed, foreign advisers were not able even to get top management to regard many problems as requiring its attention. This whole area of internal administration has to be seen as an enormously difficult problem of cultural change and not merely one of technical assistance.

The above remarks are not meant in criticism of OCI's work within PlanOrg in 1949–50. Some of the sources of frustration experienced may seem outrageously simple to people who have not tried to operate in such an environment. For several months, for example, it proved impossible for OCI advisers to secure a list of projects that had been approved by the High Council. (Without such a list the advisers did not know what PlanOrg's program or financial obligations would be.) PlanOrg's top management did not get around to preparing any meaningful budget during the nine months of its first year (1949), nor did it prepare any for the next year in advance of its start.

Part of PlanOrg's ineffective start must be put down to some highly political appointments to its internal policy-making authority, the High Council. By May, 1950, less than a year after the Council's establishment, Mr. Thornburg could write in his private diary:

> Today (Plan Organization) is so nearly completely dominated or victimized by either political or private personal interests ... that ... there probably is little to choose between the Plan Organization and any government organization.
>
> ... It does not seem realistic to expect more than a slight relief from political interference by giving such an organization statutory autonomy. The front is simply too long and too thinly protected to withstand rapacious invaders. The real answer appears to be in raising the standard of government and political behavior to a level at which a constructive undertaking in the public interest ... can successfully discharge its mandate. . . . The time has come to concentrate all the constructive and forward-looking forces of the country, together with all the legal authority,

weight of public opinion and foreign collaboration which is available, on the eradication of the sources of public maladministration.

This is the same conclusion Millspaugh had come to in 1927. It is the same one the Iranian and foreign economic planners came to in 1961. But no one has yet found the path out of this swamp. It is plain enough that raising the standards of public administration is a top-priority goal in Iran, a precondition for so much else that needs doing. But as the painfully slow and ambiguous results of the massive Point IV and U.N. efforts in Iran have shown, public administration is not an easy field in which to score gains. There are too many bad habits and vested interests to challenge, too much cultural rejection to overcome if the initiative and techniques of reform come from foreigners. And if it be said that improved performance could be induced by shocking bureaucrats out of their evil ways and raising new standards through decisive intervention from the highest political authority, one can only report that there had been no effective intervention during the past two decades. The Shah, not generally regarded as personally corrupt, is nevertheless surrounded by corruption in which some of his closest associates and family members are widely believed to be involved. He has also felt sufficiently obligated to certain military and civilian officials who supported him during and after the Mossadegh episode so as to have been unable to resist their pleas for favors or insist on minimum standards of conduct.

But the Shah's weak stand on public corruption is not the main reason that it would have been unwise to abandon the "separate agency" concept of development in 1950. In point of fact it *was* possible (as later events were to show) to insulate PlanOrg in adequate degree from the muddy stream of Iranian politics and administration. The condition for doing so was to endow PlanOrg with non-political leadership and a forceful executive. PlanOrg was not to realize this condition until the Second Plan. Before then, people persuaded the Shah to gamble on an attempt at reform. The main thrust of the changes was a turning over of all executive functions to the ministries, the strengthening of PlanOrg's role as a central planning body, and a decentralization of both ministry and PlanOrg administration to build up stronger organizations in the provinces. The designation of General Ali Razmara as Prime Minister in July, 1950, was the launching of the campaign.

But eight months later Razmara was assassinated in a Tehran mosque. The government's ill-fated negotiations over a revision of the oil concession with the British had already begun, and nationalist emotions were rising. By April, 1951, Dr. Mossadegh had begun his three-year tenure as Prime Minister. When the oil industry was nationalized, oil production came to a halt, cutting off PlanOrg's main source of revenues. Inevitably, PlanOrg's program, which had never really gained momentum, stalled almost completely. It did not become active again until 1955.

Summary and Conclusions

It is worth summarizing a number of points about Plan Organization and its program as illustrated by its first two years of life. The points are important mainly because they concern issues that were still unresolved ten years later. The issues represent a mixture of "pure" problems involved in planning and technical assistance and the special difficulty of conducting such operations in Iran.

1. *The attempt to deal with the uncongenial political and administrative environment through structural solutions.* When Plan Organization was established, it had the choice of working independently or through the ministries. Its initial choices went heavily in favor of independent execution. This policy unwittingly furthered the "withering away of the state," since it is impossible to strengthen incompetent ministries by doing their work for them. Because many people were unhappy about this independent executive posture, whenever they had any hope of a reform movement improving government performance they tended to reopen the question of PlanOrg's basic structure and purpose. This meant that the basic organizational question was never settled in people's minds for any long period of time. The fact of PlanOrg's unimpressive initial performance strengthened doubts about the possibility of solving problems through structural formulas.

2. *Effect of key appointments, plus structure, on political independence.* The hopeful structural approach to development was negated by lack of sufficient care in filling key positions with per-

sonalities free of political motivations and obligations. This weakness applied more to the High Council than to PlanOrg's executive branch. As a result PlanOrg was unable to establish the position of independence from the traditional Iranian influences which its structure was intended to assure.

3. *Inability to generate momentum.* The literature of planning and development is so preoccupied with the refined choice of investment alternatives that it has neglected the question of whether or not development authorities have the elementary capacity for making any expenditures at all. The slow start made by PlanOrg at a time when public expectations were high, plus the history of the following decade, makes the question of activity—of the crude overall volume of expenditures—as important as the investment choices they represent. Obviously, one would not excuse a high volume of "nonsense" expenditures on grounds of sheer magnitude. But PlanOrg deserves much more credit than it usually gets just for generating (after 1956) a high volume of activity along reasonably sensible lines. Whether or not a better "investment mix" could have been chosen is relatively unimportant. A reasonably good expenditure is better than a perfect nonexpenditure.

4. *The importance of internal management procedures in a development agency.* PlanOrg did not begin with a rapid, routine acceptance of those internal managerial procedures and controls which are assumed to be essential in Western business and government operations. Foreign advisers strongly counseled top management to pay more attention to such matters if it wished to avoid trouble. While this aspect of PlanOrg's activity carried less of a penalty in the early days than it did later, the early period does reflect the cultural rejection of those rational Western-developed managerial procedures typically sponsored by foreign advisers and expected by foreign lenders.

5. *The role of foreigners.* Although most of the comments on the role of foreigners in PlanOrg will be based on later experience, the history of the twelve-man OCI advisory team reflects the cultural tension and functional ambiguities *inherent* in such operations. Frustrations and annoyances are not occasional individual reactions; they are constant and common to all individuals, on both sides. These frictions are tolerated by the "advisees" only because they recognize certain functional imperatives, certain things that

have to be done on which foreigners can help, or which they may actually perform even though they are supposed to be only advisers.

6. *Subsidiary structural issues.* The desire for independence from government politics and bureaucracy was anything but a clean, clear choice. Once PlanOrg was given the choice between executing projects alone or through the ministries, its initial choices ran heavily to independent execution. But independent execution obviously meant foregoing an opportunity to involve ministries in new functions and responsibilities and to insist on new ministerial practices as a condition for spending Plan funds. A Plan which had as one of its intended objectives the building up of ministerial competence did not, either in its first years or later, adopt practices which honored this objective. On the contrary, the practices adopted did much to frustrate this objective. Nevertheless, it is not clear that PlanOrg's behavior was incorrect. Failure of PlanOrg to use its "banker's leverage" to enlarge ministry competence was probably an unavoidable price of getting things done.

7. *Regional planning.* The OCI Report urged the establishment of regional offices for determining regional investment needs and for decentralized control over execution. Nothing was done on this problem until the Razmara government assumed office in July, 1950. The attempt at decentralization was too short-lived to achieve any significant results. Regional planning, and the regional distribution of investment, remained important and difficult issues in framing the Third Plan. The basic difficulty is the lack of any provincial decision-making bodies that could assume a planning function, plus central government reluctance to encourage the growth of any such bodies.

8. *Surveys and studies.* Surveys are general studies to develop lists of candidate projects, to suggest choices among them, and to identify order-of-magnitude project costs. Studies are more detailed examinations of individual projects to subject them to careful technical scrutiny and to economic justification. Plan Organization was established after two highly competent and useful general surveys had been conducted by foreign engineering firms. But once the First Plan had started, PlanOrg officials were reluctant to spend money for individual project studies. They felt they could select projects without the necessity for costly studies. Later, PlanOrg came to rely heavily on foreign consulting firms to conduct feasi-

bility studies. Because these were of variable quality and disinterestedness, PlanOrg had to develop its own capacity for critical evaluation of the expert advice it was getting from outside sources.

9. *Comprehensive planning.* Neither the First nor the Second Seven Year Plan was concerned with development objectives covering the entire economy. The first two Plans were limited to a particular set of government-executed projects that added up to something much less than the government's total investment activity. Although minor amounts of PlanOrg funds were used to encourage and finance private investment, the shift from partial to comprehensive planning was not seriously discussed until 1959, when a review of the country's development program revealed an alarming amount of uncontrolled government investment in the ministries, plus a significant amount of private investment. The call for "comprehensive planning" in the 1959 *Program Review* (see below, p. 41) repeated, without its authors' knowing it, a similar plea made a decade earlier by Mr. Thornburg.

10. *Financial planning.* The shortcomings of the Iranian fiscal system were not a serious embarrassment to PlanOrg during its first two years of life, mainly because it had not mounted a program calling for a heavy, steady stream of payments. But enough problems were visible in the government at large for Mr. Thornburg to want some additional advisers to help the government (not PlanOrg) put its financial house in order. Similarly, the problem of the government's over-all financial planning proved a major difficulty during the second half of the Second Plan.

11. *The importance of enlisting the Shah's understanding and backing.* The important moves in Iranian politics normally emanate from the Shah, directly or indirectly. When major crises arise in PlanOrg that have important political implications, the final arbiter is the Shah. The experience of the first two years, as later, showed clearly the importance of briefing the Shah on important development issues. Since the occasions for briefings normally grew out of crises that had to be handled diplomatically, the approach to His Majesty was through private audiences by influential people. In general, the main problem of PlanOrg in its relation to "top management" (i.e., to His Majesty) was not that he interfered too much in secondary problems but that he did not support planning strongly enough when intervention was necessary.

This chapter has explained the conception of the development effort that underlay the First and Second Seven Year Plans. The essence of the approach was a development program carried forward by a special agency authorized to execute projects directly if in its judgment this seemed more effective than working through the regular ministries. The Plan consisted of spending-allocations for Plan Organization; it said nothing about specific goals for the country, about the investment or development activities of other branches of the government, or about the private sector. The Plan's spending-allocations represented a particular set of projects (many of them not fully worked out before the Plan started) that commended themselves to the engineers who were largely responsible for suggesting them and to the administrators and politicians who approved them. To finance this program most of the oil revenues were earmarked by law for PlanOrg's exclusive use. From every point of view, then, the first two plans were limited to special programs of government investment; they were not comprehensive development plans embracing the whole economy. The tactical reasons for taking this independent approach have been explained.

By the late 1950's responsibility for planning strategy had passed into the hands of a new set of people, and new problems occupied the stage. When the time came to prepare the Third Plan, the underlying philosophy of the First and Second Plans was abandoned and a major attempt was launched to introduce comprehensive economic planning. The following chapter recounts why this change took place and what success it had.

CHAPTER III

 From a Development Program to
Comprehensive Planning

The Boom of the Late 1950's

The four-year crisis over oil nationalization, with its attendant political repercussions, had brought the first Seven Year Plan to a standstill almost before its start. After the Shah's restoration in 1953 and the resumption of oil production late in 1954, it was decided to terminate the uncompleted First Plan and to start again with a second Seven Year Plan, to begin in September, 1955. Mr. A. H. Ebtehaj was appointed Managing Director of Plan Organization. It was Ebtehaj who had played a key role in starting Iran on the road to planning right after the war.

During the four years of Mr. Ebtehaj's leadership, Iran's development effort achieved a success never won before or since. Plan Organization itself succeeded in mounting a high level of development expenditures. Rather unexpectedly, the rest of the government also embarked on an unprecedentedly high level of expenditures. These two sources of high government spending, combined with liberal bank credit and easy access to foreign exchange, quickly generated a major boom in private investment, mainly in urban housing and industry, both heavily concentrated in Tehran. The boom also generated excesses that took the form of rising prices and falling exchange reserves. When the government finally ran out of foreign exchange in 1961 and needed help it had to take the IMF's (International Monetary Fund) standard medicine—a Stabilization Program that involved carefully spelled out fiscal and monetary restraints. It was stiff medicine: the boom was followed by a recession of at least equal depth and duration (1961–64).

In 1957–58 Mr. Ebtehaj—assisted by the World Bank, Harvard University, and the Ford Foundation—was able to establish a competent group of economic analysts within the Plan Organization.

The group consisted of young, well-trained Iranians, strongly supported by an international team of foreign advisers. In 1958 the first task of the new Economic Bureau was a thorough review of PlanOrg's program, set against the wider needs of the economy, short-term and long-term. This program review took a year to complete. Its published report[1] (the 1960 *Program Review*) played an important part in broadening the conception of Iran's development effort. Two of the more important conclusions were (1) that a sound development effort would require much closer co-operation among key government agencies and (2) that future planning should be comprehensive and not partial. When the Shah directed the Economic Bureau to prepare the Third Plan, he made clear that the horizon should no longer be limited to a PlanOrg program alone but should embrace the whole economy, i.e., all government development activities plus activity in the private sector. Thus the stresses and strains produced by three economies each of which had begun to gallop—the development plan, the rest of the government, and the private sector—were proving an unmanageable troika. Economic events were pushing the executors of the plan into a posture of political co-operation and control which its architects had considered unworkable.

The Economic Bureau devoted nearly three years (1960–62) to erecting the framework of a comprehensive development plan. The sectoral chapters of this book report how this work was done and the development strategies and tactics used. The work went forward in a steadily deteriorating political and economic climate. In September, 1962, when the Third Plan began, it was, unfortunately, still in a state of massive unreadiness: in the unraveling atmosphere of 1960–62 few of the necessary surveys and project design studies had been completed. Even if the Plan had been ready there was every reason to doubt that it could be implemented as intended, given the political facts of life sketched in Chapter I. This is an *ex post* comment; at the time the decision in favor of comprehensive planning was made, and while the effort was in hand, those involved

[1] *Review of the Second Seven Year Plan Program of Iran,* a publication of the Division of Economic Affairs (originally the Economic Bureau) of Plan Organization, March 10, 1960, 120 pages plus Appendix (hereafter called the *Program Review;* without italics or capitals the phrase refers to the exercise, not the publication).

41

in the task lived on the hope that the political situation, for all its weakness, could support an effort that would at least be worth the effort. So it is worth reviewing why the attempt was made. The findings of the 1959 program review provide the starting point.

The Main Findings of the Program Review

The program review brought into focus a number of problems that quickly came to engage the serious attention of the few Iranian authorities interested in giving such attention to economic problems. Its findings were also of great interest to key external agencies, notably the World Bank, the International Monetary Fund, and foreign embassies. The problems uncovered reflected a woeful lack of control over the main economic forces at work in the country. PlanOrg was not responsible for any of these forces except its own program. Nevertheless, the review clearly implied that the existing conception and organizational arrangements for carrying forward the development effort were too narrow and should be changed.

The symptoms of trouble were classic. Government investment activity outside the approved Plan had risen to unexpectedly high levels, foreboding trouble with public finance. It was known that much of this non-Plan investment was being financed by foreign debt but no one knew how much was owed or to whom. When the program review succeeded in drawing up a list of these debts it became clear that much of the uncontrolled borrowing consisted of medium-term suppliers' credits that would require heavily bunched debt repayments over the next few years. Another shadow came from the ordinary budget: it had grown much faster than the government's willingness to finance it by taxation. Instead, oil revenues intended for Plan Organization were diverted to the current budget. (For two years the Ministry of Finance successfully resisted an effort to persuade it to undertake systematic financial planning.) PlanOrg's loss of oil revenues came at a time when the cost of its own rather open-ended program threatened to spill over the agreed spending limit by about one-third. In the private sector, a fast-growing banking system had readily acceded to demands for credit that grew faster than the economy could absorb without putting pressure on prices. Inflation never became serious but constantly threatened to become so. A less ambiguous symptom appeared in 1958: the foreign exchange reserves began to fall.

In the face of these conditions it was inevitable that the International Monetary Fund should insist that Iran adopt a Stabilization Program if it wanted stand-by help from the Fund. The World Bank supported the move because it was not enthusiastic about lending to Iran under the fiscal and monetary conditions it saw developing in the late 1950's.

When the PlanOrg economists had finished taking the economy's pulse they left the monetary situation to the central bank and the IMF and turned their energies on two problems central to their next major task, the preparation of the Third Plan. These two problems were the development of comprehensive planning and the introduction of some measure of financial planning into the government's fiscal management. Apart from its role in ordinary budgeting, financial planning was needed to estimate the amount and sources of funds likely to be available to the government during the Third Plan for financing both the Plan and the ordinary budget.

As noted, one of the fiscal problems that had developed during the Second Plan was the unexpectedly rapid growth in the ordinary budget without an equal growth in the means of financing it. Although much of this growth was undisciplined and excessive, the planners recognized that a national development program would require a fairly rapid increase in the government's current expenditures, e.g., in agricultural services, in education, in public health, in road maintenance, and on through a long list of government services whose expansion could be regarded as necessary parts of a development program. The idea became accepted that expansion of the government's development services should be financed from Plan funds, with the ordinary budget carrying only the level of expense needed to maintain the level of activity in existence at the start of the Plan. Thus 109 government agencies were classified as either "development" or "nondevelopment" agencies, or agencies with self-balancing accounts. The government's ordinary budget, prepared and administered in the Ministry of Finance, would be responsible for all expenditures of the fifty-two nondevelopment agencies and for that portion of expenditures by the thirty-five development agencies represented by their end-of-Second-Plan expenditures. The expansion of development agencies would be financed from Plan funds by deducting them from PlanOrg's share of the oil revenues and transferring them to the Ministry of Finance for disbursement through normal procedures.

The practical design of these financial and budgetary proposals required a new and quite different relationship between Plan Organization and the Ministry of Finance. The working out of this relationship was the most difficult organizational problem of the Third Plan. Apart from the general need to improve the government's financial projections and budgeting, there was a specific need to establish much tighter links among economic planning, long-range financial planning, and annual budgeting if there was to be any hope of making or carrying out a comprehensive Plan. Why this was not a straightforward administrative matter is partly explained by Iran's budgetary tradition.

Iran's Budgetary Tradition

Ever since the first Millspaugh mission in the early 1920's Iranian budgeting has been conducted by the Ministry of Finance. Its traditions are purely financial: the main purpose has been to control the over-all volume of expenditures to prevent the government from running out of money. It has not been used to justify programs or to set priorities. The Ministry has been effective in realizing its limited money-control objectives and the country has built up a fairly conservative fiscal tradition. However, this tradition has not included the development of careful planning, selection, and costing of activities in the spending agencies. The main tradition has been simply, "Thou Shalt Not Spend." Indeed, right down to the 1950's it was customary at each year-end to reward Finance Ministry officials with bonuses that varied inversely with the amount of money that had been turned over to the spending ministries! Needless to say, this system contributed to the spread of corruption and to the creation of semi-autonomous organizations (bongahs) that stood outside the regular budgetary process.

Since the start of the U.S. Point IV program in 1952, with its heavy emphasis on improving the government's administrative and financial competence, much effort has gone into the improvement of budget work. Point IV has tried to help by providing technical assistance at both ends, the Ministry of Finance and some of the key ministries. While there has probably been progress, it has been incredibly slow and modest. By 1960, the Ministry of Finance had shown so little interest, understanding, and competence in proper budgeting or financial planning that American advisers and several Iranians had come to believe that these functions should be transferred to a new specialized agency in the Prime Minister's office. Many patient and knowledgeable people had simply given up on the Ministry of Finance as a budgeting authority, since there was no one in the Ministry who really understood the task and who was willing to take the tough positions vis-à-vis the spending ministries that effective budgeting always requires. Ministry officials were satisfied with issuing an annual budget call, adding up the ministries' summary claims, and presenting the total to the government. The traditional attitude in the Ministry of Finance has been that its job stops with raising money; it is up to "the government" to decide how to spend it. The Ministers of Finance never conceived of their Ministry as that part of the government charged with preparing the Cabinet's spending proposals for presentation to the *Majles.*

The budget discussed up to now has, of course, referred to the central government's ordinary budget, a budget in which no distinction has been made between operating and capital expenditures. The "development budget" (the Plan Organization budget) was not part of the national budget. Since Plan Organization was financed outside the regular government's normal revenues and was free of many normal government regulations, it developed its own budgeting procedures. Between 1957 and 1960 Plan Organization's Budget Bureau, with some excellent personnel and strong help from foreign advisers, was able to establish some degree of budgetary planning within Plan Organization itself. An annual budget was prepared and published, showing proposed expenditures each quarter by individual projects. The budget emerged from rudimentary discussions with Plan Organization's spending offices after study of responses to an internal "budget call" issued by the Budget Bureau. The Finance Division was not supposed to authorize disbursements except for projects that were an approved part of the budget.

There were two main problems in making Plan Organization's budget process an effective control, even in that island of enlightenment and modernity. One was to see that the budget, once made up, was in fact respected, that it served its intended purpose as a control over programs and spending. The other problem was to achieve the cash-flow necessary to see that money was available when the budget said it would be needed. For various reasons the Economic Bureau took upon itself the task of policing PlanOrg's budget. It did so by establishing a formal committee to try to prevent personally inspired changes in the program and by sporadically investigating the cash-flow problem when it had to know what the cash outlook was in order to judge what level of expenditures could be financed and what foreign loans should be sought.

The reduction of Plan Organization's share of the oil revenues and the expansion of its program created cash shortages no one had expected. Initially these shortages were covered by short-term accommodations from Bank Melli and long-term foreign loans. But these borrowings never caught up with PlanOrg's need for cash during the last three and one-half years of the Second Plan. Consequently the agency lived on a hand-to-mouth basis. It was this chronic cash shortage that led an IMF official to write, in the spring of 1961, that "to all intents and purposes Plan Organization is bankrupt."

The continual shortage of cash naturally affected the execution and planning of projects. PlanOrg projects were being carried out by many different types of agencies—foreign contractors, domestic contractors, ministries, welfare organizations, independent *bongahs,* and so on. Some of these had other funds that could be shifted around while the agencies waited for payments from PlanOrg. Some could borrow from domestic banks, some from foreign banks. Some could get advances from the Ministry of Finance. Projects that had none of these alternatives never got started or just ground to a halt. It was often difficult to explain to people why they could not be paid when they knew that "there was money in the budget." Alas, there is never money in budgets.

It is doubtful if anything in Iran was quite so disruptive of programs and so demoralizing to people as the persistent absence of cash that was supposed to be available in certain amounts at certain times. Uncertainty over future cash availability was a major reason why so few surveys and studies for the Third Plan were undertaken before the Plan began. While Plan Organization could have done more than it did to protect its cash position, the problem stemmed primarily from poor financial management of the government's over-all revenues. This shortcoming affected countless government agencies and their programs. The causes of this financial mismanagement were political and cultural, and ran much deeper than anything technical assistance could remedy. A major tactical problem in designing the Third Plan was how to organize a budgeting operation that could overcome the weakness of the government's financial performance.

There were three possibilities. One was to leave things as they were, with the ministries submitting their capital budgets to Plan Organization and their ordinary budgets to the Ministry of Finance. The second was to set up a new Budget Bureau in the Prime Minister's office—in effect, to take the budget function away from the "hopeless" Ministry of Finance and make a fresh start (with appropriate technical assistance). The third alternative was to set up a new joint budget committee on which both PlanOrg and the Ministry of Finance would be represented (this was the "if-you-can't-beat-'em, join-'em" solution). In more than a year of staring at these choices and endless internal discussions the planners could make no clear decision. They were torn between (1) wanting to choose an alternative that would turn over certain functions to the government and thus move the planning agency closer to the rest of the government and (2) wanting to retain control to assure a minimum competence in the budget process. The planners finally recommended to the government that Plan Organization be given authority over a new instrument of control, an annual Development Budget. It would work thus: the *Majles* would enact a basic five-year appropriation at the time of approving the over-all Plan. Specific programs and projects would be proposed to PlanOrg by the executive ministries and *bongahs* and approved proposals would be formulated in project agreements between PlanOrg and the sponsoring agency. There would then be an annual Development Budget prepared by PlanOrg on the basis of annual spending estimates submitted by the executing agencies. After the Development Budget had been approved by the government it would be incorporated, in summary form only, in the government's over-all budget. Neither the Ministry of Finance nor Parliament would have power to review the Development Budget in detail. PlanOrg would retain control over disbursement of development funds to the executing agencies.

In a social and political milieu where the formal intentions of plans and budgets are subject to erosion or evasion there seemed good reason to leave control over development expenditures in the institution which had the greatest stake in the progress of the development effort, which had some of the best government personnel, and which was most open to the help and pressure of foreign influences, personal and institutional. The possibility that reasonable budgetary procedures might be developed outside Plan Organization in time to handle Third Plan expenditures was too unlikely to justify doing anything else.

The Main Features of the Third Plan Law

The Third Plan Law adopted the substance of the 1961 recommendations on budgetary arrangements, although, in the Iranian tradition, it left certain key points vague and open. The Third Plan was described simply as a government spending program, financed by the earmarking of 140 billion rials of oil revenues.[2]

[2] The Third Plan Law established the legal basis of the Third Plan on the same limited basis as the Second Plan: the law says nothing about economic objectives for the country, makes no mention of economic policies, and does not refer to the 1,500 pages of documents called the "Plan Frame" and regarded by the planners as the Third Plan. Thus there is no publication which one can refer to as the Third Plan; there is only a fifteen-page law. The 1,500 pages of the Plan Frame (mimeographed and distributed in English and Farsi) were intended as an outline or first draft of the kind of comprehensive Plan document familiar in Pakistan and India. The final document never got written, because many of the details never got worked out and nobody much cared whether or not a finished document appeared.

The Third Plan Decree (which became the law after *Majles* approval) was approved by the Council of Ministers only two weeks before the Plan began. The sectoral spending targets for the 140 billion rials which the Cabinet thought of as "the Plan" were not ready at the time the decree was approved: Plan Organization was given two months to prepare these targets, "with the approval of Ministries and other Government institutions," for submission to the government and incorporation in the Law.

The Third Plan did not greatly change Plan Organization's form. The main substantive change was the clear insistence in the Law that all projects should be executed by the ministries, under PlanOrg regulations and accounting controls. All bodies created by PlanOrg in the course of executing the Second Plan were directed to be turned over to appropriate ministries.

In 1965, midway through the Third Plan, spending was way below targets. A more rational, more politically acceptable relationship between PlanOrg and the rest of the government went hand in hand with a disappointing economic performance.

48

These 140 billion rials were broken down into annual expenditures. The annual expenditures were to be controlled by an annual development budget drawn up by Plan Organization for approval by a new outside authority, the High Plan Council. The annual development budget would finance the capital cost of approved development projects plus an unspecified portion of the growth in the ordinary budgets of the "development ministries."

The government's ordinary budget was to be drawn up, as before, by the Ministry of Finance, which was directed to "keep the Plan Organization informed." Government agencies were forbidden to "invest capital" without the consent of the High Plan Council. However, "investment" was defined as the expenditure of funds for the purposes spelled out in the Plan. The definition seemed to leave ministries free to make investments in fields not covered by the Plan, provided only that they could get the funds. A special article forbade government agencies from contracting any kind of foreign loans (including suppliers' credits) unless they first received the joint permission of the Ministry of Finance and Plan Organization. (A special arrangement acknowledged the virtual independence of the National Iranian Oil Company from the normal planning arrangements: they regarded "planning" as a game in which they could only lose; so they declined to play.)

On a straightforward reading, the Third Plan Law seemed to provide greater co-ordination between the country's development and nondevelopment expenditures than existed under the Second Plan. It appeared to settle the respective budgetary functions of Plan Organization, the Ministry of Finance, and the NIOC. It seemed to assure adequate financing for the Plan by setting aside increasing proportions of the (increasing) oil revenues each year and by putting a ceiling of $7\frac{1}{2}$ per cent on the annual increase in the government's nondevelopment expenditures.

In Iran, however, law is weaker than personalities. Much weaker. One cannot expect that the ship of state, once set on course, will hold to it. Two weeks after the Council of Ministers approved the Third Plan at 140 billion rials, the Prime Minister announced that the Plan was being scaled down by about one-third. A year and a half later, in April, 1964, a new Prime Minister announced that the Plan was being increased to nearly 200 billion rials. He also announced an intention to transfer to Plan Organization the entire budgetary function of the Ministry of Finance. The transfer was subsequently made. All one could say is that a year and a half after the Third Plan had begun it was suffering from symptoms familiar in Iranian politics. For a few years, under the force of Mr. Ebtehaj's personality, Plan Organization and the development effort had been partially insulated from these traditional influences. But if a strong Managing Director had proved an economic success he had failed politically. After his removal Plan Organization had been brought closer to the mainstream of the country's political life— at considerable cost to the development effort.

One cannot help wondering whether, in Iran, the game of planning is worth the candle. Two Danish authors who were members of the Harvard Advisory Group had as much difficulty as others do in answering this question. Their net judgment is that, while the attempt to launch a comprehensive plan would undoubtedly fail, the drawing up of the Plan affected, irreversibly, the thinking of many people in government. They also hoped that much of the technical assistance work of the past decade in the field of public administration would produce lasting results. Witness this paragraph:

It should be noted [the advisers wrote] that the situation has improved remarkably over the recent years—perhaps not so much in executing a government policy as in establishing some prerequisites for executing a government policy at all. The income tax administration is bad, but not as bad as it was five years ago. A number of improvements have been introduced in the field of budgetary administration, which, when considered together, give promise of the possibility of developing an effective budget system. Efforts have been made to improve the accounting system of the government's industrial and commercial enterprises with a view to making it possible to prepare operating statements.... The accounting procedures of the ministries are being gradually improved. These and many other administrative and managerial improvements, which take place quite inconspicuously (and with the assistance of United Nations, United States, and other foreign advisors), do not contribute very much to a planned economic development in the short run but will undoubtedly—*if continued*—have a substantial impact over a five- or ten-year period.[3] [Italics added.]

[3] P. Bjørn Olsen and P. Nørregaard Rasmussen, "An Attempt at Planning in a Traditional State: Iran," *Planning Economic Development*, ed. Everett E. Hagen (Homewood, Ill., 1963), p. 249.

My own view is not as hopeful, precisely because my reading of the Iranian political system suggests that the kinds of gains cited by Olsen and Rasmussen are *not* likely to be continued. On the contrary, such "gains" are more likely to prove temporary as the procedures underlying them get captured "by the dominant forces of the system," to use a phrase from one of the most perceptive analysts of public administration in developing countries.[4]

The central question in administrative reform is what pressures are most likely to alter the traditional forces that still dominate the system. They may flow, in varying proportions, from the rapid spread of education at all levels; from the explosion of communications and transport; from technical assistance; from the large number of foreigners working in the country; from a radical shift in the sources of political power; or from the growth of a middle class made up of commercial, industrial, and professional people. Most of these modernizing forces are strong today. So far they have not affected significantly the traditional conduct of politics. Does traditional behavior draw some mysterious strength from history that makes it highly resistant to the forces that should be modifying it, or can we assume, on grounds of faith and history elsewhere, that the new forces are gradually and imperceptibly transforming the traditional society in ways that will eventually support instead of frustrate economic planning? The latter possibility—the caterpillar-and-the-butterfly model of modern Iran—is a comforting and hopeful view because it assumes that almost any modern activity, from educating more Iranians overseas to the preparation of balance sheets for government companies, will assist the transformation of attitudes and mores necessary for Iran to become a modern society. This image may be correct, but it draws its strength from faith and from the history of other cultures, not from Iran itself. Iran's own history is far more ambiguous. The last two or three decades suggest that instead of creating the needed transformation the chemistry of progress in Iran may lack some vital catalyst—that inside the chrysalis the caterpillar is not only still alive but may not be turning into anything new. Whichever view is correct, Iran today is no more ready to support comprehensive economic planning than it was ready to support an independent development program.

[4] Fred W. Riggs. See his article, "Prismatic Society and Financial Administration," *Administrative Science Quarterly*, June, 1960, pp. 1–46.

Conclusion

It would be a mistake to draw purely cynical conclusions from the apparent failure of both a "nonpolitical" and a "political" Plan Organization, i.e., of partial and then of comprehensive planning. Failure is a relative term. Both solutions have probably been better than the absence of any kind of organized development effort. At minimum, a country that receives as much money from oil revenues as from all other taxes combined has to have some kind of trustee arrangement for using these funds. Even arrangements that work very imperfectly are probably better than the alternative of turning over the oil revenues to the Ministry of Finance for distribution through the ordinary budget.

It would be better, of course, if Iranian politics permitted the country to have an effective, sustained development program on either the partial and independent pattern of the Second Plan or the comprehensive and co-ordinated pattern intended by the Third. The laws of Iranian politics make it unlikely that either approach will lead to the desired result. At present there is no solution that will "make planning work." The only solution (short of restructuring the political behavior) is for people to adjust downward their expectations of tidiness, rationality, and efficiency and to hope that the spending of the oil revenues will somehow produce many of the benefits that some other countries win from a more effective use of less abundant resources. In short, Iran must live with the myth of a planning effort that does not work and the beneficent reality of an Unseen Hand.

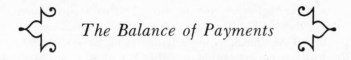

CHAPTER IV

The Balance of Payments

Most developing countries have severe problems with the availability of foreign exchange and the management of their balance of payments. Iran is no exception. But its difficulties are not the usual ones. In particular, shortages of foreign exchange do not constitute a limitation to the size of the development effort.

The typical pressures which development generates on the balance of payments are these. Stepped-up private and public investment raises the demand for imported capital goods and for raw materials. Rising consumer incomes create intensified demand for imported consumer goods. Both sources of increased spending may raise home demand for goods ordinarily exported. The net result of these forces is a high income-elasticity of demand for imports and a persistent trade deficit that can be financed only if capital inflows are available, i.e., grants or loans from abroad. The trick of containing these developments within manageable, orderly limits is one Iran has still to learn. Fortunately the bounty of its exchange earnings gives Iran room for maneuver, and a capacity for recovery from crises, that is rare. Since it is also rare to find an Iranian Government willing to heed the warnings of its few able economists, most of the maneuvering is curative, not preventive. In short, Iran does periodically experience foreign exchange shortages; but these take the form of short-term crises that should not have occurred.

Iran's Normal Trade Deficit and Its Financing

As soon as the development program began to gather momentum in 1956, imports expanded rapidly, more rapidly than the country's capacity to pay for them. By late 1960 the country was in serious trouble and painful corrective measures had to be introduced. To understand these difficulties, one must first get a feeling for some of the normal relationships underlying Iran's foreign trade. These relationships are clearly visible in Table 1, a simplified presentation of Iran's balance of payments for eight years following Mossadegh's fall. At that time Iran had completely run out of any foreign exchange reserves,[1] had imposed the tightest possible controls so as to hold imports to the country's minimum level of needs, and had exerted itself to expand exports so as to minimize the trade deficit. Historically, it is normal for Iran to run a trade deficit (except in years of recession, such as 1961–64). Ever since World War I this deficit has been financed by oil revenues. But late in 1950 these ceased for nearly four years. So the picture given at the start of Table 1 is one where Iran is "all even," with the trade balance as favorable as could have been expected and no foreign exchange reserves. During the succeeding years, what happened?

A. *Imports* (i.e., ordinary nongovernment commercial imports) expanded rapidly, without a break, though the rate of expansion naturally slowed down. By the middle of the Second Plan (1959) the level of imports was roughly double what it had been at the start of the Plan three years earlier.

B. *Exports* stagnated, bumping along without any significant change in over-all value. In Iran, oil is traditionally not treated as an export, a term conventionally reserved for the non-oil items. The reason is that Iran has never received direct foreign exchange

[1] "Relations with Great Britain had been broken in October of 1952. After January 1951, no serious efforts were made to resolve the oil question, and the situation had deteriorated to the extent that the Senate was disbanded and the majority of the Majlis resigned. The dollar was selling on the black market in Tehran for Rls. 132 although the official rate was 32.5. Bank Melli was without foreign exchange for legitimate transactions. The confidence of the people of Iran in their government and banking system was at a low point. Rial notes had disappeared in such numbers, because hoarding was so widespread, that the Bank could not cash government salary checks. Import and export trade was at a standstill, and even government factories were idle part of the time for want of spare parts that had to be purchased abroad. Government employees had not been paid for several weeks in Tehran and for several months in the provinces" (quoted from a January, 1955, U.S. Government dispatch in Audit Report No. 825, "Counterpart Fund Withdrawals through March 31, 1958, for Budgetary Support in Iran," June 7, 1958, p. 1).

TABLE 1
Iran's Balance of Payments for Eight Years, Beginning in 1954ᵃ

	1954	1955	1956	1957	1958	1959	1960	1961ᵇ
					(million $)			
A. Imports (nongovt.)	138.2	206.7	229.6	280.2	370.7	440.5	473.7	484.1
B. Exports (non-oil)	108.3	82.1	89.6	98.4	86.3	96.8	95.7	106.0
Trade deficit	29.9	124.6	140.0	181.8	284.4	343.7	378.0	378.1
C. Other foreign exchange payments (excluding debt service)								
1. Plan Organization	–	30.3	34.0	53.1	63.3	59.5	52.9	47.2
2. Net services	5.4	6.9	18.1	12.0	3.7	10.3	7.1	7.7
3. National Iranian Oil Co.	2.1	6.1	18.0	19.3	21.1	20.1	19.5	15.7
Subtotal	7.5	43.3	70.1	84.4	88.1	89.9	79.5	70.6
D. Trade deficit plus other nondebt payments	37.4	167.9	210.1	266.2	372.5	433.6	457.5	448.7
E. Oil earnings								
1. Earned tax revenues	18.5	79.8	140.2ᶜ	207.8ᶜ	265.8ᵈ	244.9	258.7	285.0
2. Rial purchases by foreign companies	11.9	46.7	40.5	48.2	74.2	74.2	76.8	70.7
Total foreign exchange from oil	30.4	126.5	180.7	256.0	340.0	319.1	335.5	355.7
F. Foreign exchange deficit from earnings $(D - E)$	7.0	41.4	29.4	10.2	32.5	114.5	122.0	93.0
G. Debt repayments (govt. loans only)	–	8.8	3.2	–	77.2	39.8	53.3	29.6
H. "Earned" exchange deficit plus debt repayments $(F + G)$	7.0	50.2	32.6	10.2	109.7	154.3	175.3	132.6
I. Foreign aid and loans	50.0	71.8	86.8	116.5	57.2	80.0	91.8	76.2
J. Increase (− decrease) in reserves	43.0	21.6	54.2	106.3	−52.5	−74.3	−83.5	−66.4
Four-year totals			225.1				−276.7	
Eight-year net change					−51.6ᵉ			

ᵃ Excludes military imports, loans to the Ministry of Defense, and U.S. military aid. Year begins March 21.
ᵇ Estimated.
ᶜ Includes small exports by NIOC.
ᵈ Includes $25 million bonus for concession granted to Pan American Oil Co.
ᵉ Financed by borrowing from IMF, increases in short-term indebtedness, and exporting gold.
Sources: Rearrangement of data from various official authorities.

payment for each ton of oil exported. It receives only a royalty payment from the foreign concerns which produce and export the oil, plus certain additional foreign currencies arising out of the oil companies' need to purchase rials to meet their expenditures in Iran.

The excess of imports over exports is the Trade Deficit. The dramatic increase in this deficit between 1954–55 and 1959–60 is clear from the table.

The Trade Deficit, however, did not reflect all the foreign payments Iran had to make. There were substantial additional payments, shown under C. Much the largest were the import requirements of the Plan Organization in carrying on the development effort. These amounted to 10–15 per cent of total private imports. Second largest of these "other" foreign payments were those made by the National Iranian Oil Company, which carries on a heavy investment program of its own. Finally, a fairly modest amount of foreign payments must be made for Iranian embassies abroad, study abroad, interest on official loans, hiring of foreign technicians, banking and insurance premiums, and similar miscellaneous nontangible items. The total of all these "other" foreign exchange payments is almost as great as the country's annual earnings from exports. If we add these "other" requirements to the Trade Deficit we arrive at line D, representing a larger Net Payments Deficit (i.e., net of debt repayments). Does the oil industry earn enough foreign exchange to cover this Net Payments Deficit? Line E shows how much foreign exchange has been generated by the oil industry. This is broken down into the two main sources of foreign exchange generated by this industry: (1) the oil royalties, much the larger share; and (2) rial purchases, which in 1956–60 were bringing in 75 per cent as much exchange as the country's total exports (these were years of exceptionally heavy investment in new facilities by the Consortium). Alternatively, one can say that the Consortium's rial purchases were then adding 20–35 per cent extra foreign exchange on top of the oil royalties.

Line E shows that in no year between 1953 and 1961 did the oil industry earn enough foreign exchange to cover the Net Payments Deficit. The result is line F (D minus E), which represents the net deficit resulting from all economic activities involving foreign exchange during the year in question. This figure excludes debt repayments and new debt taken on, as well as foreign aid and all other purely monetary exchanges. But these monetary items cannot be ignored; in particular, debt repayments have a top priority claim and must be included among each year's claims for foreign exchange. So we must add line G to line F, giving us a Gross Payments Deficit that includes debt repayments. The resulting line H is the total deficit the country has had to cover. There are only three ways of covering such a deficit: (1) drawing on reserves of foreign exchange or gold which were accumulated in earlier years, (2) getting gifts of foreign exchange, or (3) going into debt, either long-term or short-term. Since Iran began the post-Mossadegh period with no reserves of exchange or gold, it has had to rely heavily on foreign aid and foreign loans. Line I shows that aid and loans during each of the first four years were larger than the over-all payments deficit, resulting in a build-up of $225.1 million in foreign exchange reserves during these four years.

Beginning in 1957 the total payments deficit jumped to much higher levels and substantially exceeded the amounts of aid and new loans received during each of the next four years. The cumulative short-fall for this period was $276.7 million, which was financed only by rapidly using up accumulated reserves. Indeed, the four-year deficit was $51.6 million greater than the surplus built up during the preceding four years. In theory, Iran should have run out of foreign exchange, and more. And in fact it had: by the end of 1960 the country was bumping along from day to day with the Central Bank understandably anxious to hide from the country the fact that at times it had only enough exchange to cover essential payments for ten to fifteen days ahead. Under these circumstances an emergency air prevails, and key government officials (and many private importers) scurry about trying to make new foreign loans to pay off those coming due, to change the terms of existing debts, to arrange for prepayment of the quarterly oil revenues,[2] and to see that all foreign payments are limited to those that are absolutely essential.

[2] The oil revenues accrue as shipments leave Iran, but payments to Iran are made quarterly by deposit of convertible sterling to Iranian Government accounts in London.

How did the situation reach this state? Not because no one realized what was going on: the trade and payments statistics were certainly good enough to have warned what was happening. Nor was it because there were no Iranian officials who recognized the danger signals and argued for more prudent policies toward imports and the casual assumption of foreign debt. The 1958–61 "payments slide" was essentially one more symptom of the general condition of Iranian politics during this period: the few sensible people who understood were not in positions of political control, and the people in positions of control either did not understand or would not listen. If real trouble developed, the authorities seemed to think, new loans could always be arranged, or the American Government would buy the country back from the brink, or the oil revenues might be pushed up by pressuring the Consortium for higher prices. As a last resort officials could resign and turn the mess over to someone else. All these remedies were tried. The Iranian talent for ingenious maneuver under pressure succeeded in confining the financial crisis and avoided the rupture of relations with her principal foreign creditors (the World Bank and the IMF) which clearly threatened.

This is not the place to review the specific steps taken to bring the country back from the foreign exchange crisis of 1960–61. We are interested mainly in the fact, size, and source of the trouble and what Iran's balance of payments can tell us about the outlines of the economy. The main source of the mounting payments deficit clearly lay in the rising trade deficit, which we traced to the uncontrolled expansion of imports and the stagnant level of exports. But is it obvious that Iran should have held imports down to a much lower level? Did not a new and large development effort *justify* a significant expansion of imports over traditional levels and did not the tripling of exchange earnings resulting from oil nationalization *support* this higher level?[3] The question is one of degree, one of "yes . . . but." The key indicator of the limit to which

[3] Oil royalties have a direct and an indirect effect on foreign exchange resources. The direct effect is the royalties themselves. The indirect effect is the ability of a country to use future oil royalties as collateral for foreign loans. Since the royalties accumulate in London banks this stream of future payments is relatively certain and secure. Exchange earned from ordinary commercial exports, whose earnings are less predictable, less certain, and less easily collected, are not lodged with a trustee bank in a politically safe "third country."

an expansion of imports might be carried in such circumstances is the level of foreign exchange reserves (including gold, something Iran holds but does not produce). If these fall below a "safe" level (perhaps three to four months of imports at current rates), then adjustments are called for.[4] But other measures were also useful for judging how large a trade deficit was reasonable. In particular one could ask whether the post-Mossadegh trade deficit was really any larger than had been considered normal during other periods. One way of judging this is to compute the percentage by which imports have exceeded exports during earlier times. This figure for a number of representative periods is shown in Table 2.

TABLE 2

Excess of Imports over Non-Oil Exports, Selected Periods

Period	Percentage[a]
1900–5[b]	82
1910–14	61
1925–29	63
1935–39	16
1946–48	97
1955–60	263
1957–60	363

[a] Yearly average.
[b] 1904 omitted as figures were not available.
Source: Current rial values of imports and exports as taken from *Iran Today,* p. 203–a, based on Customs publications.

These figures make clear that the size of the post-Mossadegh trade deficit was indeed of an entirely new order of magnitude. Our review of the over-all balance of payments showed that even the new, higher level of oil earnings plus the resort to foreign long-term borrowing was insufficient to support it.[5] In plain language, Iran was now living beyond her means.

[4] There is much room for technical judgments as to what holdings of gold and exchange should be considered part of the reserves and what level of reserves should be considered safe. The three-to-four month rule of thumb affords a temporary cushion in the event an imbalance develops between imports and the means of paying for them. The existence of a cushion permits remedial action to be taken in an orderly way instead of in a crisis atmosphere.

[5] The systematic use of long-term foreign loans is something Iran came to adopt only after 1956, when the first World Bank loan was negotiated by Mr. Ebtehaj to finance the early part of the Second Seven Year Plan. Historically, Iranian leaders and deputies have been extremely suspicious of foreign loans for fear

The notion of living within one's means is the same for a nation's balance of payments as it is for an individual consumer or an enterprise. The limit of prudent spending in any period is not determined directly by one's current income. It is set by one's debt-service capacity. This, in turn, is determined by one's income (or "earnings"), both present and future. In 1960 Iran's planners thought the present and prospective growth of imports was higher than it could pay for out of (1) current and prospective exchange earnings plus (2) sustainable capital inflows (i.e., additional debt). This judgment emerged from the simple arithmetic of a few reasonable assumptions applied to the eight-year period 1960–67 (the remainder of the Second Plan plus the period of the Third). These were the main assumptions and calculations:

1. *Exports* were assumed to rise by 5 per cent per year. This was thought reasonable, since the oil royalties alone (which account for nearly two-thirds of foreign exchange earnings) would rise by at least 5 per cent. The assumption of an over-all increase of 5 per cent in export earnings therefore included an assumption that non-oil exports would rise about the same rate as the oil royalties.

2. *Imports* were treated under three alternatives: (A) that they remain constant at the 1959 level; (B) that they be allowed to increase at the same rate as national income; and (C) that they be allowed to increase 40 per cent faster than national income (a figure that seemed to fit the slender data for 1958–59).

3. *National income* was assumed to increase, on average, at 6 per cent annually. If the income-elasticity of imports is taken at 1.0, then imports would also rise at 6 per cent; if the income-elasticity is taken at 1.4, imports would rise at 8.4 per cent annually.

Table 3 shows the results of one of these calculations (i.e., imports held constant at the 1959 level). The decline in Foreign Exchange Payments (col. 2) is explained by the tapering off of debt repayment and interest charges on foreign debt outstanding in 1959. It is mainly this factor that would convert the payments position from

they would be used by foreign creditors to extend foreign control over Iranian politics and the economy. Foreign borrowing had got off to an unhappy start under the Qajar kings, who mortgaged the country's main tax source (the customs receipts) against loans used to finance personal expenditures, usually trips to Europe (cf. Chapter I above).

a deficit into a surplus during the last three years of the period. On the other hand, if foreign borrowing were not cut off in 1959 but were allowed to continue at the then-estimated rate of $100 million the results would be as shown in cols. 4 and 5: the situation

TABLE 3

*Projected Balance of Trade with No Increase in Imports
and 5 Per Cent Increase in Exchange Earnings*

			Deficit or surplus assuming:		
	Foreign exchange earnings	Foreign exchange payments	No inflow of capital	\$100 mn. annual inflow 10-yr. maturity	15-yr. maturity
Year	(1)	(2)	(3) *(million $)*	(4)	(5)
1960	531	711	−180	−96.0	−92.6
1961	558	707	−149	−80.4	−73.9
1962	586	673	−87	−33.2	−23.8
1963	615	665	−50	−10.4	1.8
1964	646	654	−8	18.0	32.7
1965	678	650	28	41.0	58.0
1966	712	648	64	64.6	83.8
1967	748	641	107	95.8	116.9
8-yr. cumulatives			−275	−0.6	102.9
Average annual deficit or surplus			−34.3	0	12.8

Source: Economic Bureau, Plan Organization (Memorandum No. 13 on the Third Plan, February 23, 1960) .

would be decidedly improved. The trouble with this optimistic conclusion was the assumption that imports, if left free, would remain at the 1959 level. A very different picture emerged from calculations (not shown here) assuming two different income-elasticities of demand for imported goods, 1.0 and 1.4. The main conclusions were that the rise in imports implied by an income-elasticity of only 1.0 would require continuing annual capital imports to finance them, and that even if the gross capital inflow could be held to $100 million of loans per year, the over-all payments deficit would progressively increase over the 1959 level. Why? Because the financing of current trade deficits through continuing capital imports entangles a country in an increasing level of purely financial repayments that leaves less and less of each year's loan available for financing trade. Table 4 makes this clear; it shows that anyone who borrows $100 million every year at 6 per cent with each year's loan repayable in equal installments over ten years will find that after the seventh year his new loans are not even sufficient to finance the repayments and interest on his accumulated old ones, much less help him finance a trade deficit. (If a fifteen-year amortization period is used, the break-even period is not reached until the tenth year.)

By the 10th year (Table 4) the borrower has assumed $1,000 million of additional debt which requires, that year, a debt-service payment of $133 million. Whether or not this rapid increase in debt is bearable depends on what the money was used for. If, to take one extreme, the $100 million each year was used only for importing consumer goods, then no foundation was laid for import-substitution or export-promotion. If, on the other hand, the $100 million borrowed each year was used wisely, then it has been used, in large measure, to reduce imports or expand exports, or both, and thus to make room for (1) the additional debt-service requirements resulting from the loans and (2) additional imports once the debt-payments begin to decline. Until the structural changes of the import-substitution or export-promotion begin to take effect, some way has to be found to meet the rising debt-service requirements. There

TABLE 4

Schedule of Annual Amortization and Interest Payments If $100 Million Is Borrowed Each Year at 6 Per Cent with 10-Year Maturities

Year	New loan	Principal and interest	Excess or short-fall (−) of new loans over annual payments
		(million $)	
1	100.0	16.0	84.0
2	100.0	31.4	68.6
3	100.0	46.2	53.8
4	100.0	60.4	39.6
5	100.0	74.0	26.0
6	100.0	87.0	13.0
7	100.0	99.4	0.6
8	100.0	111.2	−11.2
9	100.0	122.4	−22.4
10	100.0	133.0	−33.0

are only two possibilities: (1) reduce current imports or (2) take on new debt to pay off the old. Table 4 shows the arithmetic of this second solution; it shows that the solution cannot work very long.

The preceding argument was used in 1960 to try to educate government leaders to a realization that the 1960 trade and investment policies were incompatible with the 6 per cent growth rate of national income targeted for the Third Plan. The country would not be able to finance the level of imports to which such a growth rate would lead if the existing liberal import policy continued. The planners were saying: restrain the growth of imports, both directly by prohibiting nonessentials or by making them more expensive by raising tariffs, and indirectly by curbing the volume of investment and hence the demand for imported capital goods and raw materials. The energetic 1961 import curbs, the IMF-sponsored Stabilization Program of 1961–62, and the associated recession of 1961–64 produced the painful but needed relief for the balance of payments. On the receipts side, foreign exchange earnings (from oil) bounded ahead nearly three times as fast as the 5 per cent rate the planners had conservatively assumed. The years 1962–64 were years of modestly rising exchange reserves and a net reduction of foreign debt. But by 1965 the recession gave way to a new boom, reserves began to fall, and observers wondered if Iran were about to repeat the wasteful "boom and bust" cycle of 1959–64, a cycle whose earliest and clearest impact was on the country's international liquidity and its balance of payments.

The Structure of Imports and Exports

Space prevents anything more than a general description of Iran's main imports and exports and how these have behaved during the development years since 1948. The outstanding fact, of course, is the huge growth in imports (from about $170 million in 1948 to about $850 million in 1965). This growth has been made possible almost entirely by the higher levels of exchange earnings resulting from oil nationalization in 1951 and the unexpectedly rapid growth of oil production in the 1960's. The rise in non-oil exports has been generally slow. (Whether the acceleration in 1964 and 1965 will hold remains to be seen.)

Imports

Although all major categories of imports have shared in the expansion of the past decade and a half, the rise in capital goods has been much larger, in absolute terms, than in either consumer durables, nondurables, or raw materials and finished goods. Between

1948 and 1960 over half the rise in total imports consisted of capital goods. Indeed, if no increase at all had been allowed in consumer durables the total increase in imports would have been cut by only 10–15 per cent. Thus, the biggest opportunity for holding down imports, at times when these seemed excessive, has lain in the capital goods sector, through control over the volume of investment (any such policy would have gone hand in hand with restraints on other categories as well).

The country is fortunate in that it does not normally have to import its staple foodstuffs, especially wheat, the leading grain. Sugar and tea have traditionally been the largest food items imported. The Third Plan is trying to build up domestic production of both rapidly and by 1963–64 appeared to be having some success. Even more success had been achieved in textiles, traditionally much the largest item of consumer nondurables. The importance of a reasonable amount of import-substitution in this field is evident in the fact that sugar, tea, and textiles accounted for about 60 per cent of all consumer nondurables in the mid-1950's.

Consumer durables have traditionally been much smaller than the nondurables (roughly only 25–35 per cent as much). Over half the category is regularly accounted for by automotive vehicles. But despite an overly liberal import policy on automobile imports until the early 1960's this item never accounted for more than 3–5 per cent of total imports (except in one or two years when it went to 10 per cent). So there was only modest room for protecting the balance of payments by limiting vehicle imports. Tea imports have traditionally been larger, besides offering greater possibilities for import-substitution.

Exports

By 1958–61 non-oil exports were sufficient to pay for only a third or a quarter of Iran's imports; by 1965, only a sixth. Oil paid for the rest—oil and foreign borrowing. In one sense this means that the $100–$130 million of non-oil exports are relatively so small that not even a substantial expansion can make nearly as much difference as small changes in the volume (or unit value) of oil exports. And for more than a generation the latter have been far easier to achieve. But oil may not hold up the level of imports forever.

What are the leading non-oil exports? Four things, mainly: raw cotton, handmade carpets, dried fruits, and coarse wool. For many years these four items have accounted for about two-thirds of non-oil exports. Thus Iran is almost exclusively an exporter of primary products, of products generated by the agricultural and mining sectors (this becomes overwhelmingly true when oil is included among the exports). The only "manufactured" item among the four major non-oil exports is carpets. The Persian carpet is of course hand-woven of wool, so that this major export is only one step removed from the class of primary products.

The important role of sheep and goats in the country's economy is easily seen from the export list: wool, hides, hair, and casings (intestines) all come from the country's flocks of sheep and goats. These are exported with little or no processing and upgrading. If to these four items (which themselves regularly account for 15–20 per cent of non-oil exports) we add carpets, we find that 30–40 per cent of non-oil exports are based on sheep and goats. (Good use is made of products produced at time of slaughtering—hides and casings.) Clearly, Iran's capacity to export is significantly affected by the size of her goat and sheep flocks, one of the most important forms of capital in the country. Furthermore, the most important part of the annual output from this stock of capital which is demanded by the home market, the meat, does not move into export markets; therefore the high income-elasticity for meat consumption at home will have the effect not of reducing exports but of increasing them, since there is little home demand for the nonmeat by-products.

If we add cotton to the sheep-and-goat products (including carpets), we account for between 50 and 60 per cent of total exports. And if we add the only other traditionally large item, fruits (which means dried fruit and nuts, mainly pistachios, and dates), we account for 70 to 80 per cent of the total. The establishment of the mill textile industry in the 1930's, and its rapid expansion during the late 1950's, has called for large increases in the output of cotton by the agricultural sector. Fortunately output has kept pace so that cotton exports have not suffered. Agricultural experts believe that Iranian cotton cultivation has a high supply-elasticity. Consequently, Third Plan output was assumed to grow fast enough so that by 1967 Iran would have enough cotton not only to supply a textile industry large enough to make imports negligible but even to expand cotton exports by 20–40 per cent. Experience to 1966 supports this judgment. Whatever question marks surround the future of cotton exports arise out of conditions in the world market, not in the drawing off of inelastic supplies by the expansion of home demand.

Iranian orchards produce many kinds of fruits, a term that includes nuts. However, Iran's export potential will be limited for some years to come to the small number of traditionally important items: dried raisins, dried apricots, dried prunes, dates, walnuts, almonds, and pistachios. The quality of Iran's citrus is too low to find a place in international markets until that defect is overcome. High internal transport costs combined with high production costs (reflecting low yields) make it unrealistic to look for any significant widening of fresh fruit exports for many years. Indeed, Iran will have all it can do to hold and expand the markets for its traditional dried fruit-and-nut products. For dried fruits the main problem is not production but proper processing, grading, packaging, and market-promotion. In recent years Iranian dried fruits and dates have tended to lose ground to other Middle East producers in the sense that others have tended to capture the increased markets produced by Europe's prosperity. The Second Plan tried to do something about this problem. So does the Third. Much will depend on the government's ability to mount an effective initiative— arranging technical assistance and credit for private investments, remedying the almost total lack of commercial information and representation abroad, enforcing objective grading and labeling standards, and avoiding the temptation to get into the processing and selling business as government enterprises. The outlook for pistachios is promising; the country's ability to meet the sharply increased pistachio export target of the Third Plan will depend mainly on the ability of growers to step up tree planting early in the Plan (it takes five years between planting and harvesting a first crop).

I have said little about any but the large, staple exports. There is little prospect that rice, tragacanth, gums, cumin, oilseeds, or timber will become major exports. The main hope for a major newcomer on the export list is minerals.

Mining has been carried on in Persia since ancient times but never on a large scale. Some twenty to twenty-five minerals have been produced in recent years but only five or six are important, and not very important at that—i.e., lead, zinc, copper, chromite, and coal. For the near future, chromite has the greatest promise.

Mineral output is a typical case of primary production that finds most of its markets abroad. Since Iranian mining costs are high and most deposits are located far from the ports, the f.o.b. costs are high. Many mines are therefore marginal suppliers, able to make sales only when world prices have been lifted above their long-run level by temporary disturbances in world markets. As a consequence, Iranian producers of copper, lead, and zinc have for some years had to rely on sales to the U.S.S.R.[6]

The government has a major role to play in mining activity, and the expansion of this sector depends heavily on strengthening the government's ability to perform its many roles.

The major problem of Iranian mining today is the development of more information about the country's mineral resources. There are two dimensions to this problem, one horizontal, the other vertical. The former requires a greatly stepped-up exploration effort. For the Third Plan main reliance is being placed on the establishment of a Geological Survey, a special office charged with the responsibility of mounting a greatly accelerated program of exploration. In 1960 a five-year program costing $3.9 million was signed with the U.N. Special Fund; but the actual start on the Survey dragged on inconclusively for two to three years while the Iranian Govern-

---

[6] These sales have been made under annual contracts negotiated between the Russian buying agency and individual producers. The Russians have declined to negotiate central master contracts with the Iranian Mining Syndicate (the private employers' organization), preferring to pick out one producer each year to negotiate with, then signing up other companies on the same terms. Russian prices have generally been somewhat above world prices for the three minerals they have bought—lead, zinc, and copper. Quantities are modest, so that the Russian market is open only to those few Iranian companies large enough to have contracts. Sometime in the mid-1950's the U.S. Battle Act was applied to Iranian copper, which could then no longer be offered to the U.S.S.R. if Iran wished to receive U.S. economic and technical assistance. Largely as a result of this U.S. policy almost every Iranian copper mine was in or near bankruptcy in 1960 (perhaps 10 to 15 mines were involved, all small). Russia had supplied a modest amount of equipment for a few Iranian mines, most of it concentrating equipment. In 1960 there was no program of Russian technical assistance, and no Russian investment, in any Iranian mines.

ment tried to find its share of the money and to work out organizational and personnel problems. The vertical dimension to exploration requires the introduction of drilling to determine the size of ore-bodies. Iranian mining companies have not yet adopted the practice of drilling ore-bodies to determine their depth. Underground mining has almost always stopped at the water table, a reflection of the primitive state of technology. Consequently no one knows how large some of the good surface deposits may be. Until this is known, no one can be persuaded to invest the large sums involved in applying modern methods, including the smelting operations necessary to eliminate the waste material that is now hauled to the ports at very high expense.

High transport costs are likely to remain a serious handicap to Iranian mining. Most mines are located far from the Persian Gulf. Many are remote from the railway and from major highways. Even when ores finally reach one of the three ports from which they are now exported (Khorramshahr and Bandar Abbas on the Gulf and Bandar Pahlavi on the Caspian Sea), they must bear a longer sea haul than ores from many other world suppliers. For example, sea freight to Europe costs $14–15 per ton for Iranian chromite as compared with $6–7 for Turkish chromite, the main competitor. In between the expensive land and sea hauls are port handling facilities so primitive that loading costs are among the highest in the world. Only high-grade ores can stand the double handicap of high transport and high loading costs. Although Iran does have some high-grade deposits (e.g., lead, zinc, chromite, and iron ore), there are many deposits of indifferent grade which can be worked profitably only during periods of high world prices or under the special terms of the Russian contracts.

Of all the minerals the outlook for chromite is much the brightest. Large, high-grade deposits have recently been opened up within easy truck haul of Bandar Abbas. When modern loading facilities become available at that small port (now being modernized in a controversial project), it is reasonable to expect the 1960–61 exports of 40–50,000 tons to rise to 150–200,000 tons and possibly higher. (In 1958 Turkey exported 200,000 tons; a year later, following a devaluation and/or a new subsidy, her exports rose to 800,000 tons.) By the end of the decade it is entirely possible that lead, zinc, and chromite exports might each be running $4–5 million, which, with minor contributions from copper, gold, antimony, manganese, iron ore, and salt, might put total mineral exports at $10–12 million or roughly three times their value in 1960. If one could take a more optimistic view of the government's ability to provide effective support over the broad field of activity needed to advance Iranian mining, one might increase these figures by 50 or 100 per cent and project mineral exports of the same order of magnitude as cotton, carpets, or fruits today. But even on the most optimistic assumptions for all non-oil exports put together, their total will be dwarfed by oil for at least the next generation. And if anything should occur to cut off the oil exports Iran's prospects for development, instead of being much better than most, would suddenly become much worse. Neither the foreign oil companies nor any responsible Iranian Government is likely to forget this fact.

CHAPTER V

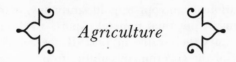

Agriculture

Introduction

When the Third Plan was being written, nobody guessed that the most important, most expensive program in the agricultural sector would be something not even mentioned in the Plan. It was not that the planners forgot about land reform or belittled its importance. Among Iranian and foreign technicians there was general agreement that in the long run land reform was a necessary condition of higher productivity over much of the country. But it was anyone's guess how much national output might be raised without land reform, or how much and how long land reform might disrupt production.[1] The planners were not blind to the importance of this question; they simply avoided it. They knew that it was too political and too controversial a topic for their views to count for much. So they looked the other way and devoted themselves to technical and economic problems that would sooner or later need attention whether land reform came or not.

When the Shah and a crusading Agriculture Minister suddenly embarked on a dramatic nation-wide land reform just before the Third Plan started, the effect was to co-opt all the resources of the sector—the administrative energies and the development funds—for this program and to make everyone forget the programs the planners had planned. Nobody reads the Third Plan for Agriculture as an account of the important things that happened in the sector during the Third Plan. The main purpose of this chapter is to review that plan as an outstanding model of sectoral planning. Such a review is instructive even though the Plan may prove little more than a "piece of paper." No matter. There is much to be

[1] In neighboring Iraq, agricultural production has fallen markedly since the land reform of 1958, with little sign seven years later that the system had yet begun to recover.

learned about Iranian agriculture and about planning even from pieces of paper.[2]

Human considerations aside, agricultural development plays a number of important technical roles in the total process of a country's growth. Without higher agricultural production there may be food shortages and higher prices in the towns, shortages and higher prices for a wide range of industrial raw materials coming from agriculture, reduced exports or higher imports (or both), a too-slow growth of the urban labor force, and poor markets for the few industrial products rural people buy. Thus for technical as well as human reasons, the importance of agricultural development needs no arguing. The real questions are what to do and how to do it. Part of the answer consists simply of expanding the government's general-purpose services into the rural areas—e.g., more and better schools, more and better clinics and hospitals, more and better roads. The core of rural development, however, is the raising of agricultural productivity. If productivity increases, then all things become possible. Higher productivity is thus the great precondition that underlies not only rural advance but also urban advance, insofar as the two are connected.

Until the land reform of 1962–63 (about which more later) the institutional setting of Iranian agriculture was dominated by a system of absentee landlords most of whom lived in cities and towns and left the daily administration of their villages to resident bailiffs, the *katkhodas*. A relatively high proportion of land was owned by a small number of landlords. However, there were many districts where ownership was not in the hands of a single individual but had been split up into shares (usually among family and friends), much like ownership in a Western corporation. The largest and most progressive landlord was the Shah, who tried to set an example by selling off much of the crown lands to the peasants. Prior to the start of land reform in 1962, it is doubtful that 10 per cent of the peasants owned the land they worked. Ninety per cent were share-croppers who divided the fruit of their toil with their landlords.

[2] Much the best account of planning for Iranian agriculture in the 1960's is the study by J. Price Gittinger, *Planning for Agricultural Development: The Iranian Experience,* published in 1965 by the National Planning Association (Washington, D.C.). The study will be useful to agricultural planners in many countries.

The distribution of this income was governed by complex customs that varied considerably from district to district.[3]

An important fact about Iranian agriculture is that it is not predominantly subsistence agriculture. For several decades now it has been oriented to cash sales in markets beyond the village. It is hardly surprising that poverty often forces peasants to sell their marketable surpluses at poor prices, that they are usually in debt,[4] and that more often than not they still live in poverty-ridden closed communities beyond the reach of elementary government services for education and health. Yet everywhere the immemorial isolation and ignorance of alternatives are crumbling, probably at an accelerating rate each year. Universal military conscription, the rapid spread of autobuses and truck transport, and the feedback from the large amount of rural-urban migration are the main modernizing influences. Not surprisingly, landlords differed in their attitudes toward the intrusion of these modern influences in their villages, influences which often threatened their labor supply and the security of their social and political authority. As many landlords realized, the era of Iran's historical pattern of land tenure, with all its implications for social and political relationships, was fast drawing to a close. This fact brings us back to the central question of what to do and how to do it, for the raising of agricultural productivity is anything but a purely technical problem. Rural life (including its production activities) is so deeply rooted in intractable institutional, social, and sociological problems that technical improvements, even if they can be devised and carried to the field, may get no hearing or have weak effects.

[3] For details, see Ann K. S. Lambton, *Landlord and Peasant in Persia,* published for the Royal Institute of International Affairs by Oxford University Press in 1953. Her subtitle, "A Study of Land Tenure and Revenue Administration," is fully as important as the main title. The book, heavily oriented toward the historical explanation of rural institutions, has one recurring theme: through the centuries, Persian rulers have almost invariably found it next to impossible to find enough cash to pay the officers and troops on whom their rule depended. Always this fiscal problem was resolved in the same way, by assigning land or the produce of land to military personnel. Although no longer necessary on fiscal grounds, the practice is not unheard of today.

[4] Relatively little written material exists on the structure of Iran's agricultural credit. See Lambton, *Landlord and Peasant in Persia,* p. 380, and the report entitled *Country Seminar on Agricultural and Cooperative Credit, November 14–26, 1959* (Tehran, Agricultural Bank, September, 1960).

For the past decade and more land reform was the dominant institutional issue in Iranian agriculture. The past political power of the landlord class in the *Majles* had much to do with the government's traditional inability and disinclination to make any significant moves in this area. In 1961, however, the *Majles* was not in session and the country was being ruled by decree. Into this legislative hiatus came a crusading Minister of Agriculture determined to seize his and the country's opportunity for land reform. We will return to this event after a look at the sector and the problems involved in its development.

The Broad Composition of Agricultural Output

Only a small proportion of Iran's total land area is used for growing crops in any year—under 4 per cent. Over two-thirds of the country's surface is wasteland (desert, mountains, and potentially arable land not now used; the latter area is much larger than the land now under crops, including fallow land). Of the cropland now in use two-thirds lies fallow each year. One advantage of chemical fertilizer (just beginning to be used) is that it can greatly reduce the proportion of arable land in fallow.

The amount of land devoted to major crops, and the relative values of these crops, is shown in Table 5. Two-thirds of the cultivated land is planted in wheat and barley. These two grains account for 45 per cent of the total values produced directly from the land (i.e., excluding livestock). Wheat alone accounts for 35–40 per cent, of the total value of all field, orchard, and garden crops. Rice and cotton take up about the same amount of land, but rice is a much higher-value crop (it also costs more to grow). All in all, field crops account for 70 per cent of all agricultural crop values. Fresh fruit (of which grapes are the largest item) is as important as all other garden and orchard products combined. Vegetables and melons are no more important than pistachios, almonds, and walnuts.

As in other Middle Eastern countries, Iranian livestock is dominated by sheep and goats. Over half the annual value produced by livestock comes from milk (60 per cent from cows, 20 per cent from sheep, 15 per cent from goats, 5 per cent from buffalo). A high proportion of this is converted into *mast* (yogurt) and cheese, consumed in the villages and does not enter the cash economy. But after Plan

Uses of Land and the Values Produced, Late 1950's

	Land use by crops		Relative values produced
Field crops	*(hectares)*	*(%)*	*(%)*
Wheat	3,100,000	51.66	24
Rice	270,000	4.50	8
Barley	910,000	15.17	4
Cotton	310,000	5.17	4
Pulses	130,000	2.17	1
Others (total)	120,000	2.00	4
Tobacco	15,000	0.25	n.a.
Sugar beet	43,000	0.72	n.a.
Other grains	43,000	0.72	n.a.
Miscellaneous[a]	19,000	0.31	n.a.
Subtotal			45
Orchards and gardens			
Fresh fruit ⎫			10
Dried fruit ⎬	930,000	15.50	3
Nuts ⎭			3
Vegetables and melon	230,000	3.83	3
Subtotal			19
Livestock			
Milk			21
Meat			8
Wool and hair			2
Eggs			2
Poultry			1
Others			2
Subtotal			36
Total	6,000,000	100.00	100

[a] Including vegetable oilseeds, gums, jute, tea, alfalfa and other forage crops, and henna and dyes.
Source: Adapted from *Program Review*, pp. 23–24.

Organization, with W.H.O.'s help, established the country's first pasteurized milk plant in the mid-1950's, four or five private milk plants were started within as many years.

Iran has normally enjoyed a favorable trade balance in agricultural products; except in years of crop failure, it exports more food and fiber than it imports. Indeed, three-quarters of all non-oil exports come from the agricultural sector (rugs and minerals account for the remaining quarter). The only foodstuffs Iran regularly has to import are sugar, tea, and, more recently, vegetable oil. Small quantities of spices, citrus fruits, and bananas are imported, plus unimportant amounts of luxury foodstuffs, mainly for foreigners.

Table 6 summarizes the relative importance of export and domestic markets for each major export food crop. The data are for 1958 and show export tonnage in the numerator, the part remaining within the country (consumption plus stocks) in the denominator. These ratios show not only the relative importance of exports to each crop but the amount of leverage small changes in domestic demand may have on exports in that crop. It is not surprising, for example, that the rise in domestic demand for pistachios in 1960–61 resulting from prosperity should have forced up both the domestic

TABLE 6

Relative Importance of Export and Domestic Markets
for Major Agricultural Exports, 1958[a]

Item	Ratio	Percentage[b]
	(thousand tons)	
Barley	$\dfrac{10}{940}$	1
Rice	$\dfrac{3}{489}$	1
Oilseeds	$\dfrac{6}{156}$	4
Tobacco	$\dfrac{0.5}{12.5}$	4
Ginned cotton	$\dfrac{42.5}{27.5}$	155
Dates	$\dfrac{35}{95}$	37
Raisins	$\dfrac{39.5}{22.5}$	175
Shelled almonds	$\dfrac{6}{12}$	50
Unshelled pistachios	$\dfrac{2.5}{1.5}$	167
Walnuts	$\dfrac{2.1}{3.9}$	54
Wool (cleaned)	$\dfrac{8.4}{11.6}$	72

[a] Exports in numerator, domestic uses in denominator; their sum equals total production. Skins and hides, gum tragacanth, and sausage casings are other important agricultural exports. No production figures are available, only export figures; it is believed that for all three products exports exceed domestic use by wide margins—i.e., the percentage figure would exceed 100.

[b] Rounded.

Source: Derived from Table 12, *Agriculture Plan Frame* (1961), p. 70.

and the international price, since small shifts in domestic demand decreased the amounts available for export—and Iran is among the world's largest suppliers. Iran's ability to increase its cotton exports by 22 per cent and at the same time to supply its expanded domestic textile industry will clearly depend on its ability to expand total cotton output. If this expansion is not realized, Iran will see all or part of its most important non-oil export melt away and/or a sharp rise in the domestic price of this key raw material.

Goals and Programs: The Choice of Objectives

The over-all goal of the Third Plan was to maintain the 6 per cent annual increase in national output achieved during the late fifties. The agricultural sector weighted its own objectives so as to support the over-all target. This weighting involved a balancing of three primary targets (and half a dozen secondary goals) which the agricultural planners selected for the sector: (1) *increasing output* to support the over-all growth rate, (2) *improving the levels of living* of rural people, and (3) *improving the distribution of income* within the agricultural sector. The weighting process determined how the planners used their energies and the specific content they gave to the programs that emerged.

Conflicts among objectives were reflected in choices among programs. It was here that compromises were forced on individual objectives to attain some reasonable balance. For example, the desire to achieve a better distribution of income within agriculture implied that special steps should be taken to improve production in the poorest, least-favored, lowest-productivity regions of the country. But with the extremely limited personnel and institutional resources available for government programs, the production-orientation of the Plan argued for throwing these resources into the most promising regions—which were also those already enjoying the highest incomes. So the poorer regions would just go on being neglected during the Third Plan, since there was no possibility of helping them and meeting national production goals at the same time. On the other hand, the Plan restricted the use of credit for large-scale agricultural machinery, which would have favored the large landlord, and tried to encourage the most rapid possible increase in village co-operatives, whose main beneficiaries would be peasant farmers. The horticulture program for improving orchard productivity tried to direct extension agents to concentrate their efforts on the smaller growers. Most important of all from the point of view of income distribution was the attempt to do something about land tenure (not "land reform"), a massive institutional problem about which the Second Plan had said nothing. But the Plan's tenure objectives were still kept subordinate to the overriding goal of raising production. Although few people doubted that the country would eventually have to undergo a drastic overhaul of its traditional tenure arrangements, most observers felt that Iran was not ready to carry through any major land distribution program on an orderly basis. Consequently they felt that a major land distribution campaign would seriously disrupt production for an unpredictable number of years. When in 1961–62 the Third Plan was put aside in favor of land reform the action represented a reversal of the relative importance of production and distribution objectives within the sector.

As for the third "primary objective," improving levels of rural life, no direct steps were proposed to serve this end. Instead, rural life was judged able to take care of itself in view of the general improvement in agriculture's terms of trade during the Plan (i.e., since demand would increase somewhat faster than agricultural production could be increased, agricultural prices would tend to rise relative to other prices). In particular, a free price for wheat was recommended, a break with the government's long-standing policy of formally requiring sellers to offer a substantial proportion of their grain to the government at a low fixed price. Thus the old policy of subsidizing urban consumers at the expense of the growers was to be abandoned, with farmers benefiting either from the expected price increases or higher outputs induced by the higher incentive, or both.

The emphasis on increasing production in the sixties has to be seen against what had been happening in the immediately preceding years. The best estimate of agricultural progress during the second half of the 1950's was that total output had been growing at 3–4 per cent yearly. Reliable statistics were nonexistent; so this was an informed guess. The rate was roughly equal to the average for the whole Middle East; it meant the food supply was increasing a little faster than population. A series of good growing years had

had much to do with this modest progress. There were several reasons why the apparent rate of progress already being experienced could give little comfort:

1. The key factor in rising demands for food and fiber was not the rate of *population* increase (though this was indeed very important and the rate was rising). The key to demand was the rate at which *national income* was increasing. With so many people eating at low nutritional levels higher incomes implied a high income-elasticity for food in general and a very high one for several individual food items.

2. With higher incomes people could afford more of the more expensive foods—fruits, vegetables, nuts, dairy products, meat, tobacco, rice (Iranian rice is very good but quite expensive). So a national income scheduled to rise at 6 per cent implied important structural changes in demand which production plans should try to anticipate.

3. The acceleration of industrialization meant a surge in demand for many agricultural raw materials—cotton, oilseeds, sugar beets, tea, flax, jute.

4. Entirely apart from the problem of keeping up with demand so that prices would not have to rise much, something had to be done to raise the incomes of agricultural people. This was important from the point of view of welfare and for the creation of greater purchasing power among the largest class of people in the country.

5. The volume and composition of agricultural output has important repercussions on the balance of payments; although price changes in both world and domestic markets were an important influence in guiding investment and production decisions, a development plan could help solve many of these problems faster and better than market forces working alone.

One of the planners' first and most difficult tasks was to give quantitative expression to the demand factors just cited. The work required building up quantitative targets for about thirty-five major product groups. This task was done by making estimates of (1) how much of several food categories people would be likely to eat at 1967 levels of income, (2) the quantities of specific agricultural raw materials that would be required to meet the 1967 production targets for industry, and (3) reasonable export targets for crops entering foreign markets.

The fixing of realistic targets is a compound of imagination, ingenuity, and energy. Rarely are there any accurate published statistics to help. Since future targets are derived by applying a growth factor to existing quantities of production and consumption, planners had to build up the best picture they could of present production and use for each of the thirty-five products. In the absence of reliable published data the planners had to go out and track down unpublished statistics.

Once the bench-mark estimates had been made, the "growth factor" appropriate to each product had to be estimated again. This was a product of informed judgment. But once the estimate was made the planners had the two "fixes" they needed: production and consumption at the start of the Plan and consumption at the end of the Plan. The gap between 1962 production and 1967 consumption showed how much additional output might be disposed of *if it could be produced.*[5] The largest part of the Plan is concerned with the institutional, technical, policy, and financial steps necessary to achieve those increases in production which seemed possible of achievement.

Table 7 identifies the thirty-five commodities for which targets were established, shows relative values per ton, indicates estimated production in 1962 and 1967, the percentage growth estimated to be desirable and/or possible, and measures how adequately the estimated 1967 output would meet estimated consumption in that year.

[5] For planning purposes the assumption was made that prices in 1967 would be the same as in 1962: income-elasticities were critical, price-elasticities and cross-elasticities were assumed away at the start. As we shall see, it looked impossible to increase the production of some commodities enough to satisfy estimated 1967 demand from home output; the supply-elasticities were simply too low. In the Plan, targets were for production, not consumption. In some cases the two would coincide, in others not. Since the Plan was more concerned with programs to expand production than with price and import problems, it made sense to express targets in terms that compared production at the start and end of the period. But in each case there was a judgment as to whether the expected increase in production would be sufficient to meet 1967 demand at constant prices. The amount by which production would fall short of demand at constant prices was expressed as a percentage of that demand, giving a measure of the gap that would still exist in 1967 (col. 4, Table 7).

TABLE 7

Agricultural Production Targets, Demand Estimates,
and Growth Rates, 1962–67

Relative prices[a]	Commodity	Forecast production, 1962	Target production, 1967	Estimated demand, 1967[b]	Plan gap[c] (% of 1967 demand)	Total growth, 1962–67
		(1)	(2)	(3)	(4)	(5)
100	Wheat	3,000	3,800	3,700	+3[d]	27
65	Barley	1,000	1,100	1,280	14	10
90	Rice, paddy	500	700	750	7	40
65	Other grains	65	73	–	–	12
155	Pulses	150	165	–	–	10
	Forage crops[e]	–	–	–	–	–
90	Cottonseed	190	245	f	f	129
280	Sesame	13	27	f	f	108
215	Flaxseed	14	30	f	f	114
400	Vegetable oil	34	55	92[f]	67[f]	62
900	Tobacco	18	25	25	0	39
1,200	Tea	12	19	23	17	58
22	Sugar beets	1,350	1,900	1,900[g]	0[g]	41
17	Sugar cane	250	500	500[g]	0[g]	100
170	Refined sugar[h]	320	550	550[g]	0	72
900	Cotton, ginned	95	125	125	0	32
140	Apricots, dried	12	15	i	i	25
200	Dates	130	143	i	i	10
240	Raisins	62	64	i	i	3
95	Oranges and tangerines	45	67	170	6	49
95	Other citrus	70	93			33
60	Grapes, fresh	260	300	380	21	15
140	Other fruit, fresh	850	950	1,470	29	12
200	Olives	13	15	f	f	15
257	Almonds, unshelled	36	36	i	i	0
1,300	Pistachios, unshelled	6	10	i	i	67
250	Walnuts, unshelled	7	7	i	i	0
250	Other nuts, unshelled	22	23	i	i	4
65	Vegetables and melons	970	1,350	1,350	0	39
	Mutton and lamb	175	191	245	22	9
	Beef and veal	95	100	95	+5[d]	5
	Milk[j]	1,700	1,940	2,280	15	14
	Eggs	46	55	65	15	20
	Poultry	18	30	23	+87[d]	67
	Wool, cleaned	20	22	i	i	10
	Agricultural production index (1962 = 100)	100	122	–	–	22
	Food production index (1962 = 100)	100	121	–	–	21
	Per capita food production index (1962 = 100)	100	107	–	–	7
	Crop production index (1962 = 100)	100	127	–	–	27
	Livestock production index (1962 = 100)	100	113	–	–	13

[a] "Average postwar prices" per ton, using the price of a ton of wheat = 100.

[b] Demand is estimated at constant prices on the assumption that the Gross National Product grows at 6 per cent per annum during the Plan period. See text for explanation of how demand determinations were made.

[c] The plan gap is the difference between the 1967 target and the estimated 1967 demand at constant prices. It is expressed as the percentage of the 1967 demand represented by the difference between the 1967 production target and the 1967 demand. Thus, for rice, the 1967 target is 700,000 tons, and the estimated demand is 750,000 tons. The short-fall of the target production compared to the estimated demand is 50,000 tons, which is the plan gap in absolute terms. The plan gap expressed as a percentage of 1967 estimated demand is 50,000 ÷ 750,000 = 0.067, which is rounded to 7 per cent.

Different Products, Different Growth Rates

The figures of Table 7 are useful mainly in showing the great differences in the rates of growth anticipated for different products and to show the extent to which 1967 supplies were expected to meet demand.

Products that would grow relatively fast (faster than 6 per cent annually) are oilseeds, oranges and tangerines, rice, pistachios, poultry, tea, and tobacco. At the other end of the scale were products whose output will grow only half as fast, or even more slowly: barley, pulses, dates, raisins, grapes, fresh fruits, olives, nuts (other than pistachios), meat (other than poultry), and wool. In most cases, the slow growth rates reflected not weak demand but inability to do any better. Over-all, total agricultural production was expected to grow at about 4 per cent annually, or only about two-thirds the 6 per cent growth rate expected of national output. Production of industrial crops was to grow somewhat faster than food crops and much faster than livestock.

---

d Per cent of excess of production over estimated demand.

e Very little is known about either the total area planted to forage crops or about total production. Estimates of production by competent observers vary as much as tenfold.

f Demand for oilseeds, olives, and vegetable oil is extremely difficult to estimate, as explained in the text for the oilseed program. The total demand for vegetable oil assumes constant or somewhat greater prices for all domestically produced oilseed. Note that flaxseed produces linseed oil, which is inedible. The demand projection for vegetable oil includes 80,000 tons of edible oil and 12,000 tons of linseed oil.

g Demand projections for sugar beets and sugar cane are based on refining capacity for domestic raw materials. The demand projection for sugar includes sugar from both domestic sources and sugar refined from imported raws. There will continue to be a demand at constant prices for more sugar than is refined from domestic raw materials. In 1967, sugar from domestic sources will fall 235,000 tons short of estimated total demand, or 42.7 per cent. See text of sugar program for further explanation.

h Production figures for refined sugar include sugar produced from imported raws.

i Demand for dried fruit, nuts, dates, and wool depends heavily on world market conditions. For these commodities the outlook is favorable, and it is likely that any amount of Iranian production could be marketed at suitable prices if international quality standards are met.

j Primarily cow (60 per cent), sheep (20 per cent), goat (15 per cent), and buffalo (5 per cent) in 1962. These proportions are expected to change slightly by 1967.

Sources: Table 3, *Agriculture Plan Frame*, 1961, pp. 47–48, and footnotes to that chapter.

Note: The U.S. Department of Agriculture has estimated 1965 production of selected crops as follows [cf. the 1967 target figs. in column (2)]:

Wheat	2,901	Oranges and tangerines	45
Barley	1,000	Vegetables and melons	1,100
Rice, paddy	925	Eggs	40
Sugar beets	800 (1964 actual)	Milk	1,700
Cotton, ginned	140		

Thus the following items seemed seriously *behind* the 1967 targets: wheat, barley, oranges and tangerines, eggs, and milk. The following seemed likely to reach the 1967 targets: rice, ginned cotton, and perhaps meat (the USDA estimate for 1965 represents an unusually uncertain figure, and there is a probability of overslaughtering forced by three bad crop years).

Predicting Future Price Changes

The "Plan Gaps" (column 4, Table 7) showed that the 1967 output of several commodities would still be short of estimated demand, indicating that price rises or continuing imports should be expected, or both. The largest gap threatened in vegetable oil and its raw materials, although this outlook was clouded by uncertainties surrounding the rate of growth in demand for vegetable oil itself. Tea, sugar, grapes, other fresh fruits, mutton and lamb, milk, and eggs were important dietary items whose prices were likely to rise by 1967 (tea and sugar are the only ones of these where the price pressure was likely to be relieved by imports). In addition, there were eight items (various dried fruits, nuts, and wool) which depend heavily on export markets; in all cases world demand was expected to be sufficiently strong to take whatever supplies of acceptable qualities Iran could produce.

Three items were expected to be in surplus *if prices remained at 1962 levels*—wheat, beef and veal, and poultry (the latter presented the only sizable surplus). Poultry prices seemed likely to fall, inducing more people to eat more chicken, a response helped along by rising prices for the country's favorite meat, mutton.

The production targets shown in Table 7 represented a marriage of demand estimates and production increases which the planners felt attainable given a reasonable administrative effort. However, the type of development expenditures that characterized the Third Plan differed markedly from those used in the Second. The latter had poured large amounts of money into a few major irrigation projects, to the relative neglect of investment in the research and training projects on which the spread of more scientific farming depends. To symbolize this difference, it appeared that the $150 million spent on the Karaj and Sefid Rud dams in the Second Plan would have had an almost undetectable influence on national agricultural output (this was one reason the Karaj hydroelectric dam, originally an irrigation dam, was redesigned as a water-supply dam for Tehran). In contrast, the Third Plan hoped to achieve a 13 per cent rise in national wheat and barley output at a cost of about $14 million for producing and distributing certified seed of improved varieties. This result would be achieved on the assumption that not more than a third of the wheat-barley acreage could be brought under the improved seed; on land using the improved seed production would rise about 40 per cent from that innovation alone.

Again, estimates showed that the huge Dez project in Khuzestan (the two dams and associated canal networks would eventually cost about $200 million) would require about fifty years to pay for irrigation's share of the multipurpose investment. In the province of Fars, on the other hand, the rapid adoption of diesel pump-irrigation by several hundred individual owners was estimated to return the original investments ($10–$15,000 per well, with pump) within approximately three or four years. With the huge sums spent on Dez an impressive amount of small-scale irrigation could have been developed in different parts of the country. This does not prove Dez was a poor project; but it could not score high on grounds of objective economic data.[6]

6 The Dez multipurpose dam was only one of five major projects making up the Khuzestan regional program, a grandly conceived long-range plan for re-awakening what had once been Iran's most fertile region. The scheme was proposed to Plan Organization and His Majesty in 1955 by Messrs. David E. Lilienthal and Gordon R. Clapp, principal officers of Development and Resources, Inc., of New York. Upon approval of a contract, D & R established an Iranian corporation, Khuzestan Development Services (KDS), which carried on the operations in Iran pending eventual transfer of responsibility to an all-Iranian regional authority patterned on the TVA.

KDS's relations to Plan Organization and to the Iranian Government were governed by the personal relations between Messrs. Lilienthal and Clapp on one side and Mr. Ebtehaj and the Shah on the other. It was only with the establishment of the Economic Bureau and the launching of the Program Review in 1958, and the necessity of seeking foreign financing for the Dez dam, that the whole costly Khuzestan program was subjected to professional evaluation *by people representing the Government of Iran.* This evaluation came at a time when Plan Organization was trying to contain its skyrocketing program within manageable limits. The Program Review meant careful scrutiny of all projects that might reasonably be scaled down or stopped, and especially the more costly projects.

The net result of judgments formed over the next three to four years was that KDS was handling economically doubtful projects extremely well under difficult financial, administrative, and political conditions. By "doubtful projects" I mean that by measurable economic tests alone the KDS projects seemed to be sucking up large amounts of money that could have been used to greater advantage in other ways, both in the Khuzestan region and elsewhere. No prudent investor would have gone ahead with any major KDS project. The real question was how much money Iran should commit to projects on the basis of little more than faith in the eventual generation of *indirect* economic benefits that could not be objectively evaluated at the time. In a society with few well-conceived projects and large funds for investment it seems foolish to put undue weight on economic

It required the economic analysis of the Program Review and the preparation of the Third Plan to develop, in Tehran, an awareness of the much higher returns to be had from small-scale agricultural projects than from the expensive investment in large-scale construction which had soaked up such a large proportion of Second Plan funds. In theory, less money should have been spent on dams and much more on research, training, and small-scale irrigation projects scattered over many districts. However, the opportunity-cost of the "misallocations" of the Second Plan may have been considerably less than the economists feared, simply because the government might have proved incapable of doing much in the areas the economists wanted to support. The Third Plan was predicated on a belief that a considerably greater effort was feasible.

Despite the Second Plan's relative neglect of the basic research and experimental work necessary to frame detailed programs with confidence, enough work had been done so that the following kinds of general statements could be made at the time the Third Plan was being drawn up:

Improved seed (with varieties unchanged) was capable of raising *wheat and barley* yields by nearly 40 per cent as compared with traditional seed qualities.

Rice yields could be raised about 50 per cent by using chemical fertilizer; on the other hand, chemical fertilizer was not felt to pay for itself on most of the dryland crops (especially wheat and barley).

Improved horticultural practices (thinning of trees, pruning, chemical fertilizers, spraying and pesticide control) could raise *citrus yields* 500 per cent within three to four years.

Better management of *date groves* could raise yields threefold; *apricot orchards* could become five to six times more productive with similar changes.

The yields of *deciduous orchards* (apples, pears, peaches, plums, and cherries) could be increased, on an average, five to ten times by

---

arithmetic. It is probably wiser to abandon doubtful arithmetic and accept reasonable speculations for what they are.

What actually happened was that the more questionable uncommitted projects were cut out (the PVC plant) or postponed (the diversion dam) or scaled down (the 125,000-hectare irrigation project was converted into a very successful 20,000-hectare pilot project, emphasizing research and training).

such rehabilitation measures as top-working of the soil, disease control, chemical fertilizer, proper pruning, and similar steps.

The use of chemical pesticides and better pruning could double *grape yields*.

Production costs of *vegetables* could be cut by one-third through planting better varieties and by using chemical fertilizers and small power equipment for soil preparation and spraying.

With no increase in acreage, *cotton output* could be increased by one-third through the use of better seed and improved cultural practices (e.g., row planting, weed control, timely sowing). By 1967 it was expected that 80 per cent of the 300,000 hectares under cotton would be planted to improved seed, which would provide a 20 per cent rise in the cotton crop. The use of chemical fertilizer could raise yields another 30 per cent, but only a third of the area could be brought under fertilization by 1967.

Well-bred *dairy cows* could yield 100 per cent more milk than randomly bred cows. If imported heifers were used, milk yields could rise not 100 per cent but 500 per cent.

These are the kinds of "minor" innovations which collectively make up the scientific revolution in agriculture. The rates of return on such investments are exceedingly high, the pay-out is fast, and the amount of private investment required of landlords and small cultivators is within their reach. The two key factors in mounting this agricultural revolution were (1) communicating the necessary technical information to the landlords and cultivators who make production decisions and (2) providing ready access to capital so that a shortage of credit would be no bar to purchasing the necessary supplies and equipment.

To diffuse information and credit major reliance was placed on the rapid expansion of the extension service and the Agricultural Bank. But a wide range of other administrative improvements and institutional buildups were also necessary. In the last analysis, therefore, the success of the Agricultural Plan depended on the least dependable aspect of Iranian life, the administrative capacity of the central government. There was reason to hope for enough success to justify and defend the program; but the goals assumed that the administrative effort would go reasonably well. If the administrative effort bogged down, the Agriculture Plan would fall on its face.

Some Key Programs

1. *Plant production.* The crucial role to be played by better seed and (later) improved varieties focused responsibility on the Seed and Plant Improvement *Bongah,* the unit of the Ministry of Agriculture charged with developing and testing new varieties and multiplying seed and orchard stock. The amount of certified wheat and barley seed, for example, to be put into farmers' hands had to rise from 19,200 tons in 1962 to 100,000 tons in 1967. Research led by a U.N. expert had developed markedly improved varieties of both wheat and rice. However, nature limits the speed with which the supply of improved seed can be expanded: the first year is devoted to growing *foundation seed* on the *Bongah's* own land; the second to producing *registered seed* that can be distributed to commercial seed growers under contract to the *Bongah;* the third to producing *certified seed,* the first generation of seed to be put in the hands of farmers. This was to be done not by selling it to them for cash but by offering to exchange good seed for bad, which is then taken out of the capital stock and "extinguished" by consumption. The same procedure was to be used for cotton and vegetable seeds. Experience in the late 1950's had shown that farmers were eager for improved seed. The bottleneck was the government's inability to supply it.

2. *Fertilizer program.* It was only after 1955 that chemical fertilizer began to be used at all in Iran. Its modest spread during the Second Plan was probably wise, since comparatively little technical work had been done on the responses of various crops to different types and amounts of fertilizers under different soil conditions. Such information was important because the planners wanted to develop simple, accurate recommendations that would minimize the risk of misleading or confusing farmers when they were being introduced to a major innovation. Early experimental evidence had suggested that fertilizer more than paid for itself on irrigated crops (including orchards) but was much less effective on dryland crops. The construction of the country's first fertilizer plant at Shiraz, designed to produce about 80,000 tons of ammonium nitrate and urea, would provide the most important all-purpose basic type. But

before specific plans could be made for importing other kinds of fertilizers not produced in the country and before deciding on what simple mixtures to recommend, more technical information was badly needed. Fortunately early in 1961 a four-year Soil Fertility Project was launched by the Ministry, with strong technical and financial support from the Food and Agriculture Organization and the U.N. Special Fund. On its work depended the ability of the Ministry to identify and prepare standard mixtures for use in each of the six to eight fertilizer regions into which the country was to be divided.

3. *Animal products.* Because demand projections indicated that over the next few years demand would increase faster than supplies, meat prices were expected to rise. Traditionally, Iranian tastes have run heavily to mutton and lamb (which includes goat, an increasingly important element in the country's flocks). Beef and veal are not important items of consumption, with supplies almost entirely a by-product of mortality among dairy and draft animals. Milk consumption has been rising rapidly in cities; so too has the consumption of poultry and eggs.

The short-run key to expanding meat production was the expansion of feedstuffs, with disease control a secondary source of increase. The longer-run outlook was dependent mainly upon the country's ability to upgrade its seriously depleted pastures through a program of range management. Today, there is so little understanding of the basic problems of range management in Iran that little progress is likely for several years. Also, a program of range management involves telling people (including the highly independent nomadic tribesmen who own perhaps 25 per cent of the country's livestock) where they may and may not allow their animals to feed. Thus any program to control grazing promised to be administratively difficult and politically unpopular. For these reasons the Plan contained no pasture program. Where feed supplies *could* be increased in the next few years was not on the range but at commercial feed lots near urban slaughterhouses.

The additional feedstuffs would come partly from increasing the amount of irrigated land now devoted to forage crops (production is now extremely low, because there has been no cash market for forage crops) and partly by trying to make sure that the main by-products of sugar production (beet pulp and molasses) were not thrown away but were successfully diverted to the new private urban feed lots that were proposed. Oilseed cake, a waste product of oilseed pressing for the vegetable oil industry, was a third new feed source, especially useful for poultry feeding.

Poultry production promised to expand far more rapidly than any other branch of animal products. The target for 1967 was set 67 per cent above 1962 production, with eggs up 20 per cent. These figures compared with increases of only 9 per cent for mutton and lamb, 5 per cent for beef and veal, and 14 per cent for milk. The rapid increase in poultry production seemed possible because of the rapid spread of commercial poultry farming during the late 1950's, especially around Tehran. Thus an institutional base of established commercial producers already existed. Also, the gestation period of "capital" in poultry-raising is much shorter than with other forms of livestock, permitting a much faster growth rate. The key problem was an adequate supply of day-old chicks. One government hatchery, operated by the Livestock *Bongah,* would aim at supplying one million chicks annually, to be used as breeding flocks. Private hatcheries would supply about ten million (in 1961 the government hatchery was built but not yet operating; no private hatchery yet existed). The rapid expansion of poultry production was expected to relieve somewhat the increasing deficit in traditional meat supplies as changing prices and tastes pulled people toward greater use of poultry.

It had been estimated that disease was reducing annual meat production about 25 per cent through deaths or reduced weights. An energetic program might expect to reach half the fifty million sheep and goats by 1967, giving them vaccination against sheep and goat pox and making available drugs effective against internal parasites. Fortunately Iran has in the Razi Institute the best facility in the Middle East for producing animal vaccines and drugs. Thus there was hope of expanding the production of needed vaccines and drugs. There was less confidence that the extension and veterinary services could get them distributed as widely as hoped. But there seemed little doubt of the productivity of this program if it could be carried off administratively.

Milk production, like poultry, was expected to come almost entirely from commercial sources surrounding a few large cities, not out in the villages. The forage program also depended on the development of feed lots around cities, not on the ability to distribute forage crops to villagers or to persuade them to grow such crops. The whole livestock program, therefore, relied on tactics heavily weighted toward urban, or suburban, operations where fairly centralized administrative steps, linked to commercialized operations headed by urban entrepreneurs (dairymen, poultrymen, feed-lot operators) could overcome some of the administrative difficulties of reaching out into the villages. The latter and more fundamental effort would take much longer. While the Third Plan would greatly accelerate work with important long-run implications (e.g., expansion of insemination and breeding stations, the beginning of a range management program), it recognized that the need for rapid production increases required primary emphasis on other tactics.

4. *Water resources.* It will surprise many who know Iran that so little has been said about the development of water resources. Only a relatively small program was contemplated for this important field. The main explanation was the weakness of the personal and institutional resources for making any larger attack on the complex of problems involved in water—the definition of water rights, fixing water charges, the surveying of water resources and optimum methods of exploitation district by district, and the like. It was tempting to try to get around the weakness of the Irrigation *Bongah* by simply making credit available and leaving it up to private entrepreneurs to develop their own water resources. But even in those limited districts where deep wells constituted the answer to irrigation needs, any such program threatened to produce patterns of water use that were highly undesirable for both technical and economic reasons—wells wrongly sited, improperly spaced, and overpumped, with consequent depletion of the underground water resources. These dangers explain why knowledgeable people were so anxious to get technical surveys done before launching credit programs to support a larger private effort.

Tactics and Agencies for Program Execution

The main purpose of the Agricultural Plan was to achieve short-run increases in production. The best hope of doing this was to concentrate the injection of new resources in those regions with the best natural endowments of soil, water, and climate—i.e., in those regions where productivity and incomes were already highest. This conscious decision to neglect some of the large, unpromising regions in favor of others also involved a "threshhold" concept, a notion that if new banking, co-op, extension, irrigation, fertilizer, and other resources were to be developed in co-ordinated programs, then progress could be achieved only if the human agents involved in the program worked in close touch with one another. Effective supervision, mutual stimulation and understanding, rapid communication and decision-making would all depend on this "critical level" approach. Dispersion of thin resources over large areas in an effort to give equal treatment to many needy areas could only dilute everybody's efforts. To serve this concept further, it was proposed that in twenty-five districts falling within the chosen regions a local Agricultural Development Center would be established. This facility would provide offices for local employees of the Ministry of Agriculture, the Agricultural Bank, and other agencies represented in the area. The main hope was not for lower costs but for higher levels of co-operation, stimulation, and convenience. Unfortunately, nothing ever came of this proposal.

A second tactic was the reliance on campaigns. In any given district, extension agents would limit their objectives in any year to one or two major innovations, such as the introduction of chemical fertilizers, improved seed, or the establishment of new crops. Training conferences, literature, and supplies would focus on the campaign objective for that year. By this device it was hoped to simplify and dramatize the efforts of all those involved in trying to introduce changes. Needless to say, the mounting of campaigns involves a considerable planning effort by agricultural administrators. Whether this proposal, like that for the twenty-five district agricultural centers, would ever move off paper was doubtful.

With information and credit the twin pillars of the agriculture program, the key institutional problems for the immediate future were building up the Extension Service and the Agricultural Bank. Both agencies would have to nearly double their personnel between 1962 and 1967; the Extension Service would grow from 1,400 to 2,700, the Bank from 1,600 employees to 2,800. Even by the beginning of the Plan, however, both institutions were seriously behind in their training programs despite the availability of ample funds to support them. Both institutions became so quickly and deeply involved in servicing the land reform program of 1961–62 that nobody had time to think about training new personnel for the Third Plan. By 1962 land reform had almost completely displaced the Third Plan as a guide to the Agricultural Bank's operations.

Table 8 is perhaps the best way of conveying an understanding of how the credit program was to be used in support of the Plan's production and other objectives. Seventy per cent of the increase in loanable funds was to remain in the Bank for direct lending; only about 30 per cent was to be re-lent out to the credit co-operatives. However, the Bank was not to have unrestricted use of the funds made available to it: nearly two-thirds of its funds were allocated to ten "earmarked" or reserved funds established to guide Bank operations along lines that supported national production objectives.

Building up the Extension Service has been a special concern of the U.S. technical assistance program ever since Point IV started in Iran in 1953. In Iran, as in the United States, the key element in educating local farmers to new techniques is the demonstration plot,

TABLE 8

Agricultural Credit Allocations by Program

Type of credit and development program	Allocation	
	(million Rls.)	*(million $)*
Loan capital as of 1962	5,000	66.7
Loan capital to be added during the Third Plan:		
Reserved credit		
Fruit, nuts, vegetables	1,500	20.0
Tea	100	1.3
Sugar beets	250	3.3
Oilseeds	150	2.0
Milk	400	5.3
Poultry and eggs	250	3.3
Forage production	200	2.7
Wells	800	10.7
Ghanats	500	6.7
Forestry	300	4.0
Subtotal	4,450	59.3
Direct credit not assigned to reserved credit accounts	2,550	33.7
Capital loaned to cooperatives	3,600	48.0
Total new capital	10,600	141.3
Total loan capital as of 1967	15,600	208.0

Source: Table 8, *Agriculture Plan Frame* (1961), p. 190.

91

a reserved area where a co-operating farmer agrees to try the new methods proposed by the agricultural agent. These plots "speak for themselves" as villagers observe and talk about the new seeds, new varieties, new methods of sowing and cultivating, fertilizer applications, and—above all—as they appraise the final crop. The social structure of a village obviously plays a major role in determining whether or not an agent is permitted to enter and go to work, and whether or not villagers feel it worth their while to undertake the initial risks and added costs which more modern methods may involve. This is especially true where the landlord may not share costs but will share benefits. A village owned by a landlord suspicious of government agents may be shut tight against extension work. Even where absentee landlords might be sympathetic the communication links between them and their local representatives (the *katkhodas*) may be so slow or infrequent that the spread of new information by extension workers may be painfully slow and uncertain. For these reasons, special emphasis was to be put on "distributed areas," regions where land is owned by small cultivators at least some of whom could be expected to take an interest in new methods and all of whom feel the full force of individual incentives.

To expand the Extension Service as recommended in the Plan would require increasing the 1961 budget of $3 million to $8–9 million (under Iranian conditions it cost $3–5,000 per annum to support one agent including overheads). There was good reason to doubt the government's willingness to move to this much higher level of support. The 1960 *Program Review* was so impressed with the low salaries and skimpy budgets for agricultural work that it concluded gloomily, "So far as agriculture is concerned, the minimum basic research and educational work for reasonable development cannot be done under existing budgetary and employment conditions" (p. 32). Agents' salaries were by no means the only problem. Inadequate facilities and allowances for transport, fuel, and equipment and supplies frequently prevented agents from making their influence fully felt.

Land Reform and the "White Revolution" of 1962–63

The recent history of land reform stems from His Majesty's 1950 decision (he was then thirty years old) to distribute his private lands as a demonstration of what he thought all large landlords ought to do. To carry out his intention the Shah in 1952 established a special private bank, the Bank Omran. This bank has administered the Crown Lands distribution program, has extended loans to the peasants to help them operate their new land, and has held the mortgages covering the distributed land. (Although the Shah is often said to be "giving his lands away," it is more accurate to say that he has been selling them off.)

During the late 1950's the attempt to extend land distribution beyond the Shah's Crown Lands program was mainly an American objective. The strongest source of pressure for doing anything on this front came from Point IV, which had supplied several advisers to Bank Omran to help it administer the Crown's program. In 1960 there was a flurry of excitement when an ambitious land reform was introduced into the *Majles*. An emasculated bill was passed, unsupported by any provision for enforcement. The lack of enthusiasm for land reform by influential political leaders and the absence of any organized pressure for it from the peasants were coupled with increasingly frequent charges of corruption and favoritism in the conduct of the Crown Lands distribution program. It was partly because of this history that the framers of the Third Plan had decided not to deal directly with land reform. They limited themselves to some hopeful statements about what might be done to improve the cultivator's security within the existing pattern of land ownership. The Plan also outlined the main steps that any orderly approach to land reform would have to take: an accurate mapping of the country's arable land area, unambiguous registration of land titles, the settlement of the many disputed titles, and, above all, the adoption and enforcement of policies on the size of permitted holdings.

The planners' ink was no sooner dry on the Third Plan frame than events took a completely unexpected turn: the government launched a program of land reform that surpassed anything most observers could have believed possible. And it was not long before this sudden and apparently serious interest in land reform was caught up in a much wider set of reforms which the Shah personally carried to the country in a bold move to isolate conservatives and traditionalists and enhance his own popularity.

The move for land reform began in the fall of 1961, not six months after the reform government of Dr. Ali Amini had assumed office. The program was not so much the work of the Prime Minister as of the Minister of Agriculture, Dr. Hassan Arsanjani, probably the strongest man in the Cabinet. In 1961 and 1962 the country was being ruled by decree; the *Majles* had been dismissed indefinitely pending new elections. Consequently a land reform bill had to get by only the Council of Ministers, not the *Majles*. The new law was approved by the Council of Ministers early in January, 1962.

The law applied to all landlords owning more than one village (land titles were considered too vague to use acreage limits for the definition of maximum holdings).[7] Landlords were given forty days to select the one village they were allowed to retain. The peasants were to remain on the land they were currently working. In distributed areas the government would establish multipurpose cooperatives to supply whatever productive services the landlord had formerly provided. Instead of paying a landlord when the crops were in, peasants would pay the government according to a fifteen-year schedule of amortization payments. Properties were to be valued, somewhat vaguely, either by reference to the landlord's previous tax payments (though everyone recognized that most tax returns had been fraudulent) or to traditional sharecropping arrangements. In most districts the compensation formula yielded landlords well under 25 per cent of the current market value of their land.

Arsanjani moved swiftly and decisively. For an initial pilot project he chose a district in Azerbaijan that was regarded as a particularly feudal area, the Maragheh district. Making wholesale transfers into the area of the limited personnel of the Extension Service and the Agricultural Bank, the crusading Minister was able to begin the initial distribution in March, less than two months after

[7] Iran is thought to have some forty to fifty thousand villages. At the time of the land reform it was said that some two hundred families owned upwards of one hundred villages each. This would account for roughly half of the villages. Another ten thousand villages were said to be owned by landlords owning "over five" villages (presumably this meant over five but fewer than one hundred). Another seven thousand villages were owned by landlords owning from one to five villages. These figures, quoted from press releases, are open to question. But they are the only figures available.

the law was signed. In May, villages near Ghazvin and Resht were added (Prime Minister Amini was an important landlord in the latter region). Early in September it was announced that over 100 villages in Azerbaijan had been distributed in the first six months of the program. In the same month a huge earthquake devastated hundreds of villages in a large region southwest of Tehran. Arsanjani announced that the affected villages would be distributed. He also moved to extend distribution to a southern province, choosing an area in Fars not far from the city of Shiraz. It was here that the government encountered its first forcible resistance to the program. A government land reform official was assassinated and the government put the region under martial law. Between November, 1962, and the following March nearly 100 soldiers and citizens were killed in the struggle over distribution in Fars. Government force inevitably triumphed: Fars came under the program as other regions had. By April, 1963, the government claimed to have taken over two million acres of land from the nation's landlords. In January, the government had announced the distribution would be extended to *Vaqf* lands, trust land held mainly by religious institutions. With this whirlwind start it began to look as though the Shah really was determined, as Dr. Arsanjani said, to break the landlords' hold on the country and to create a free peasantry as a new force in the land.

Major problems had to be expected in a year convulsed by the plunge into land reform. There were formidable technical and organizational problems. A country with a brief tradition of failure in organizing agricultural co-operatives had suddenly to create hundreds of new ones to assume central responsibility for many functions formerly provided by landlords. The political problems of dealing with the landlords proved manageable, largely because their main instrument of political power, the *Majles,* had been dissolved and the country was being ruled by decree and the army. One of the most vexing problems was how to meet the huge and sudden financial demands of land reform. Compensation of landlords was less of a problem than finding capital for the hundreds of new co-operatives. Arsanjani estimated that some $200 million would be needed to finance the program. The only way the government could find such a sum without printing it would be to do what it had habitually come to do when it needed money it did not have: divert the oil revenues.

The mounting problems of the land reform program came on top of an overload of ordinary government problems. After fifteen months of trying to reform the government Prime Minister Amini, never strongly supported by the Shah, found the Council of Ministers unable to agree on a budget. Dr. Amini resigned in July, 1962. His successor was Mr. Assadollah Alam, a large landlord who has been a close friend of the Shah since schooldays. The weakness and inexperience of most members of the new government indicated that His Majesty once again intended to assume a more active role in the conduct of affairs. The National Front, the chief critic of the regime (particularly for its failure to hold free elections and to end government by decree), had been progressively silenced during 1961–62 by suppression. Indeed, when the land reform program was launched in March, 1962, it was dubbed a fraud by "the only leader of the National Front not in jail."[8] For the peasants in the countryside 1962 was a year of soaring hopes; but in Tehran it was a year of political disintegration, collapsing morale among the modernists, and mounting financial and administrative confusion.

Arsanjani stayed on in the Alam Government and the Shah continued to identify himself closely with land distribution, traveling to the distribution areas to hand out deeds to the peasants. Late in the fall the Shah announced a sweeping program of reforms that included five other major steps in addition to land distribution. The entire list was to be submitted to the nation in January as an "all-or-nothing" referendum. The six items included in the referendum were:

1. Land reform.
2. The abolition of traditional sharecropping arrangements and the substitution of cash wage contracts whenever peasants worked for landowners.
3. The nationalization of all forest lands.
4. A massive rural literacy program, with the establishment of a teaching corps of some 50,000 youths.
5. A uniform nation-wide profit-sharing scheme under which

[8] *New York Times*, March 13, 1962, p. 4.

employers would be required to distribute 20 per cent of their annual profits to their employees.

    6. Revised electoral laws to assure free elections.

Miraculously, the results were announced within twenty-four hours of the poll: over five million votes had been cast in favor of the Shah's program, only five thousand votes against. Voters obviously liked the Shah's role as champion of the worker and peasant at the expense of the landlord and merchant-industrialist. There were many who predicted that this bold referendum, like many earlier attempts at reform, would soon be forgotten. But many also wondered if the regime would be allowed to forget its momentary enthusiasm for reform even if it wanted to do so.[9] A government can trifle with the fundamental appetites of its subjects only so long, and so often, before some reckoning seems to be inevitable—if no "White Revolution," perhaps one of a different color.

After a year of rapid land distribution Dr. Arsanjani resigned, in March of 1963. Why he did so is not clear. It is true that some members of the government, led by the Finance Minister, felt that land distribution had been proceeding about twice as fast as they thought it should. Others say that Arsanjani began to sense the overwhelming problems the program was generating and wanted to resign while he was still a hero. Still others say that he could not get on with certain individuals in the Cabinet. In any event he resigned, and became Ambassador in Rome. It soon became clear that his successor as Minister of Agriculture, General Riahi, intended to proceed more slowly. Whether he would proceed at all only time would tell.

One fact was clear: during the eighteen months before the Third Plan was due to begin everyone concerned with agriculture had his attention focused on a very different set of problems from those necessary to make a success of the Third Plan. This is not important. A serious land reform program, even a hastily devised one,

---

[9] By the summer of 1964 little or nothing had been done on reform items number 2, 3, and 5 above. However, the rural teaching corps had been established (it has since been quite successful) and a national election for *Majles* members was held in September, 1963. The government organized this election on new and somewhat more democratic lines than has been traditional in Iran.

may be more important to the country's agriculture (not to mention its politics and social structure) than a systematic development plan. This judgment has to be made on faith and social values. No one could say for certain whether land distribution would help or hurt production over the years it would take to establish new social relationships and new institutions. But a program that petered out in confusion and loss of conviction promised nothing but tears and trouble—for the peasants, for the Shah, and for the nation.

The history of modern Iran suggests that confusion and drift are all too likely to be the fate of the momentous reform begun by Dr. Arsanjani. Land reform, like so many reforms in Iran, cannot be assessed except in terms of Iranian political behavior. Seen from this perspective, no Iranian land reform is likely to achieve its aims until there have first been much more fundamental changes in the political system than have yet occurred.

CHAPTER VI

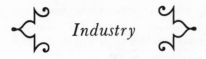 *Industry*

Introduction

In almost every country, industry is the glamor sector of economic development. People look to industrial development to provide much-needed employment; to generate higher individual and national incomes; to relieve the balance of payments by import substitution; to open up markets for the primary products of agriculture, mining, forestry, and fishing; to give the country greater economic independence; to generate new tax revenues; and to furnish an important source of national pride. Curiously, one of the most important benefits of sound industrialization is often low on the layman's list, i.e., to lower the prices of industrial goods for consumers. By and large, these hoped-for benefits of industrialization are sensible and realistic—provided a country makes sensible choices.

Although Iran's industrial progress before World War II was modest, apart from oil, and was confined almost exclusively to state-run enterprises, the postwar period has seen an impressive flowering of private entrepreneurship. This is the result of buoyant demand flowing from the government's generally high level of infrastructure investment, the ready availability of foreign exchange to finance the import of capital goods, the development of arrangements for extending public funds to assist private projects, and the emergence of a substantial number of industrial entrepreneurs. These were men who had either accumulated funds in foreign trade, were shifting their energies and family funds out of an increasingly uncertain and unprofitable landlordism, or who had been recruited to industry by an engineering education. Today, Iran is not nearly as far along the road of industrial modernization as India, Mexico, Brazil, Egypt, Nationalist China, or even Turkey. But it has made more of a start than many might suspect, and has good prospects.

99

In any country where investment decisions are primarily guided by a free market, industrialization follows a similar path. Iran is already well launched on this path. An understanding of this standard pattern of industrial growth helps bring order to the details of Iranian industrialization and provides an explanation of why, at a given time in history, certain projects look attractive, others unattractive.

The classic pattern of industrialization in free economies consists of a clustering of the early projects in three types of industries— essential consumer goods, simple capital goods providing materials for construction activities, and extractive industries oriented to export markets. This pattern summarizes and reflects the conditions of demand and supply for industrial products in the early years. Because incomes are low, consumer demand centers on such essentials as foodstuffs, textiles, footwear, tobacco products, and simple pharmaceuticals. The two main factors explaining the specific consumer industries that will spring up are what its climate is and what a country's farmers grow. The demand for capital goods, like that for consumer goods, is much wider than the country's capacity to supply. But there is one large class of capital goods that can usually be supplied more cheaply from home production than from imports—construction materials and simple items of equipment and furnishings closely associated with construction. While a development effort with any momentum to it will generate a diversified and widely based construction boom, a large proportion of it is likely to be located in a few urban centers. This tendency applies particularly to housing, commercial and government buildings, and factories—predominantly urban forms of construction. As in the case of consumer goods, the main determinant of which capital-goods industries start first will be the availability of domestic raw materials, mainly from mining and quarrying. The third great class of industries often found in the vanguard of industrial growth centers on the export of rich natural resources for sale in world markets. Oil, minerals, timber, and fisheries products are the leading examples. For oil and minerals, especially, the initial capital and management come from abroad. The home country benefits from employment and, particularly, from large foreign exchange earnings and tax payments.

The three classes of first-stage industries all depend heavily on domestic raw materials, particularly primary raw materials, i.e., those that come from the ground, from nature. The consumer-goods industries are based on agricultural raw materials, the capital-goods and natural-resource-export industries depend mainly on nonagricultural or inorganic raw materials (timber and fisheries are obvious exceptions). But the early industries today, unlike the Lancashire cotton industry of 150 years ago, depend heavily on natural resources—including land capable of supporting a reasonably efficient agriculture. Other common features of these early industries are a fairly simple technology and capital requirements moderate enough not to lie beyond domestic financial capabilities, after allowing for possible foreign help.

Once pioneer industries have been established, their subsequent expansion also follows predictable patterns. Typically, the industrial sector will grow along three axes: (1) horizontally, through the straight-forward replication of existing units in given industries; (2) vertically, along lines of forward and backward linkages that are suggested to existing firms by technological relationships and acted upon when the most attractive linkages become financially feasible and attractive; and (3) "exogenously," i.e., by the establishment of new industries that spring up from outside the system in the sense that they neither duplicate, nor stand in any close technical relationship to, existing industries. A country's first steel mill, its first chemical fertilizer plant, its first auto assembly plant is of the latter type. Once established, such exogenous projects set in motion further expansions based on the principles of horizontal and vertical growth.[1]

An understanding of the classic pattern of industrial growth was of limited use to those in Plan Organization responsible for leading Iran into its industrial future. Even questions of policy and ideology, far more important than general philosophy, got relatively little attention—mainly because the basic policies affecting industry had been set, tolerably well, by Reza Shah twenty-five years before any formal planning existed. Also, Tehran does not have an atmosphere where political debate is encouraged and where the habit of

[1] For a somewhat fuller description of industry's classic growth pattern, see the author's article, "Industrialization: A Standard Pattern," in *Finance and Development*, December, 1966, pp. 274–82.

public discussion is widespread. Consequently the main concerns of postwar planners had to do with technical, administrative, and institutional questions. In industry after industry planning was dominated by the attempt to answer four simple questions: (1) what is the present and prospective size of the market? (2) do domestic raw materials exist in adequate quantities and qualities to support a project? (3) what is the minimum economic size of plant for the industry? and (4) what is the present capacity of the industry? These questions lay at the heart of industrial planning in the postwar period. In addition, the early years of industrialization always involve a large attempt at institution-building around the edges of industry to support its growth: credit institutions, statistics-gathering-and-publishing offices, geological surveys, cartographic offices, tariff authorities, productivity centers, trade associations, professional associations, educational programs, bonded warehouses, a bureau of standards, assay laboratories, and the like. These are overwhelmingly government functions; in the Iranian political and administrative environment these inherently difficult tasks became more difficult, more uncertain, more fragile.

With this background we are nearly ready to turn to the making of the Third Plan for industry. First, however, a brief summary of Reza Shah's industrial policies and accomplishments, and the approach used in the 1950's under the First and Second Seven Year Plans may be helpful.

The Reza Shah Period

Apart from oil, modern industry in Iran dates from the mid-1930's, when Reza Shah launched a vigorous program of industrial investment as part of his program for modernizing the country. Except for a few private textile mills in Esfahan, the industries started in the 1930's were almost all government-owned. They included the beginnings of what are today the three major factory industries in the country—textiles, sugar, and cement. By 1946, when studies for the First Plan were begun, the government owned and operated thirty-four industrial and mining establishments plus thirty-nine tea factories and rice mills.

The size of Reza's industrial effort was more impressive than its long-term results. By the 1950's few of the government plants were well run and almost the only profitable ones were those enjoying a monopoly (e.g., sugar and tobacco). For the past fifteen years there have been a series of attempts to reorganize, rationalize, re-equip, and, since 1956, to sell off the government plants. These efforts have not come to nothing, but they have not come to much. At the one time when political support for disposal might have permitted it, the plants were offered on unrealistic terms (i.e., cash sales and no arrangements for allowing private buyers to avoid taking surplus labor). Later, when Plan Organization's star went into decline, the few public officials who gave the problem any thought thought it easiest to leave things as they were.

The 1950's

The most interesting and significant industrial development of the 1950's was the emergence of a private sector on a much larger scale than anyone had expected. The growth was especially marked after 1956; the next four years saw private industrial investment climb rapidly from around $60 million per year to an estimated $120 million. This was not an orderly and soundly based expansion. Quite the contrary. The boom was partly the product of an alarmingly liberal policy of industrial credit, a policy administered by the Ministry of Industries and Mines entirely outside the Second Seven Year Plan. Those who believed in monetary orthodoxy, conservative capital structures, and well-conceived projects lamented the loose standards that underlay much of the investment during this boom. For myself, I am not distressed that the country went on this "binge"—but glad it is over. Table 9 shows, for thirteen representative products, the impressive increases in output that occurred during the brief four-year period after 1955 (significant further increases occurred in 1960–61, especially in sugar, vegetable oil, and textiles, both cotton and woolen). The breadth of industrial growth was much wider than is suggested by Table 9. (See the chart, p. 116.)

By the end of the Second Plan, in September, 1962, industrial production probably accounted for 13–14 per cent of domestic production, a much higher proportion than it would have been thirty years previously. The oil industry was contributing another 12 per cent to gross domestic output.

103

Table 9

Production of Main Industrial and Mining Products
in 1955, 1959, 1962, and 1965

Product	1955	1959	1962[a]	1965[a]
Cement[b]	131	700	750	1,430
Sugar[b]	75	110	n.a.	200
Vegetable oil[b]	–	20	45	100
Tea[b]	7	8	11–12	15
Glass[b]	4	5	n.a.	5.5
Soaps[b]	15	35	n.a.	n.a.
Chromite[b]	10	46	110	n.a.
Iron ore[b]	14	30	10	n.a.
Cotton textiles[c]	34,000	160,000	260,000	350,000
Hand-woven textiles[c]	40,000	40,000	40,000	n.a.
Woolen textiles[c]	2,000	2,100	6,000	6,500
Matches[d]	300,000	400,000	n.a.	n.a.
Cigarettes[e]	6	7	n.a.	n.a.

[a] 1962 and 1965 figures taken from the Third and Sixth Annual Reports of the Industrial and Mining Development Bank, covering March, 1962–March, 1963, and March, 1965–March, 1966. For many industries (including cement and cotton textiles) 1962 was a year of depression, with operations below 1961 levels; by 1965 "boom" conditions had returned. (The IMDBI's annual reports, in English, provide the best source of data on recent industrial developments.)
[b] In thousands of tons.
[c] In thousands of meters.
[d] In thousands of boxes.
[e] In billions.
Source: Third Plan Frame, Industry and Mining (May, 1961), p. 5.

A brief résumé of industrial development under the first two Seven Year Plans is a necessary preface to the main concern of this chapter, i.e., how the Third Plan was made. Relatively little need be said about the First Plan in view of its interruption by the oil nationalization crisis. The entire $15 million spent on industry went into a half-dozen government factories, most of which had been started before the Plan started. The Second Plan was still limited almost exclusively to investment in government-owned plants but was much more ambitious than the First. Like its predecessor, the Second Plan consisted purely of financial allocations. It did not contain any physical targets nor any statement of the philosophy underlying the allocations. Nevertheless, the Plan's approach to industrialization seems to have been guided by five unwritten objectives:

1. To assure the availability of essential consumer goods, free of the disruptions caused by international events. This policy found

expression in Article 1 of the Plan law, where the government stated its intention of producing "public necessities within the country." This policy underlay the large investments in sugar and textiles.

2. To lay the basis for a greatly broadened pattern of industrialization by starting the domestic production of iron and steel.

3. To assure the availability of cement, perhaps the most important construction material for civil works.

4. To demonstrate to private investors the feasibility of certain industrial and mining projects by making initial investments in industries not previously carried on in the country. This policy underlay the proposed Plan Organization projects in paper, polyvinyl chloride, olive oil extraction, a few canneries, some of the mining projects, and the cane sugar experiment in Khuzestan.

5. To assist private investment by giving suggestions, technical assistance, and credit or credit guarantees. To exercise these functions Plan Organization was authorized to establish a bank or similar specialized agency.

Plan Organization's industrial program did not hold at all closely to the original allocations. Projects that got started early naturally established themselves as preferred claimants for the unexpectedly scarce funds. Among these projects were the rehabilitation of two large textile factories and the construction of two new ones, the building of a new textile finishing plant to serve the three large mills (in Shahi and Behshahr) and the construction of two new cement mills. All these projects cost substantially more than their original estimates—some of them, like the two cement plants, about double the expected cost. Consequently, in 1959 when, as part of the general cut-back in Plan Organization's program, the industry allocation was reduced from 15 to 8 per cent of the total Plan, the need to complete the textile and cement programs tied up two-thirds of the reduced funds available to the sector. Indeed the constant shortage of cash in PlanOrg after 1958 imposed repeated financial crises on all these major projects, demoralizing everyone involved in their execution—planners, contractors, consultants, and suppliers and their embassies. Yet the plants got built: by 1961 the government owned four large integrated spinning and weaving mills capable of producing 110 million meters of cloth annually (a third of the country's requirements) and the two new cement plants successfully furnished the cement for the Sefid Rud and Dez dams, the main reasons the two plants had been built.

Ironically, one of the main accomplishments of the planners was to prevent the expenditure of the large funds allocated for the country's first steel mill. This is a story that deserves its own telling.

The Steel Project

The Second Plan's proposal for an integrated iron and steel plant involved the country in a classic case of planning and project evaluation. The case involved major technical, political, financial, and international commercial considerations. Had the project gone forward along the lines being proposed in 1958–59, as it very nearly did, the country would undoubtedly have become entangled in a costly mistake, not one that could have been written off and forgotten but one the economy would have had to carry on its back for years and years. It is one of the ironies of economic decisions that the bigger the mistakes, the less likely it is that they can be written off. Too many people are usually involved to make closure feasible.

In the late 1930's Reza Shah's dream of starting his country's first steel mill resulted in a definite project's taking shape. An administration building was built at the plant site at Karaj. A small mill was designed and manufactured by a German supplier and paid for in advance. The war prevented the equipment from reaching Iran, which had thus paid for something it never received. When the steel project was taken up again in the mid-1950's Iranian officials returned to Germany. A consortium of German steel-plant suppliers (headed by the prewar supplier) was requested to design a larger mill for Iran's expanded postwar needs, and to say what it would cost. The design studies and financial estimates resulted in a series of reports to the Iranian Government extending over two years from August, 1955.

Apart from the trans-Iranian railway, which cost some $80 million in the 1930's (perhaps $500 million in 1960 values), the 1957 steel project would have been the largest project of any kind ever undertaken in the country. The provision of about $35 million in the Second Plan was only a beginning. One rough estimate showed the project might run to $150 million or more, including the necessary investment in coal mines, coking facilities, railway extensions, and the social overheads required in building a new town. So the question of whether Iran would be wise to sign the agreement proposed by the Germans was serious business. It was also heavily loaded with nationalistic feelings, suspicion of foreign advisers, with twenty years of history, and with all the issues of personal prestige and venal temptations that large contracts involve in Iran. The project was anything but a matter of straightforward economic analysis for PlanOrg's newly established Economic Bureau. Economic analysis had to fight hard even to get a hearing.

The details of the steel project are not important. What is important is the process by which these huge investment decisions get made in Iran, and elsewhere. Perhaps the main point to make is that no investor should ever put himself unreservedly in the hands of machinery suppliers for the crucial data on which a decision should rest. Suppliers can normally make plausible arguments for projects that involve purchase of their plant and equipment. It is therefore always essential to test the completeness and honesty of large projects put forward by suppliers. This can be done by establishing internal procedures for project evaluation that invite professionally skeptical critics (such as economists) to look at what the politicians and engineers propose to do, and to engage qualified technical advisers (usually consulting engineers) to pass judgment on engineering questions (i.e., questions of design, input requirements, and location). It is of course much easier to insist on an independent professional appraisal of a project if people other than the supplier and the buyer will be required to finance it. This necessity is what finally saved Iran.

The 1957 proposal from the Germans was not sufficiently convincing on some key technical and market questions to erase certain doubts which PlanOrg management entertained about the project. PlanOrg, having carried the project to a very advanced stage, and the Shah and others, having announced that a steel contract was about to be signed, found it rather late in the day to test these doubts by stepping back and arranging for an independent feasibility study. Instead Mr. Ebtehaj tried to persuade the German consortium to prove its faith in the project by taking a share of the capital. The Germans agreed to participate to the extent of 20 per cent of the f.o.b. value of equipment they supplied. The terms on which they did so would have required Iran to repurchase the German equity at guaranteed prices before the plant got into regular commercial production. Furthermore, the equipment would have had to be purchased from the consortium without international tendering, a practice that invariably costs the buyer dear. When the Iranian authorities perceived that the German offer of participation was nothing of the kind and countered with a demand for a genuine sharing of risks, the consortium said it would agree provided its government would guarantee its investment! This the German Government refused to do until it had satisfied itself on many of the specifics that still bothered certain people in Tehran. These were points that could be answered only by an independent feasibility study. But the government had made so many irresponsibly optimistic statements that it could not face the embarrassment of reversing itself and going back to the kind of independent technical and economic studies that it ought to have sought in the first place. Fortunately Iran was in no position to go ahead with a $150 million steel mill without international financing, including, in all probability, a loan from the World Bank. The latter would certainly not consider lending without a thorough feasibility study. Equally important, Iran had pledged itself not to undertake the steel project without first securing the Bank's approval. This pledge was part of a 1959 Bank-PlanOrg agreement to prevent the development program from getting out of hand through the un-co-ordinated sanctioning of new projects that would take the Plan way over an agreed limit representing Iran's financial and administrative absorptive capacity.

The World Bank was asked to nominate a number of steel-industry consulting firms in whose findings they believed Iran and the Bank could have confidence. From these Iran chose Kaiser Engineers and Constructors of California to conduct what was euphemistically called an "Implementation Survey," a politically dictated phrase with a go-ahead ring. It was announced that the Kaiser study "would answer various questions about how Iran could best proceed with the steel project." The Kaiser report, submitted in 1961, advised Iran not to commit itself at that time to an integrated iron and steel project until much more work had been done evaluating alternative raw material sources within the country. The report did suggest that a modest start, beginning with a rolling mill making the structural shapes that constituted the country's main requirements, would be feasible. This would be based on imported steel billets and the melting down of domestic scrap. It would not manufacture steel or iron; it would fabricate end-products. As a result of the Kaiser findings, the previously chosen site at Chamsabad was closed down and a more intensive study of the iron and coal deposits in Kerman was launched.

The Iranian and foreign economists who played such a large role in preventing the signing of a steel contract with the German suppliers feel they saved Iran from building a white elephant. They feared that the particular project then under consideration might cost the country millions and millions of dollars in wasted capital and in annual operating subsidies from the government budget. There are other Iranians, some innocent nationalists, others little better than thieves, who saw the halting of the steel project as another chapter in the long history of foreign interference with the legitimate aims of the Iranian people.

The moral of the story is not that underdeveloped countries should not build steel mills. The moral is: don't build bad ones. In Iran, this distinction got lost in a fog of historical, political, cultural, and commercial influences. It thus became nearly impossible to insist on testing the project for soundness without appearing to be against any kind of steel project. Although several Iranian economists saw this project in much the same light as their foreign advisers, the latter were in a stronger position to press for a ventilation of the key issues before it was too late.

What did the interested and thoroughly knowledgeable German suppliers really think about this project they had proposed? Their attitude is probably well summed up in a private comment made by one of their sales representatives in the region: "We have our private doubts about the project, but sooner or later someone is going to sell Iran a steel mill. We would like it to be us." This was not to be. In the fall of 1965 the Iranian and Russian Governments announced an agreement whereby Russia would lend Iran nearly $300 million to help build a 500,000-ton Russian-supplied iron and steel mill, plus a heavy-machinery plant alongside it. The mill would be based on the Bafq ore deposit and would be located northeast of Esfahan. Iran would repay the loan in kind with natural gas. This would require construction of an eight-hundred-mile, forty-inch pipeline from southern Iran to the border at Astara, at an estimated cost of $450 to $500 million. Not nearly enough details have been made public to allow a judgment as to whether or not this complex of major projects is a sound one.

Planning and Anti-Planning in Petrochemicals

The petrochemical industries produce a wide variety of chemical products whose common denominator is the use of oil or natural gas as their primary raw material. Iran has huge reserves of both but a market only for oil. For years large amounts of gas have had to be wasted, since much is unavoidably produced in the course of producing oil. In looking about for industrial projects to help develop the Khuzestan region, what seemed more natural than to look for petrochemical projects that might use this wasting resource? By 1958 two such projects had become part of the Second Plan. One was Iran's first chemical fertilizer plant, being designed by Belgian consultants as a Plan Organization project to cost about $23 million. The second was a $10 million polyvinyl chloride (PVC) plant, proposed to Plan Organization by Development and Resources, Inc., the American company in charge of the Khuzestan development program on behalf of Plan Organization. Both plants, plus a privately owned chlorine-caustic soda plant, were to be located at Ahwaz. As matters turned out, neither plant was built: politics killed the fertilizer project, economics and finance killed PVC. When the fertilizer plant was killed in the summer of 1959, PlanOrg itself was mortally wounded.

PVC is one of the many powders from which plastic products are made—everything from plastic pipe and siding for houses to rainwear, penholders, and domestic tableware and washbuckets. As with many projects, a PVC plant has to be built to a certain minimum size or it might as well not be built at all. Speaking loosely, the larger the scale of the plant, the lower the production costs. The consultants knew that Iran's consumption of PVC would be so low that they would have to build the smallest plant possible and still keep production costs in some reasonable relation to the landed cost of PVC made in the much larger foreign plants. The recommended plant had a capacity of 4,000 tons per annum; this would probably make it the smallest PVC plant in the world. In 1958

Iran's total consumption of PVC products was about 300 tons per annum. Over half the latter was imported as finished goods: imports of PVC powder for fabrication by Iran's young and small plastics fabricators were much smaller. A considerable job of market development would have to be done, to say the least. The entire market would have to be domestic, since there was plenty of PVC capacity in the world and none of the foreign producers or distributors had any interest in tying themselves to a small, distant, and high-cost producer when they could get all they wanted at much lower costs.

The KDS experts who were sponsoring the PVC project were fully aware that Iran did not then have a market for 4,000 tons of PVC. But they bet on a long shot: they thought a market could be created. To develop the market while the plant was being built, KDS organized two trade fairs (in Abadan and Tehran) to familiarize people with PVC products. It also built and put into operation a $500,000 PVC compounding and fabricating demonstration plant in Tehran to show the twenty to twenty-five plastics fabricators how to make more and better PVC products.

There were some people in Tehran who seriously doubted there was any chance of expanding PVC consumption to 4,000 tons for many years to come. When in 1959 the plant was dropped from the Khuzestan program because a shortage of funds forced a cutback, the decision was made largely because of the weakness of the market outlook. The project illustrates the general problem of deciding how much to risk in introducing new industries ahead of the market. If a project is indeed ahead of a market, poor timing will eventually be overcome when the market finally catches up to the investment. But it is not safe to assume that every plant is ahead of some market. It may simply be out in the desert with a product nobody will ever want.

It is not enough to judge the PVC project solely in terms of the market outlook for PVC. The project was originally proposed not because of the market potential for PVC but because technical features of the PVC production process fitted in with a certain conception of how chemical industries get started in countries with low industrialization. The American chemical engineer who originally proposed a PVC plant did so because its manufacture would bring into existence five fundamental building-blocks of the chemical industry (chlorine, caustic soda, ammonia, hydrochloric acid, and nitric acid). Demand for all five of these chemicals arises relatively early in the process of almost any country's industrialization. A chemical project that created these early building-blocks looked attractive on grounds of creating external economies that would encourage investment in technically related industries whose creation could reasonably be anticipated. The assumption was that Iran could count on markets developing for more and more of these basic chemicals, and could plan the initial units with a view to later expansions, expansions which would constantly improve the economics of the initial project(s). On this view, the government could afford to take some early risks and low returns (even losses), knowing time would make everything all right.[2]

The imaginative if somewhat speculative planning that conceived of this technically linked chemical complex came to nothing. Early in 1959 the PVC plant was eliminated from the Second Plan because the Plan had to be cut back to keep it down to an agreed size. That was enough to persuade the private promoters of the (technically linked) caustic soda plant to move their plant farther south, near their main customer, the Abadan refinery. However, Ahwaz still looked like an ideal site for the country's first fertilizer plant. Then suddenly, in mid-1959, came an announcement that stunned everyone in PlanOrg. The Ministry of Industries and Mines had signed

[2] There was no one in planning circles who knew enough about the chemical industries to have a sound judgment as to what might reasonably be started. The planners needed the advice of specialists. The International Finance Corporation was persuaded to send a two-man survey mission for a preliminary study of chemical industry possibilities. The team spent the month of June, 1961, in Iran. Its findings were summarized in a pamphlet published by the IFC, *Potentialities for Private Investment in the Chemical Industry in Iran* (Washington, D.C., September, 1961).

These experts did not find enough "conclusive evidence" to advise the start of any project. However, they did recommend further study in seven areas: fertilizer mixing, fertilizer manufacture, paper and paper products, viscose rayon, pharmaceuticals, glass, and sugar. The pamphlet contains a useful review of the country's small chemical industry, the main chemical-using industries, and the main chemical projects then being discussed.

The IFC experts had the following comment on PVC: "At one time the Government was seriously considering the establishment of a PVC plant. However, a comparison of the requirements of the country with a minimum economic size plant indicated that PVC production in Iran would not be economically feasible for many years to come. It is also unlikely that polyethylene and polystyrene domestic consumption would ever reach a level as to warrant its manufacture in Iran.... All that can be said for the present is that the case for the production of PVC and other polymers should be kept under review" (p. 27).

a contract with three European firms to build a large nitrogen fertilizer plant. It was to be built near Shiraz. With the same capacity, it would cost 50 per cent more than the Ahwaz plant the Belgians had already designed for PlanOrg. The Ministry had no funds for such a huge project and was not even known to be studying it. But there it was: a signed contract. PlanOrg officials were dismayed. The country could not support two fertilizer plants for several years to come. Somebody would have to back down. Officials at the Ministry, led by a bitter political enemy and critic of Mr. Ebtehaj, delighted in PlanOrg's embarrassment and their own triumph.

Superficially, it did not matter whether Plan Organization or the Ministry built Iran's first fertilizer plant. What mattered was that the plant should be a good one, that Iran should get good value for its money. As the weeks and months passed and more became known about the Ministry's plant the more it looked a bad project. It had been designed by equipment suppliers and sold to the Ministry without competitive bidding (its capital costs per ton of capacity turned out to be among the highest in the world). The location at Shiraz was nowhere near any railway and about 100 kilometers away from any source of natural gas. Shiraz was thus much inferior to Ahwaz as a location with respect to both raw materials and the distribution of output. The Ministry's tactic of committing the country to a major foreign exchange payment in moral violation of a government pledge to the World Bank and in defiance of the development plan was symptomatic of the lack of control and discipline within the government. Would an ambitious Minister dare risk his political future with such an act if he had not first cleared it with the Shah? And if this had happened, why would the Shah let one of his Ministers play such a game in violation of all the Shah's assurances that he believed in planning and financial responsibility? These were questions that never got answered.

When Mr. Ebtehaj learned of the Shiraz contract he made his continuance in office conditional on its cancellation. In Iran, this meant that the Shah had to decide whether or not to back Ebtehaj and Plan Organization or to remain aloof and let the mounting political animosity within the Government (spearheaded by the ambitious Minister of Industries) boil over and run its course. The

Shah chose the latter course. Mr. Ebtehaj's resignation was accepted. PlanOrg's autonomous position was curbed by downgrading the status of its Director and making it responsible to the Prime Minister. All the government industrial plants owned by PlanOrg were summarily transferred to the Ministry of Industries. Within months of these events the same Minister of Industries and Mines who had humbled PlanOrg was made Prime Minister. This episode reflected a mood that had come to a head in Tehran's politics. Although Ebtehaj's successor, Khosrow Hedayat, skillfully managed PlanOrg's relations with the government for over a year, the crisis over the Shiraz fertilizer plant put PlanOrg's future behind it.

The Beginnings of Industrial Finance[3]

A major task of early-stage planning for private industry is the design and establishment of new financial institutions capable of serving the requirements of modern industry. This was Iran's situation in 1956.

The period of the Second Plan had seen two radically different approaches to meeting this need. One was a highly political, all-government program of easy credit dispensed without any serious concern for the soundness of the borrower's capital structure or of the project for which he wanted a loan. The other was a joint move on the part of a few knowledgeable Iranians and experienced international bankers to establish an industrial development bank, free of government influences, that would finance (at reasonable interest rates) soundly capitalized enterprises after careful appraisal of each project. The government initiative came first with the establishment in 1957 of a $45 million industrial loan fund administered by the Ministry of Industries and Mines. Most of this fund had been committed and disbursed by late 1959, when the new Industrial and Mining Development Bank of Iran opened for business. The establishment of this bank was an institutional innovation of major importance for the long-run growth of Iranian industry.

[3] The fullest account of this subject will be found in Richard E. Benedick, *Industrial Finance in Iran* (Boston, Mass., The Graduate School of Business Administration of Harvard University, 1964).

In 1955 the Government of Iran and the International Monetary Fund agreed to revise the official exchange rate of the rial from 32 to 75 to the dollar. With this devaluation the country's existing stock of gold and foreign exchange (both used as backing for the currency) would now support a much larger money supply: the Issue Department of Bank Melli suddenly found itself with a new stock of rials that could be issued upon due order. In 1956 Parliament enacted a law using part of these windfall resources to establish two special funds to promote economic development: both Industry and Agriculture were given 3.5 billion rials (over $45 million each) with which to establish revolving loan funds. The Ministry of Industries and Mines was entrusted with making industrial loan decisions, Bank Melli acting as the disbursing agency. It took about three years for the full $45 million in this fund to be obligated. On the assumption that these loans supported investments of two to three times the loan value, something like $90 to $135 million of industrial investment was financed from the initial disbursement of the fund (spread over four to five years). Thus the fund was involved in something like 25–30 per cent of the total volume of private industrial investment during the four to five years when it was being disbursed.

The chart on p. 116 shows the distribution of loans from this fund in its first two and one-half years of existence. One is impressed by (1) the large number of loans going to what was already the country's largest factory industry, textiles, and (2) the large number of industries (fifty-four) into which funds went. Two-thirds of the funds had been earmarked for three industries, with textiles and sugar getting nearly 60 per cent. Over-all, fifteen of the thirty-four industries represented in the chart had received nearly 90 per cent of the funds. More than half the funds were given to new firms; just under half were expansion loans for existing firms. By number, most of the loans were small: over half were for $65,000 or less and over 80 per cent were for $260,000 or less. Only nine of the 256 loans in this sample were for more than 100 million rials ($1.3 million); the largest ($5.2 million) was for the Ministry's own controversial fertilizer factory at Shiraz. Five of the other eight loans over $1.3 million went into sugar milling, an industry first opened to private investment in 1959.

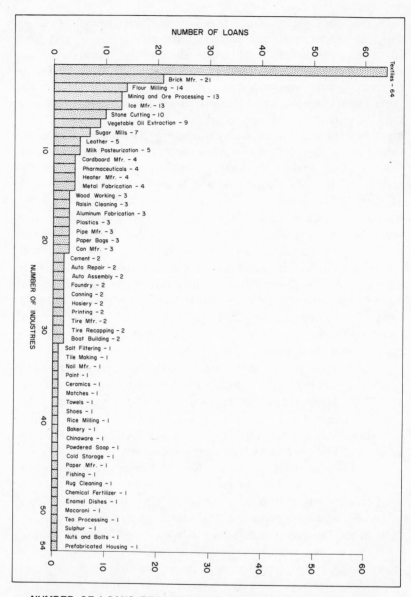

NUMBER OF LOANS

Textiles – 64
Brick Mfr. – 21
Flour Milling – 14
Mining and Ore Processing – 13
Ice Mfr. – 13
Stone Cutting – 10
Vegetable Oil Extraction – 9
Sugar Mills – 7
Leather – 5
Milk Pasteurization – 5
Cardboard Mfr. – 4
Pharmaceuticals – 4
Heater Mfr. – 4
Metal Fabrication – 4
Wood Working – 3
Raisin Cleaning – 3
Aluminum Fabrication – 3
Plastics – 3
Pipe Mfr. – 3
Paper Bags – 3
Can Mfr. – 3
Cement – 2
Auto Repair – 2
Auto Assembly – 2
Foundry – 2
Canning – 2
Hosiery – 2
Printing – 2
Tire Mfr. – 2
Tire Recapping – 2
Boat Building – 2
Salt Filtering – 1
Tile Making – 1
Nail Mfr. – 1
Paint – 1
Ceramics – 1
Matches – 1
Towels – 1
Shoes – 1
Rice Milling – 1
Bakery – 1
Chinaware – 1
Powdered Soap – 1
Cold Storage – 1
Paper Mfr. – 1
Fishing – 1
Rug Cleaning – 1
Chemical Fertilizer – 1
Enamel Dishes – 1
Macaroni – 1
Tea Processing – 1
Sulphur – 1
Nuts and Bolts – 1
Prefabricated Housing – 1

NUMBER OF INDUSTRIES

NUMBER OF LOANS RECOMMENDED IN EACH OF 54 INDUSTRIES

– RIAL REVALUATION FUND –

(First 2 ½ years)

Even if it were true that personal influence and "commissions" had much to do with loan decisions, the fact is that the Ministry made a lot of decisions and committed a lot of money in a short span of time. Despite the onset of depression in 1961, failures among borrowers have been few.[4] If it is true, as I believe, that countries with accelerating industrialization often have to choose between high loan standards and a high level of investment, then it is probably true that the revaluation fund helped development much more than it hurt it.

It was unthinkable that the mechanism of the rial revaluation fund could have served for long as the main source of industrial finance. Its staff was small, inexperienced, and weak. Its control was subject to political influences. It had no link to external capital markets and the promotional and technical advantages such contacts bring. The standard of its loan appraisals and end-use supervision served to perpetuate many bad business practices that needed reform. It was fortuitous, therefore, that a proper industrial development bank should have been organized just as the revaluati~ fund's initial stock of capital was being exhausted.

The initiative for the Industrial and Mining Development Bank of Iran (IMDBI) came from two New York investment banking firms that, with their Iranian sponsors, invited the World Bank to act as an advisory midwife. When IMDBI opened for business in October, 1959, it had a capital structure as shown in Table 10. This capital structure reflected some interesting aspects of the Bank, of which the following are the more significant:

1. The largest contribution came from a portfolio of "managed loans." These represented eighty-three loans (made originally by PlanOrg's Industrial Credit Bank and the rial revaluation fund) which the government agreed should be loaned to IMDBI to give it immediate earning assets. These loans represented all of ICB's portfolio of about sixty loans and some twenty revaluation fund loans representing about 20 per cent of the loans made with those

---

[4] It is significant that there has not been a high number of failures among borrowers from the revaluation fund despite the depressed economic conditions of the three years following 1961. However, the government has been obliged to lengthen the repayment period, reduce the interest rate, and extend new funds to certain borrowers. The original repayment periods (mostly five years) were too short even for good projects under normal economic conditions.

Table 10

Capital Structure of the IMDBI

Capital source	Rials	Dollar equivalent
	(millions)	
Equity capital:		
Iranian	240	3.1
Non-Iranian	160	2.1
Subtotal	400	5.2
Loans:		
Iranian government advance	600	8.0
IBRD	390	5.2
Development Loan Fund		
(U.S. govt.)	390	5.2
Managed loans	1,400	18.7
Subtotal	2,780	37.1
Total	3,180	42.3

. Source: *Industrial and Mining Development Bank of Iran*, pamphlet (Tehran, February, 1960, p. 3).

funds. IMDBI was to be paid a 3 per cent management fee for administering loans in this portfolio that were not over three months in arrears. This income has covered nearly three-quarters of the bank's payroll.

2. Without the managed loans the bank's capital amounted to $23.6 million. One-third of this was an interest-free thirty-year advance from the government. When in 1964 the bank needed more government funds it worked out a low-cost loan from Plan Organization. The government advance plus the managed loans meant that government funds had provided nearly 60 per cent of IMDBI's initial capital. Yet considerable emphasis was put on making IMDBI a private institution, in law as well as in fact. The experience of the first seven years shows that this pragmatic mixture of government money and private ownership and management has worked well. Around the world, most postwar industrial development banks have found that they require large capital subsidies from domestic governments if they are to reach a scale that will make an impact.

3. The United States Government and the World Bank provided substantial loans in foreign exchange. As in many other countries, the World Bank loan was expected to be the first in a series if IMDBI proved successful. IMDBI borrowers using these funds were obliged to assume the foreign exchange risk, i.e., the (rather

remote) possibility that if the rial should be devalued they would have to repay more rials than they borrowed. Borrowers from the revaluation fund had not had to carry this risk. When they needed foreign exchange they borrowed rials, bought exchange, and were obligated only to repay rials.

4. The share capital was small, about one-eighth of the total. It was owned by individuals and a handful of foreign companies interested in strengthening their information and connections in a promising country. Despite majority ownership by Iranians, it was agreed that voting power on the Board, and the bank's management, would be in foreign hands for the first five years.

IMDBI had a successful start despite the fact that three of its first five years were years of depression. It attracted an excellent staff. It completed the transition from foreign to Iranian management. It made about eighty loans totaling nearly $30 million. Defaults on its own loans were low, although nearly a fifth of the managed loans were in various degrees of default in mid-1964 (mainly for lateness in interest or amortization payments). Initially, IMDBI charged 9 per cent interest plus a 1 per cent annual service charge, for an effective interest rate of 10 per cent. (The revaluation-fund loans had cost 6 per cent, with the stagnant mining sector offered 4 per cent funds.) IMDBI's interest charges were not set by competition; they were set by management's judgment of a "just rate" under Iranian conditions and the Bank's estimated costs (including desired profits). Interest rates were reduced on both new and outstanding loans to 9 per cent in 1963 and to 8 per cent in 1964. This was in line with the Central Bank's policy of lowering rates as an antidepression measure. Notwithstanding, net profit after taxes has risen each year and prudent sums have been set aside for reserves. Shareholders have been paid dividends of 4, 6, 6½, 7, and in 1965, 8 per cent plus a 20 per cent share dividend. Most important of all, perhaps, is the fact that IMDBI had established itself, even before the Third Plan began, as the most effective institution in the country for giving life to the government's announced policy of advancing industrialization through private investment. Nevertheless, the revaluation fund continues to exist and as repayments allow it to become more active again there is a danger that Iran will have two sources of credit for large-scale industries, one a "hard-money" window (the IMDBI), the other a "soft-money" window (a ministry-controlled revaluation fund). How Iranian politics will dispose of the revaluation fund is an interesting question; there will be many people who will not want to see these funds given over to the IMDBI. At present, the IMDBI is in no way hampered by competition from cheap money offered by any government ministry: during the first half of 1965–66 the Bank approved a higher volume of loans than at any similar period in its history, amounting to a fifth of all loans made during the first five years of its existence.

The Third Plan: Aims and Methods[5]

As events turned out the Second Plan did much less for industry and mining than originally intended. It was almost exclusively a program of completing, modernizing, and constructing government-owned plants. With the relatively minor exception of credits given to medium-sized firms through the Industrial Credit Bank, PlanOrg did not attempt to play an important role in stimulating private investment. Nevertheless, there was an unprecedented boom in private industry during the Second Plan, reflecting an unsuspected readiness of the private sector to respond to favorable fiscal and monetary conditions, i.e., to cheap money and a mildly inflationary atmosphere. In designing a comprehensive industrial program for the Third Plan the main problem was how to sustain this new industrial momentum while putting it on a sounder basis. The remainder of this chapter describes how this was to be done.

It is well to fix in mind certain aspects of the planning machinery and certain of the institutional facts of life that governed what planning might accomplish.

The people charged with preparing the Industry Plan were the three Iranians and one foreign adviser who constituted the Industry Section of PlanOrg's twenty-five-man Division of Economic Affairs. These four individuals were by no means the most knowledgeable individuals in Tehran concerning industry. Nevertheless, they were the people charged with seeing that a plan got made. According to a theory that worked very imperfectly, the four-man Industry Section was to be linked, via an elaborate network of committees, with

[5] Based heavily on the *Third Plan Frame* (150 pp., mimeographed) published by Plan Organization in May, 1961.

other authorities also presumed to have some knowledge of and interest in the preparation of a Plan for Industry. The main groups were the Industry Division in PlanOrg, the Ministry of Industries and Mines, the United Nations and U.S. Operations Mission offices in Tehran, and the two industrial banks, PlanOrg's own (small) Industrial Credit Bank and the newer and larger IMDBI. These were not the only institutions but they were the more important ones. Consultations with "the private sector" consisted of a few ad hoc talks with individual industrialists, often in the course of visits to their plants. There were no employers' organizations to consult and no trade unions. That virtually no effective consultations took place between the planners and the planned was not just a matter of oversight and apathy: the absence of any institutional structuring of employers, and the thinness with which the planners' limited time and energies had to be spread over their bottomless tasks, made consulting virtually impossible.

Certain other features of the environment were important. (1) Reliable statistics on current output, investment, employment, and industrial capacity were not available. There had never been a census of manufacturing, for example (as there had been in some countries of the region). As in most underdeveloped countries, statistics of foreign trade were the best figures available. (2) Governmental machinery operated weakly, with occasional good individuals presiding over a cumbersome and inexperienced administrative apparatus with low morale and high venality. (3) Private businessmen characteristically regarded government with suspicion and mistrust, not as a source of information and technical assistance. (4) Few government people were familiar with the characteristics and problems of industry. (5) All planning activity was centralized in Tehran, with a consequent limiting effect on the planners' perspectives. Overcentralization was not a fault of the planners' approach to their task; it simply reflected the historical policy of not allowing local government and private interest groups to become strong.

The Broad Strategy

Four general policies gradually emerged in support of the overriding goal of maximizing the industrial growth rate: (1) public investment in industry would be sharply limited; private investment would be assisted "by every possible means"; (2) foreign investment and technical assistance would be actively sought; (3) whatever measures could increase managerial skills would be given a top priority; and (4) an attempt would be made to spread new investment outside Tehran and to create a new awareness within and outside government of the importance of small-scale industry. The problem of defining what was meant by "small industry" later proved troublesome.

The statement of general objectives was followed by an attempt to identify in somewhat more specific terms the main considerations that ought to govern the choice of industries to be encouraged. A government, it was said, ought to guide growth along lines of the country's comparative advantage. But not even the ablest economic advisers knew how to translate this advice into practical terms that retained theoretical respectability.[6] In practice, two tests came to dominate thinking on whether particular industries made sense for the country: (1) was there an adequate market for the product? (2) was the product something Iran could make to reasonable standards of quality and cost? If a candidate industry got affirmative answers on both questions, it was pronounced a good one for the country.

A key problem was to find standards of reasonable costs and to estimate whether a particular industry was likely to meet them. For established industries there was little difficulty: a comparison was made between the price of the domestic product (or its ex-factory cost, if you could determine it) and the c.i.f. price (without tariff) of the imported good. In a great many cases home-produced items cost more than the import. One simply had to decide how much protection domestic producers deserved in the interest of encouraging "infant industries"— i.e., industries that some day ought to be able to compete with imports without protection. The two most important factors favoring home production were heavy reliance on a domestic raw material and a high ratio of transport costs to product value (a factor which makes it difficult for imported goods to compete with local production). These two factors were never

---

[6] I have since come to believe it feasible to rank industrial possibilities by the ratio of domestic to imported costs, with industries having the lowest ratios deserving the most encouragement. See my article, "What Price Domestic Industry?," in *Development and Finance*, March, 1966, pp. 24–30.

conclusive by themselves, and other factors often counted for much (e.g., requirements for high technical skills, heavy capital investment, the size of market in relation to a plant of minimum economic size). In effect the planners made a series of ad hoc judgments about Iran's *absolute* advantage in given lines of production— absolute in the sense of comparing Iranian production costs of cotton cloth or sugar or PVC with the landed cost of imported cloth, sugar, and PVC. It was hard enough to get the data needed for rough comparisons of this kind let alone anything more sophisticated. For example, unless one knew the level of world prices for certain goods over a period of several years one had no way of judging whether a c.i.f. price for raw sugar of $86 per ton was low or high; unless one knew what metal zippers were being sold for in the home markets of Germany, Italy, Czechoslovakia, or Japan one could not judge whether or not the price at which these were entering the country was a "dumping" price (marginal production being sold at little more than the manufacturer's out-of-pocket costs).

The policy question of what degree and kind of protection should be accorded home producers did not command as much attention as one might suppose. The reason was probably that Iranian tariff policy has for years been quite sensible: home industries have been given no more than "reasonable" protection (usually much lower than 40–50 per cent on the c.i.f. price), and capital goods and raw materials have entered either without duty or at only nominal rates. It was never quite clear how duties got set or what principles were taken into account—Iran has no body such as a Tariff Commission and there are no public hearings or published studies dealing with tariff matters. Just before budget time, however, there is an annual review of the level of the commercial benefit taxes on each of the 300–400 items covered by this special form of tariff.[7]

More important than protection policy was its administration. Entrepreneurs attempting to start industries new to the country normally found themselves without any protection, or with only a

---

[7] It was explained earlier that the device of a "commercial benefit tax," set administratively by the Ministry of Commerce after intragovernmental consultations, is a way of varying tariff rates because the latter can be changed only by act of Parliament. The commercial benefit taxes are levied only on imported goods and are collected at the same time tariff duties are collected, and by the same agency.

nominal revenue duty. Since new production was almost always import-replacing (imports had proved the existence of a market) the producers were up against not only foreign producers but the domestic importers. This necessarily involved a clash for government favor between the producer and the importers. The outcome often seemed to depend on personal influence. As a matter of policy, however, most home producers could count on the government promising them some degree of protection, though they might have to wait endless uncertain months before getting a definite answer to their case. Nor could the government always be relied upon to live up to its promises—e.g., one major foreign investor who had top-level assurances of three-year protection was still waiting for such protection eighteen months after his plant began operations.

The Investment Program and Its Financing

The rapid expansion of private investment after 1956 had suggested there would be an adequate volume of such investment if sufficient financing could be made available. Since much of the investment consisted of imitative entrepreneurship representing the expansion of existing industries, the problem in these fields was to prevent overinvestment with its attendant distress among investors and waste of the country's capital and entrepreneurial energies. Consequently in the more important industries estimates were needed of capacity that would exist at the start of the Plan, of how much consumption would grow during the five and a half years of the Plan, and thus of how much additional capacity would be needed by the end of the Plan. Formidable difficulties are involved in trying to get tolerably good figures—the kind that lie behind such a simple table as Table 11.

The expansion of the larger existing industries for which information sometimes existed was only one part of the picture. Some way had to be found of giving shape and form to the total sector. The seven categories finally chosen were those shown in Table 12. The categories were somewhat arbitrary and involved different bases of classification; but they did not overlap, so that no double-counting was involved. The important point was the necessity of establishing categories to organize (1) people's thinking and (2) the financial

TABLE 11
Expansion of Major Existing Industries, Third Plan[a]

Industry	1962 estimated capacity	1968 estimated capacity	Investment needed	
			(million $)	*(million Rls.)*
Cotton textiles[b]	400,000	430,000	19.80	1,500
Woolens[b]	7,200	9,000	11.88	900
Cement[c]	1,100	1,700	18.56	1,405.5
Vegetable oil[c]	50	90	8.71	660
Sugar[c]	230	315	29.04	2,200
Dried fruit and nuts[c]	80	102	9.90	750
Date packing[c]	40	80	1.98	150
Carpets[d]	1.3	1.6	9.90	750
Leather[e]	1,250	1,700	6.25	472.5
Glass[c]	28	43	4.10	311
Food preservation[f]	50,000	80,000	6.93	525
Total			127.05	9,624.0

[a] Net investment in fixed assets plus working capital; excludes depreciation.
[b] In metric tons.
[c] In tons.
[d] In billion reels; export.
[e] In pieces.
[f] Units.   Source: *Industry Plan Frame* (May, 1961).

TABLE 12
Major Types of Industrial Activity

Activity	Investment[a]	
	(million $)	*(million Rls.)*
1. Expansion of 11 major existing industries: cotton, wool, cement, vegetable oil, sugar, dried fruit, dates, carpets, leather, glass, canning	127.05	9,624.04
2. Establishment of major new industries: iron and steel, paper, wallboard, synthetic fiber, petrochemicals	221.00	16,740.75
3. Medium- and small-scale private industry	242.15	18,342.86
4. Expansion of government industries: fertilizer, tobacco, tea, fisheries	15.90	1,204.43
5. Mining	47.50	3,598.13
6. Replacement	178.80	13,544.10
7. Miscellaneous		
a. Surveys	15.00	1,136.25
b. Support of foreign technicians	7.00	530.25
c. Increase in ministry budget	5.80	439.35
Total	860.20	65,160.16

[a] This investment is the total gross investment in fixed assets plus working capital.

allocations. This task took longer than one might suspect—several months.

The degree of precision and definiteness behind the figures of Table 12 varied wildly from category to category. The $127 million for expansion of the eleven existing industries about which something was known was a tolerably good figure, built up from individual estimates (themselves of greatly varying solidity) for each industry. But the $221 million for five "major new industries" was full of huge uncertainties. It included $150 million for an iron and steel project alone, something that, politically, could not be left out of the Plan at the time it was being written even though the feasibility study then in progress was expected to recommend *against* any project for basic iron- and steel-making during the Plan period. For tactical reasons it was wiser to include in the Plan Outline a big steel project so that the government would not have to admit that this project had been abandoned before it had the backing of a World Bank-approved study advising its abandonment or postponement pending proper technical studies. The other "major new industries" involved smaller amounts but not smaller uncertainties. Each required detailed feasibility studies before anyone could know whether or not it really made sense. Even when the Plan was nearing completion not a single feasibility study (except steel) was in progress.

The figure of $15.9 million for four government industries represented a fairly specific investment program of the tobacco factory, some bold gazing into a crystal ball to foresee fertilizer developments, and the arbitrary denial by the planners of an absurdly high bargaining request from a fisheries company that had a record of proven incompetence and suspected corruption.

The $47.5 million for mining was much too high: it represented a maximum should a lot of unpromising government projects prove feasible, plus an estimate of the level of private activity. The figure simply represented bad planning that could not be made any better.

The figure for replacement (depreciation) was arrived at by making an extremely crude estimate of the current value of fixed industrial capital in the country at the start of the Plan and assuming arbitrarily that 6 per cent would need replacing each year. The resulting figure of $178.8 million was about 20 per cent of gross investment; this is a much lower proportion than one would expect in a developed country with a large, long-established industrial sector.

Omitting the miscellaneous category we have now accounted for five of the six categories in Table 12. There remains the largest and most important item: medium- and small-scale industry. This figure is a residual after deducting from the total all the other categories accounted for above. It represents an annual net investment in fixed assets of about $44 million per year. The planners had no idea at all how this amount would be distributed among various industries, which they could not identify (and did not need to). Here was planning that was completely financial, with no physical content at all. Under Iranian circumstances, this was much the most sensible approach. In effect it left the physical planning to the future: the investment-regulating mechanisms would prick out a line of sensible decisions as the Plan unfolded.

The original hope was that a much-improved system of industrial licensing might provide not only a reasonable control over the intended distribution of investment but also the source of data for keeping abreast of what was actually happening to capacity in various industries. (The government had an investment licensing system, but the planners found it difficult to learn how or whether the system worked—except for textiles, where it worked well.) The proposal to build up this improved licensing system was not a particularly controversial one among those involved in industrial planning. But the more they tried to work out the details of a simple, workable licensing procedure, and the more they got to understand the mores of government administration, the less promising this method of regulation looked. Eventually the conclusion was reached that investment could be better controlled through the credit institutions than through a licensing authority. The Plan would simply set up the best investment target it could for the ten to fifteen largest private industries and leave it to the two main industrial credit banks (the IMDBI and the ICB) to allocate credit to deserving applicants up to the suggested limits. In these major industries (involving perhaps half of all private investments) bank officials were likely to have better information on the supply-demand balance in each industry than officials of either the planning agency or the Ministry. For the minor industries no targets would be set. The hope was that the credit institutions (the ICB, mainly) would learn enough about an industry in the course of investigating each loan application to avoid creating overcapacity.

Government Money for Private Industry

The investment figures of Table 12 represented the value of investment in fixed assets and working capital set as targets for the Plan. They did not represent the amount of government money to be allocated to these industries. The whole question of where the money was to come from (i.e., of finance) was an entirely separate matter; the distinction was not always realized, however, and people had to be educated to the difference between an investment target and an allocation of government funds. The latter would help finance the former through several channels—e.g., through direct investments, government loans for new plant and equipment, and advances to private banks for re-lending as industrial working capital. Similarly, private funds would come not only from savings generated within Iran and made available through domestic financial institutions but also from foreign investors, foreign lending agencies, and foreign suppliers of machinery and equipment. These same forms of foreign private capital would also be available for financing some of the government's direct investment. Thus the basic division of financing into "government" and "private" shown in Table 12 must be understood as a crude summary of a complex set of financing arrangements. The table makes clear the heavy dependence of all parts of the program on government financing.

The provision of government funds for private investment was the cornerstone of the Plan for Industry. The main problem in laying this cornerstone was not the one that would limit most countries, i.e., a shortage of funds. Money was no problem. The difficulties all centered on working out the detailed policies and administrative arrangements necessary to give life to the basic policy. No new public institutions were proposed; all funds were to be channeled through existing public and private banks. The job of programing the distribution of credit required (1) working out with each credit institution specific agreements governing the use of the funds to be given it by the government, and (2) strengthening weak institutions (such as the ICB) so that they would be able to make effective use of funds entrusted to them.

Since the planners were credit innovators they had to concern themselves with the practical details of their proposals. The planners contributed more imagination than experience to the field, and they needed the help that could only come from repeated meetings with experienced bankers in Tehran (and there were several). In the world of meetings that dominated planning, progress came slowly.

Another typical example of the kind of institution-building needed was the effort to turn the ICB into a serviceable agency for getting long-term credit into the hands of small industry. This was a weak organization kept going mainly by assured business from its parent, the Plan Organization. It had operated a small program of medium- and long-term loans to private industry during the late 1950's, but PlanOrg's cash shortage had meant that it had not been able to give ICB nearly as much money as originally intended by the Plan. Staff was weak, morale was low. The loan department was capable of processing four to five applications a month, all of them in or near Tehran. Since it had no branches the ICB had no way of attracting, or appraising, applications from provincial cities. Consideration was given to hiring a firm of foreign consulting engineers to serve as an enlarged and mobile loan-appraisal arm for the bank. Opening a few branches was considered, but these seemed too costly and qualified personnel too scarce. It was suggested that two- or three-man loan appraisal teams from the Tehran office make periodic visits to selected provincial towns and that Bank Melli, with 230 branches, be commissioned to act as ICB agents for receiving and screening small-industry loans. For this and other reasons the Plan recommended that Bank Melli establish a new Industrial Credit Department to lead the commercial banks into new types of industrial lending, and to achieve the geographical coverage for small-industry credit programs which only Bank Melli could provide. Nothing ever came of this recommendation, partly because no one had enough time to develop the idea in detail and to engage Bank Melli officials in serious discussions of its desirability and feasibility.

All these problems and proposals required long discussions and debates. The slowness of progress underlined how the shortage of experienced men limits the capacity for institutional growth even in fields where progress looked easiest.

Effect on Income, Employment, and the Balance of Payments

Not much attention was paid to the economic effects of the invest-ment proposals until the Third Plan was nearly complete. Only then were the proposals tested for their probable effects on employ-ment, income, and the balance of payments. It is difficult to imagine a cruder set of calculations than those which produced the results which follow. But without a research effort that was entirely out of the question, the following estimates stood as a rough measure of what the industry program would do for the economy:

1. *Additional direct employment:* it was estimated that the Third Plan would produce about one million new jobs by the end of the Plan (only two-thirds the growth of the labor force). Of this million industry and mining were expected to provide about 120,000 or 12 per cent. This estimate was built up from estimates of new employment in each of twenty industries, plus a crude assump-tion about capital-employment ratios over the rest of the sector. The twenty industries were of course the more prominent ones; they accounted for 55 per cent of the sector's new investment. To-gether these twenty industries promised to provide no more than 9,910 new jobs! The average of the marginal capital-employment ratios for these twenty industries worked out at $37,000 (the twenty industries included the vague but large allocations for "petrochem-icals," "steel," "newsprint," and "viscose rayon"). From this calcu-lation it followed that the remaining 45 per cent of the pro-gram would have to generate about 110,000 jobs.[8] This back-of-the-

[8] The planners assumed that a reasonable capital-employment ratio for this class of industries lay between $2,000 and $4,000. This figure was taken from what was known about other countries—with the Pakistan and India Five-Year Plans heavily influencing the thinking, mainly because copies were at hand. Using these limits, it followed that investment of $290 million would create between 72,000 and 144,000 new jobs, with an average of 108,000. When the 9,910 jobs from the twenty "visible" industries were added and rounded off, the estimate of new jobs came out at 120,000.

The best estimate of existing industrial employment (including perhaps 125,000 part-time jobs in carpet-weaving plus the whole artisan subsector) was around 400,000 to 450,000. The Plan would therefore increase employment in industry and mining by 25 to 30 per cent, compared with a growth in total employment of 14 to 15 per cent. Even so, the growth in industrial employment was considered disappointing. As a matter of practical judgment, however, there was doubt that the Industry Plan could reach even the low target of 120,000 because there was little conviction that the investment targets would be reached.

envelope arithmetic was a powerful reminder of the importance of "medium- and small-scale industry" in generating industrial employment. This arithmetic also seemed to justify the Plan's strategy for industry: since objectives could be reached only by a strong performance on the part of the "invisible" industries about which little was known, the important thing was to assure general conditions of buoyant demand and liberal credit availability so that the system would look after itself.

2. *Growth in national income:* by assuming, quite arbitrarily, that the marginal gross capital-output ratio in industry would lie between 3:1 and 3.6:1 it was estimated that the gross investment of $860 million would add $240–290 million during the five and a half years. When this increment was compared with the total increase in national income generated by the Plan it appeared that the industry sector would account for 18–22 per cent of the total increase.[9] Only the large agricultural sector would account for a larger addition to the national income.

3. *Effect on the balance of payments:* the net improvement in the foreign balance was defined as "the sum of the rise in export earnings plus the *net* reduction in imports." However, "net improvement" did not imply an actual improvement in the absolute figures between the beginning and end of the Plan. Net improvement was defined as the difference between what the balance of payments would look like at the end of the Plan (1) assuming the Industry Plan were carried out and (2) assuming no net investments were made in industry. (For this purpose the oil industry was not considered part of industry.)

Three industries (dried fruits and nuts, carpets, and chromite mining) had hopes of increasing their collective exports by about $10 million between 1962 and 1968. Eleven import-substituting industries might save about $56.5 million of imported industrial products; however, the foreign-exchange cost of producing these domestic substitutes might come to $20 million, affording a net saving from

---

[9] Thus industry would add to income about 50 per cent more than it would add to employment (the income-elasticity of employment was somewhere between 0.5 and 0.8). This was to be expected, since it reflected the higher marginal productivities found in industry as compared with most other sectors, and notably with agriculture.

import-substitution of around $36.5 million. Adding the $10 million of added exports gave a total net improvement on the foreign balance of $46.5 million. No great confidence was put in this figure; a range of $35 to $55 million was suggested as the possible net improvement. The rough calculations served to satisfy the planners that the net thrust of the industry program would be helpful and that most of the help would come from import-substitution, not exports.

Planning Supporting Services

In addition to providing credit, there were countless additional suggestions of things government might do to help industry. For example, there was plenty of room for improvement in the government statistical information available to entrepreneurs to help them decide on new investments. But unless one could spend the time to work out a detailed technical assistance project involving the Ministry of Industries and either the United Nations or some foreign government there was little more the planners could do than announce piously that "industrial statistics should be improved." This was not considered a viable enough problem to tie down limited planning energies on this front.

Again, there was interest in a number of measures to spread an understanding of modern management methods. For four to five years Point IV had supported a new Industrial Development Center attached to the Ministry of Industries and Mines. For the first five or six years of its life this Center suffered from leadership problems that prevented it from making any contribution to industrial planning. Nevertheless, some of the planners hoped that this Center might provide the core of a National Productivity Center. A center bearing that name had in fact been created within Plan Organization late in 1960. This was a paper organization without any conception of what productivity is or what a government might do to promote it. The center's head was a senior engineer who had managed to persuade top PlanOrg officials to establish an office for him to preside over without the matter having been given any serious thought by anyone. The existence of this National Productivity Center, ineffectual as it was, greatly complicated the problem of how to launch any serious technical assistance project for raising productivity, work which the U.N. has pursued successfully in a number of countries and which it wished to promote in Iran. Institutional rivalries and personal deficiencies put a very low ceiling indeed on the possibility of doing anything worthwhile in this field. These difficulties, which ran deeper and were messier than this summary can suggest, surrounded the Third Plan's recommendation that the government should "establish a National Productivity Center . . . with the close help of the United Nations . . . independent of any government ministry." What feasible administrative setting might be worked out (the crucial problem) was left unresolved.

These two problems of "industrial statistics" and "management improvement" have been cited to emphasize how difficult it is in Iran to implement, through government, the sensible ideas of people concerned with industrial growth. In such an environment one has to decide, time after time, whether or not it is worthwhile trying to launch some project that needs doing but whose prospects for success are so doubtful that no one plans with much faith or conviction. People tend to divide into those who think some good must eventually flow from any project with a sensible objective, and those who throw up their hands and conclude that the situation is so hopeless that nothing is worth trying. More accurately, people do not divide into two such groups: each individual becomes divided in his own mind. This is not a happy psychological foundation on which to build projects with conviction, consensus, and co-operation.

The mood of the preceding paragraph helps explain why an industrial strategy that minimized direct government programs seemed to offer the greatest hope of success. The key element in the Plan was the ambitious credit program described earlier. Two quite different elements, both in the field of technical assistance, were likewise based on government money but private administration. One was a program of subsidies for encouraging feasibility studies to generate specific investment projects. The second was an attempt to increase, through subsidies, the number of foreign technicians working in Iranian factories. (Both programs were eventually adopted.)

Special Programs for Small Industry

The first task in trying to help this sector was to convince people it was important enough to bother about, that artisans and workshops were really part of "industry." There were some whose industrial horizons stopped with a steel mill, petrochemicals, and cement plants. Rough estimates showed that small industries employed many more people, and probably produced as much of the national income, as medium- and large-scale industry combined.

The sector's size depended on how you defined it. The government had none of the laws or protective programs which define "small industry" in near-by Pakistan and India. A definition had to be made. This was finally done operationally, i.e., by describing the sector in terms of units the Plan tried to reach with some kind of assistance. There was little hope of doing anything for the largest number of "small industrialists," i.e., the urban and village artisans, because there was no way of putting the government in touch with them. There was no statistical information to guide the planners' thinking. There was no evidence that any research study, public or private, had ever been made of any of the small industries of the country. The planners therefore had to rely on their imagination and judgment to identify what it might be practicable to attempt in an environment in which there had been next to no thinking about small industry and where practically no administrative capabilities existed to mount programs in this field.

After sifting through all the program possibilities they could think of (e.g., mobile vans to demonstrate improved tools, taxing mill-made cloth to protect and assist the 40,000 handloom weavers, establishing an industrial extension service, forming co-operatives of artisans) the planners ended up with four things they thought could be tried: (1) they would establish a special credit program for this sector; (2) they would establish three industrial estates; (3) they would try to mount a special trade promotion program to boost carpet exports; and (4) they would try to organize a sample survey of small industry to learn more about these enterprises. These proposals were worked out in sufficient detail so that by reading the Plan people could get a fairly specific idea of what it was proposed to do. To illustrate the problem of planning for small industry the next few paragraphs summarize the proposals for industrial estates and the carpet industry.

1. *Industrial estates.* In a country where new industry was too heavily concentrated in the capital, where long-term industrial

capital was scarce (especially for small firms), and where private firms often had to provide their own water, power, and employee housing, any device that mitigated these problems looked helpful. So the Third Plan explained what an industrial estate is and urged that a few be built. But this was not a "Plan for Industrial Estates" in any meaningful sense of the phrase. It was nothing more than a reasonably well-shaped idea that was ready for the next stage—the crucial stage in all Iranian planning, the stage where an idea has to be carried around by "the planners" from office to office and from official to official, trying to get it understood by the people who counted, trying to find someone who could take responsibility for working through all the details involved in pushing a paper plan towards some sort of reality. Trying to carry this task forward in an administrative atmosphere in which few influential people cared very much whether or not anything happens was not exhilarating.

2. *The carpet industry.* This ancient handicraft employs more people than any other industry in the country and regularly earns $15–20 million of foreign exchange, trailing only oil, dried fruits, and cotton. Perhaps 125,000 people are engaged in the trade, many of them women and children, though in a few districts men predominate. For many years it had been forbidden to make carpets by machine in Iran, a policy aimed at reserving the home market for the ancient craftsman. In the main export markets of Europe and North America there is no evidence that Western machine-made carpets will completely displace the Persian carpet. On the contrary, the Persian carpet still holds its historical and somewhat romantic market position, endowing demand with a high income-elasticity. The outlook for the industry seemed sufficiently promising over the next generation to justify attempting a special program of assistance.

Reza Shah had tried to help the industry in the 1930's with the establishment of a government company to preserve standards of design and workmanship and to provide a government-sponsored sales outlet. In 1960 the Iran Carpet Company had about a dozen provincial offices, plus a large salesroom at its headquarters in Tehran. The provincial offices distribute designs and natural-dyed wool to the cottage weavers under the old putting-out system, with the state company a benevolent merchant capitalist. But for all this good intention the Iran Carpet Company is not a vigorous and effective preserver and promoter of the industry. It has done some good work, but it has done too little for too few. After thirty years the Company today accounts for no more than about 5 per cent of carpet exports and an even smaller proportion of domestic sales. The industry is overwhelmingly dominated by private merchants, large and small. This is by no means unfortunate; but it does suggest that the government's chosen instrument has had a very short reach.

Whether or not a government program of export promotion could improve on what private merchants were already doing was an unknown question. It was felt that a major sales promotion campaign, carefully prepared by marketing experts in Europe and North America, might be able to broaden and strengthen consumer interest in this classic Eastern product. There was fear that unless such a step was taken some of Iran's competitors (e.g., Afghanistan, Turkey, Rumania, and even Japan, where an enterprising Japanese had imported some Iranians to teach people how to make "Persian rugs") might eat further into Iran's export markets. As a basis for a trade promotion program two preliminary surveys were considered advisable. One was a survey of market tastes in the U.S. and Europe. The other, and less important, was a survey of production conditions within Iran. The planners wanted to know something about Iran's ability to expand those types of carpets that stood high in any market survey and they wanted to know more about production problems and the structure of production and distribution costs. The government had no organized information whatever about the industry. The Iran Carpet Company had a handful of dedicated individuals who were knowledgeable about the industry, but there were no studies and no one who knew how to go about making any.

To make a long story short, the hope of helping the carpet-weavers never made any significant progress. The planners did manage to enlist the interest of a good group of designers and students at the Fine Arts School in Tehran, men who in four or five meetings responded to Plan Organization's initiative with enthusiasm and good sense. Many of these designers and teachers were from the provinces; socially and psychologically they stood outside the administrative milieu of the government establishment in Tehran. In a sense, they were "unspoiled." It is symptomatic of Iranian life that the incipient enthusiasm and help of these people was cut down at its birth by the planners' inability to secure prompt approval for the two surveys they had proposed and in which the teachers and designers would have participated. Despite the budgetary allocation for surveys to produce programs for the Third Plan, the attitude of PlanOrg's top management towards surveys was so cautious that survey proposals dragged out indecisively over weeks and months until everyone's enthusiasm gave way to cynicism and the press of other work turned the planners' limited energies onto other problems.

The carpet trade will not grind to a halt because a few planners did not get their way with some surveys and because no trade promotion program was adopted. But as so often happened, there had been a chance to do something but nothing got done.

Conclusions

Over the past generation Iran has made great progress toward converting its industrial sector from a traditional low-productivity handicraft sector into the modern, factory-based activities that characterize "industrialization." This structural change began thirty years ago largely as a program of state-owned enterprises, when private entrepreneurship was exceedingly weak. A few of the government plants have proved viable but many have not. So it is particularly significant that since World War II a vigorous private sector has emerged in response to favorable monetary and fiscal conditions created by government. The key areas of government activity have been the generation of buoyant demand conditions through a high level of planned (and unplanned) investment expenditures and the provision of industrial finance through government loan programs. Some of the latter have been sound and carefully prepared, some highly political and slapdash.

The government will undoubtedly continue to sponsor, in the form of direct investments, certain major industrial projects (such as chemical fertilizers, iron and steel, and petrochemicals) that are beyond the resources of the present entrepreneurial class and the highly personal, limited sources of equity finance that are available. The government is unlikely to subject such projects to the kind of thorough economic and technical analysis necessary to avoid making occasional bad mistakes. It should be said, however, that projects sponsored by the National Iranian Oil Company, which has a natural hegemony over petrochemical projects, are likely to be better than most others. In great contrast to the powerful stimuli periodically contributed by the government's unpredictable monetary, fiscal, and credit activities has been the weakness of most of its administrative programs—e.g., any kind of direct controls, direct services, institution-building of almost any kind. It was because of this long-standing institutional weakness of the government that the planners relied primarily on helping industry indirectly through credit programs based on a fast-growing banking system.

CHAPTER VII

Manpower and Education

Introduction

In 1956, just as manpower planning was becoming fashionable around the world, the Managing Director of Plan Organization set up a Manpower Development Division and employed three or four foreign advisers to help in its work. This move made Iran one of the earliest developing countries to attempt a formal program of manpower development. Although the Manpower Division did some useful work in its four years of life, the Iranian manpower effort did not, by and large, achieve great things. The main significance of this work lies in what it has to tell us about the theory and practice of manpower planning and its relation to educational planning.

Basic Concepts

Manpower planning involves an attempt to overcome present or future imbalances in the supply of and demand for specific skills. The first thing for manpower planners to realize (as in Iran they did not for some time) is that there is no use at all in worrying about most of the skills a country will require. Most skills will take care of themselves, without government intervention. The proper concern of manpower planning is with the minority of skills that (1) are strategically far more important to economic growth than others and (2) whose creation is especially dependent on government policies and programs. In particular, manpower planning will be concerned with skills that depend on education above the primary level, and especially those requiring post-secondary study. However, one of the most difficult intellectual and practical prob-

139

lems of manpower programing is to decide what specific occupations do in fact depend upon formal study, and how much.[1]

Supply and Demand: Gearing Relationships

It is dangerous to transfer general planning concepts mechanically to the manpower field because the gearing relationship between demand and supply is much looser in the field of human resources than in most others.

This looseness explains why one is justified in treating supply activities so much more independently of demand estimates than is true in most other sectors. It explains why the supply side of manpower planning is so much more important than the demand side, even though many discussions, in their exaggerated emphasis on techniques of forecasting demands, give an exactly opposite impression. Even if very accurate demand estimates could be made (which they cannot) they would not give any more than loose guidance for the kind and amount of supply activities needed to meet those demands.

The main reason supply is so much more important than demand is that it is more difficult to deal with. The critical supply problems center on the familiar, age-old problems of educational expansion and include the following: the proper shape of a country's educational pyramid, the degree of differentiation within the system to serve special needs, developing the curriculum and teaching materials, providing the teachers, building the classrooms and laboratories, constructing the administrative apparatus, avoiding neglect of the special and especially difficult problems of the rural population, finding the money for one of society's more expensive activities. Manpower considerations—how to gear supplies to estimated demands—are implicit in many of these issues. Manpower planning can help resolve these problems; but its contribution is limited.

[1] A slightly more detailed version of this chapter appeared as Chapter V in F. H. Harbison and C. A. Myers (eds.), *Manpower and Education: Country Studies in Economic Development* (New York, 1965), pp. 140–72. An excellent discussion of the relations between manpower and educational planning appears in the pamphlet by Herbert S. Parnes, *Forecasting Educational Needs for Economic and Social Development,* written for the Mediterranean Regional Project of the Organization for Economic Co-operation and Development (Paris, October, 1962).

This follows from the inherent looseness of the gearing relationship, even if one pays no attention at all to the claims for education that do not arise from the labor market. When we add in these other claims the relationship between supply and demand becomes even looser.

This looseness of the supply-demand relationship stems from the following four considerations:

1. The unavoidable *uncertainties underlying demand estimates:* these reduce the seriousness with which estimates deserve to be taken.

2. The *nonmeasurable character of certain highly valuable skills* (e.g., for creative and risk-taking people in many fields).

3. The *inelasticities of supply,* which often make any possible supply response fall short of "requirements" set for any given date. This is an extremely important factor. It means that a country's education and training effort must often be scaled to what it can hope to do tolerably well over the next five to ten years and not to what would need to be done if demand estimates were to be satisfied. In such cases supply, not demand, is the independent variable.

4. *The highly arbitrary amounts of education and/or training required* in manning certain occupations. One of the trickiest and most arbitrary areas of manpower planning is encountered in trying to correlate education and training requirements with specific occupational titles or skills. It is easy to make general statements about the extremes of high and low skills; e.g., a "common laborer" does not need to have any education or training while a hydrologist or surgeon needs to have postgraduate education and a period of supervised training on the job. In between the extremes are vast gray areas where different levels and kinds of education and training may be considered essential or perhaps merely desirable. These variations in "ideal" gearing relationships depend on the laws and customary standards of individual countries as much as they do upon objective occupational requirements.

Classification of Skill-Producing Institutions According to the Nature of the Gearing Relationship

This discussion of gearing allows us to classify formal skill-producing institutions into three categories based on how closely their

141

activities are determined by the demands of the labor market. There are two dimensions to this relationship: (1) the *scale* on which the activity is conducted and (2) its *content*, i.e., how closely the curriculum is related to a student's future vocation or to specific occupational content. The three categories are these:

1. *The general education system*, excluding those parts of it which prepare students for particular lines of work (e.g., vocational and professional schools). In this area labor market considerations exert their weakest influence, nonlabor market considerations their strongest influence, on the scale and content of education. The gearing between the demand for and the supply of graduates is therefore looser than in either of the two following categories. But the higher one goes in any educational system in an underdeveloped country the more regard planners must have for the demand for their graduates, a regard that must influence the numbers educated and the content of their education. Since it takes so long to produce secondary and higher graduates, and since the graduates of these levels are so important for staffing development jobs, the shape of the educational pyramid which emerging countries should seek is one that yields outputs of secondary and university graduates adequate to meet estimated demands within a shorter rather than a distant time horizon. A national goal of "universal primary education," for example, would seriously interfere with the development of an educational pyramid appropriate to the needs of a country in the early stages of development.

2. *The system of vocational and professional education* is geared fairly closely to labor market demands. *Scale* and *content* are both geared explicitly to labor demand. But demand is generalized and is not tied to the job requirements of a specific employer or to temporary demands which will diminish in the future and would make foolish the establishment of long-lived institutions. Vocational and professional education assumes that certain important skills would not be produced, or not in sufficient quantities or qualities, unless special academic institutions are set up to produce them. And since the graduates of such institutions have invested in them costs which they and society can recover only if their skills are put to use, supply and demand must be more tightly geared than in the case of

general education. For many reasons, touched on later, the gearing is still quite loose.

3. *Training programs related to the needs of specific employers* obviously represent the tightest gearing of demand and supply—the size and nature of demand can be described precisely, with supply a one-to-one response, allowing for dropouts and post-training wastage. Ordinarily employers with such specialized labor requirements provide their own training. There were many such instances in Iran, all of them in government bodies.

Recent Educational Expansion and the Growth of Interest in Human Resources

The first major task of manpower planning is to work up a basic description of where the country is at the present time, in terms of manpower. This task has three parts: (1) making an inventory of the occupational skills presently found in the labor force; (2) establishing a reasonably accurate and complete picture of the country's educational system, the largest and most important skill-producing resource in any country; and (3) making an inventory of all the training institutions or programs that exist outside the educational system, including all agencies (public and private, foreign and domestic) having formal skill-producing activities. These are essential "tooling up" tasks that must be done before one can talk sensibly about what ought to be done next. By the time an explicit manpower plan was drawn up for the Third Plan these three basic inventories had been completed (it took over four years to do the work, from 1956 to 1960). But the expansion of education and training institutions certainly did not mark time waiting for marching orders from the handful of struggling manpower planners. All through the 1950's Iran's network of education and training institutions was expanding rapidly without benefit of any master plan. This growth is worth reviewing.

Recent Educational Growth

Despite the educational reforms of Reza Shah, in 1948 Iran was still 95 per cent illiterate.[2] During the next fifteen years, however, education became one of the fastest-growing sectors in the economy. All three levels of the system seem to have been growing at rates above 10 per cent a year, as indicated in Table 13. Although all levels have grown rapidly, secondary education has grown almost twice as fast as the two other levels. Notwithstanding, the 1960 enrollment rate for thirteen- through eighteen-year-olds was only 13 per cent compared with 40 per cent for primary-age children. Among urban primary-age children, the enrollment rate was 85 per cent as against only 25 per cent in the rural areas, where two-thirds of the children are. Dropouts are vaguely known to be heavy at both levels.

TABLE 13

Educational Enrollments, 1945–46 and 1959–60

Level	1945–46	Per cent	1959–60	Per cent	Per cent increase
Primary	288,000	89	1,327,000	82	360
Secondary	29,000	9	253,000	16	770
University	6,000	2	30,000	2	400
Total	323,000	100	1,610,000	100	400

The pattern of university enrollment has changed almost as significantly as the numbers, in two ways. First, in 1945 there was only one university, in Tehran. By 1960 five struggling provincial universities were in existence, with about 4,000 students as compared with 13,000 in Tehran. Second, there has been a dramatic increase in the proportion of university students going abroad for their studies: in 1945–46 25–30 per cent of all university students were enrolled abroad; in 1960 the proportion was about 45–50 per cent. The large number of students who have gone abroad, most at their own expense, testifies to the strong desire for a university education among those who can afford it. In the early 1960's the annual cost of foreign study was running around $30 million, about a third of total export earnings excluding oil. Foreign studies have not been

[2] A good summary of Reza Shah's educational reforms will be found in Banani, *The Modernization of Iran, 1921–41*, Chapter VI, "Educational Reforms," pp. 85–111.

closely geared to national needs, and a sizable (but unknown) number of students have failed to return to Iran after completing their studies.[3]

Foreign Influences

The impressive educational growth of the 1950's was not a simple expansion of the educational system as it existed in the late 1940's. The period was one of experimentation and differentiation, not according to any plan but through a series of ad hoc projects and programs. The extent of this growth, experimentation, and differentiation of the system has often been neglected by observers. The presence of large numbers of foreign advisers, in every conceivable branch of education and training, was undoubtedly the main source of innovations. In addition, foreigners, and particularly the Americans, pushed hard at purely quantitative expansion.

The largest, most pervasive source of technical assistance on manpower problems was the United States foreign aid program, both civilian and military. There was hardly an agency or program of the Iranian Government concerned with training or education that did not have its Point IV experts or U.S. contract group. There were U.S. advisers in all the ministries active in education and training, most importantly in the ministries of Education and Labor. There have been American advisers and teachers in technical schools (though fewer than French and German teachers). One of the most successful U.S. training efforts was in the field of police training, which included everything from directing traffic to riot-control and security investigation techniques. There have been U.S. university contract teams in residence at the Agricultural College in Karaj, at the National Teachers College in Tehran, and at the Institute of Administrative Affairs at the University of Tehran. This list is far from complete.

Second to the U.S. in number and variety were the experts of the several U.N. agencies—UNESCO, the W.H.O., the I.L.O., the I.C.A.B., and others—involved in manpower and education projects. Their jobs ranged from general educational planning to the training of ground personnel for civil aviation. Private sources of aid in-

[3] See the author's article, "The Foreign-Educated Iranian: A Profile," *The Middle East Journal,* Summer, 1963, pp. 264–78.

cluded the Near East Foundation (a leader in vocationally-oriented rural education); the Ford Foundation, with a demonstration vocational school in Shiraz and a major experiment in community development in the Gorgan district; and the Organization for Rehabilitation through Training (ORT), a Swiss-based agency that ran a fee-charging vocational school in Tehran, probably the best one in the country. The German Government, too, had a long tradition of supplying instructors for one or two vocational schools.

There remains the oil industry. The trade school in Abadan had long been recognized as one of the best in the country. By 1958 the National Iranian Oil Company had established a training department that had developed ambitious plans for almost all the kinds of manual, white collar, and executive training found in any large Western company. NIOC also ran the Abadan Institute of Technology. An attempt in the late 1950's to upgrade this once-British technical college into a degree-granting engineering college along American lines was weakened by confusion and conflict at the policy level.

This summary of educational expansion and the amount of technical assistance going into education and training makes clear that the subject of human resources received a great deal of attention during the 1950's. The system was growing up "like Topsy," with no government agency assigned responsibility for studying the country's needs and trying to see that they were being met. To perform this function Plan Organization established, in 1956, what was intended to be a major new office, a Manpower Development Division.

Although the Division did some useful statistical work it proved to be an ill-starred and ineffective division, progressively weakened by politics. When the first national manpower plan was prepared in 1960–61 the Manpower Division played no part in the task: the work was done by PlanOrg's Economic Bureau. In 1961 the Division was abolished.

No planners could have been more aware of the importance of human resources than the members of the Economic Bureau. The fact that the planners were able to produce a respectable program for increasing the country's supply of trained manpower was a considerable achievement. In 1961 for the first time the country had, on paper, a comprehensive general strategy for increasing the output of needed skills. But like most of Iran's planning the preparation of specific projects lagged badly. Ironically, the most dramatic and successful manpower program during the Third Plan (the Army-based Literary Corps) was not a product of that Plan.

The writing of tolerably well-co-ordinated manpower and education plans does not mean that the approach to manpower planning in Tehran was orderly, confident, and well-disciplined. Far from it. There were separate and sometimes rival groups working on overlapping parts of the over-all problem. People (including the foreign advisers) were often confused as to just what the "over-all problem" of manpower planning really was and how the parts ought to be fitted together. There was no one in the country, Iranian or foreigner, who had ever been through a full-scale effort at manpower planning and who might have given an authoritative lead. So the planners had to muddle along hoping they would muddle through.

The National Manpower Survey of 1958: Uses and Limitations

When PlanOrg's Manpower Development Division decided in 1957 to make estimates of Iran's future manpower requirements so that measures could be taken to meet them, it had to collect its own statistics. Neither Iran's young Ministry of Labor nor any other branch of the Iranian government published employment, occupational, or wage and salary information of any kind.

The successful carrying out of a National Manpower Survey in 1958 was a triumph of ingenuity, diplomacy, and patience for the two or three Iranians and their foreign advisers who were responsible for it. The Survey classified all employed members of the non-agricultural labor force into one of the 240 three-digit occupational classifications contained in the ILO's (preliminary) Standard Classification of Occupations. This was Iran's first inventory of its human skills. The Survey also attempted to deal with future demand, although these estimates were open to serious question. A separate survey of the country's present and future output of graduates from the educational system, and from training courses outside the education system, provided a basis for estimating additions to the 1958 stock of manpower for those occupations fed, in whole or in part, by the formal skill-producing institutions. These figures,

147

plus those from the Manpower Survey, pointed to surpluses and shortages in the more important occupations two and five years in the future.

The 1958 Manpower Survey revealed some interesting facts about the structure of Iran's high-level manpower, the strategic group for economic development.[4] Table 14 presents the general occupational structure of the entire nonagricultural labor force covered by the 1958 manpower survey. High-level manpower was defined by selecting from the whole list of occupations those considered critical for economic development. There were two elements to the definition: (1) an occupation had to require a large amount of formal education (usually completion of secondary school) and perhaps some additional vocational training, and (2) the occupation must have contributed to the performance of an activity judged essential to the country's development. Thus the training of *mullahs,* archeologists, musicologists, art historians, and the like would have met the first test but not the second. Inevitably there were borderline occupations whose inclusion or exclusion was arbitrary.[5]

The Manpower Development Division selected forty-six occupations as the high-level manpower group. All of these occupations lay in Group 1, the "Professional, Technical and Related" group of Table 14. This group (shown by three-digit occupation in Table 15) contained 85,700; but not all these were in occupations considered critical to development. When the latter test was applied,

[4] Ministry of Labor and Plan Organization, *National Manpower Resources & Requirements Survey, Iran, 1958,* Tehran, July, 1959, 90 pp.

[5] The above definition of high-level manpower rests entirely on acquired characteristics, i.e., on background and skill conferred by education and training. It says nothing about the contribution of natural talent (perhaps entirely untouched by education, or only barely touched by a few years' schooling) to such key occupational roles as entrepreneurship and political leadership. The main contribution of primary education to development may be its function of mobilizing for modern activities the statistically small proportion of any population born with talents especially useful for nation-building. This seems at least as important a reason for a generous expansion of primary education as the much more common argument based on the creation of a literate labor force. Functional literacy is also a less important justification for primary-school expansion than increasing the number of eligibles from whom selections can be made for entry into secondary schools and universities. Thus first-level education is primarily important as a selection mechanism for mobilizing the *natural* talent in the population so that it can be upgraded with *acquired* skills. Fortunately this perspective coincides with the normal configuration of political pressures.

TABLE 14
Occupational Structure in Nonagricultural Employment, 1958

ILO code	Title	Number	Per cent of total	Per cent of own group
1.	*Professional, technical and related*	85,700	6.3	
10–11	Physical sciences and related	9,870		11.5
12	Biological and agricultural sciences and related	1,950		2.3
13	Medical and health sciences and related	21,730		25.3
14–15	Social sciences and related	47,630		55.6
16–17	Artistic, writing, entertaining, and related	4,540		5.3
				100.0
2.	*Managerial, administrative, clerical and related*	115,820	8.4	
20	Managerial and administrative, staff	3,560		3.1
21–24	Managerial and administrative, line	15,610		13.5
25	Clerical and related	96,650		83.4
	High-level management (incl. above)	(1,610)		(1.4)
				(100)
3.	*Sales and related*	250,050	18.3	
30	Retail selling	230,450		94.0
31	Wholesale selling and related	19,600		6.0
				100.0
5.	*Mining, quarrying, and well drilling*	16,870	1.2	
50	Mining and quarrying	9,450		56.0
52	Well drilling, petroleum and gas	50		0.3
59	Laborers	7,370		43.7
				100.0
6.	*Operating transport*	44,940	3.3	
60	Ships and boats	2,940		6.6
61	Aircraft	60		0.1
62	Railways	2,400		5.3
63	Road vehicles	39,540		88.0
				100.0
7–8.	*Crafts, production processes, and related*	718,110	52.4	
70	Textile making	71,120		9.9
71	Textile finishing (except printing)	3,340		0.5
72	Garment and related textile and leather products making	100,890		14.0
73	Basketry, broom and brushmaking	4,180		0.6
74	Woodworking and related	30,180		4.2
75	Metal making and treating	19,740		2.7
76	Metal machining, fitting, assembling	48,330		6.8
				(38.7)

TABLE 14 *(Continued)*
Occupational Structure in Nonagricultural Employment, 1958

ILO code		Title	Number	Per cent of total	Per cent of own group
	77	Metal working miscellaneous (excluding machining)	31,990		4.5
	78	Electrical and electronic	15,190		2.1
79–80		Construction and related	135,730		18.9
	81	Stationary engine, lifting equipment, machinery operation	13,500		1.9
	82	Printing, bookbinding, and paper product making	9,500		1.3
	83	Ceramic and related	64,930		9.0
	84	Chemicals and related processing	3,610		0.5
	85	Felt and hide treating	5,080		0.7
	87	Miscellaneous crafts, production processes, and related	9,880		1.4
	89	Laborers in crafts, production, and related	75,330		10.5
					100.0
9.		*Services*	138,850	10.1	
	90	Protective service	13,940		10.0
	91	Domestic (institutional), personal, and related	122,950		89.0
	99	Laborers	1,960		1.0
		Total covered:	1,370,600	100.0	100.0
		Female	68,320	5.0	
		Foremen	8,820	0.6	
		Leadmen	14,400	1.1	
		Skilled[a]	342,180	25.0	
		Semi-skilled[a]	116,530	8.5	
		Unskilled	238,470	17.4	

[a] A "skilled" person was defined as one "qualified to do a particular job adequately"; all jobs except those "that do not require any special training, knowledge or skill" were included in determining whether or not a person was to be classified as "skilled." The concept of "skill" was not related to the inherent difficulty of the job and the length of time it would take a normal person to become proficient, essential elements in most systems of skill-classification. The loose definition of skill used in the Iranian Survey accounts for the untypical distribution of people among the three skill levels. It would have been better if the classification had been based on job difficulty and the desirability of formal training; but these would have required a degree of knowledge about the content of Iranian jobs that was not available and could not have been quickly gathered.

Source: Table 1, *National Manpower Resources & Requirements Survey,* pp. 1–2. Figures rounded to nearest 10 or 100.

the total was reduced to about 75,000 people. This was Iran's stock of high-level manpower; it constituted 5.5 per cent of the nonagricultural labor force, 1.25 per cent of the total labor force, and 0.4 per cent of the population. These figures would give Iran a high-level manpower ranking far above sub-Sahara African countries and just below Egypt and India.

TABLE 15

Detailed Occupations within the "Professional, Technical, and Related" Category

ILO code		Title	Number	Per-cent of total	Per cent of own group
10–11.		*Physical sciences and related*	9,870	11.5	
	100	Architects	113		1.1
	101	Engineers, civil	2,536		25.7
	102	Engineers, electrical	1,414		14.3
	103	Engineers, mechanical	1,914		19.4
	104	Engineers, metallurgical	2		–
	105	Engineers, mining	133		1.3
	106	Engineers, chemical	547		5.3
	107	Engineers, miscellaneous	964		9.8
	108	Chemists	610		6.2
	109	Physicists	17		0.2
	110	Geophysicists	109		1.1
	111	Geologists	98		1.0
	112	Geographers	5		0.1
	113	Physical scientists, miscellaneous	7		0.1
	114	Draughtsmen and cartographers	997		10.1
	115	Surveyors	402		4.1
					100.0
12.		*Biological and agricultural sciences and related*	1,953	2.3	
	120	Biologists	166		8.5
	121	Agronomists	1,252		64.3
	122	Horticultural scientists	36		1.8
	123	Foresters	405		20.6
	124	Soil scientists	27		1.4
	125	Animal scientists	67		3.4
					100.0
13.		*Medical and health sciences and related*	21,730	25.3	
	130	Physicians and surgeons	4,358		20.0
	131	Medical—allied scientists	267		1.2
	132	Dentists	842		3.9
	133	Pharmaceutical specialists	3,904		18.0
	134	Veterinarians	424		2.0
	135	Nurses, professional	610		2.8
	136	Midwives and nonprofessional nurses	6,334		29.1
	137	Therapy technicians	16		0.1
	138	Medical and health technicians	4,975		22.9
					100.0
14–15.		*Social sciences and related*	47,631	55.5	
	140	Economists	47		0.1
	141	Accountants	814		1.7
	142	Statisticians and technicians	135		9.3
	143	Political scientists	243		0.5
	144	Historians and related	12		–
	145	Anthropologists	17		–
	146	Sociologists	26		–
	147	Psychologists	25		–

151

TABLE 15 (*Continued*)
Detailed Occupations within the "Professional, Technical, and Related" Category

ILO code		Title	Number	Per cent of total	Per cent of own group
	148	Personnel specialists	120		0.3
	149	Language scientists	17		–
	150	Teachers, nontechnical subjects	40,862		86.0
	151	Librarians and archivists	301		0.6
	152	Social welfare workers	3		–
	154	Jurists, lawyers	4,213		8.9
	159	Social science, miscellaneous	796		1.7
					100.0
16–17.		*Artistic, writing, entertaining, and related*	4,539	5.3	
	160	Painters, drawers, and engravers	465		10.0
	161	Decor designers	42		0.9
	162	Sculptors and modellers	134		3.0
	164	Photographers	2,380		52.6
	165	Authors, journalists	396		8.7
	170	Theatrical directors	49		1.1
	171	Actors, entertainers	186		4.1
	172	Musicians	586		13.0
	173	Dancers	90		2.0
	174	Professional athletes	161		3.5
	179	Artistic, writing, miscellaneous	50		1.1
		Total	85,723	100.0	100.0

The high-level manpower fell into four main occupational groups (see below). A striking fact was that *over half the total supply of high-level manpower consisted of teachers, mainly elementary teachers.* This numerical domination of high-level manpower by elementary school teachers is probably characteristic of many countries during the long early years of educational "catching up," i.e., until the annual demand for teachers falls back to a secular-growth-and-replacement basis and until demand arises for high-level skills in other sectors. A second striking fact about Iran's high-level manpower was that 85 per cent of it was employed by the central government; in many fields the figure was 90–95 per cent. Thus the foreseeable demand for university-trained manpower depended almost entirely on government programs.

The main characteristics of each of the four main classes of high-level manpower were these:

1. *Physical sciences and related.* Engineers accounted for three-quarters of this family of sixteen occupations. The three core branches of engineering (civil, mechanical, and electrical) accounted for 60 per cent of the total. Engineering education (with a heavy weighting for civil engineering) would obviously hold a high priority in any early-stage program of university development.

2. *Biological and agricultural sciences.* This was the smallest of the four major fields. It was dominated by agronomists, university-trained specialists on field crops. Veterinarians would have been the second largest branch in this group if they were not included, less logically, among the Medical and Health Sciences.

3. *Medical and health sciences.* This large category of nine occupations was dominated by people in four branches: midwives and nonprofessional nurses, technicians, physicians, and pharmacists. Of these four, only the last two require university training. The fact that there were five physicians for every dentist is much more reasonable than that there should have been seven times as many doctors as professional nurses. Expansion of training for professional nurses became the top quantitative priority in the medical field for the Third Plan.

4. *Social sciences.* This was by far the largest of the four high-level groups. Teachers accounted for five-sixths of the total. Perhaps 75 per cent of these were primary teachers formally supposed to have secondary school degrees plus some teacher training (but not university degrees). The only other large groups were jurists and lawyers, a group almost the same size as the physicians. The accountant group was a fairly large one where a severe shortage was being felt and where two special training programs had been started in 1957.

A distinction has been made between those high-level occupations requiring university training (about 30 per cent of the 75,000 high-level group) and those normally requiring only secondary schooling with or without some specialized training in a specific field (professional nursing, pedagogical methods, surveying, drafting, medical technicians, etc.). The nonuniversity group accounted for about 70 per cent of the high-level total, as defined.

Manual Skills as High-Level Manpower

All high-level occupations mentioned so far have been "white collar" occupations. Ordinarily manual occupations do not qualify as high-level manpower. It is true that nearly every country has, like Iran, some system of vocational education that takes students up through secondary level; these graduates might be classed as high-level manpower. However, the largest number of entrants into even those occupations for which vocational schools exist will never have attended such schools. They will learn their skill informally, picking it up by experience. Thus there is a much looser gearing between occupational qualification and formal education and training in the manual skills that in most of the high-level occupations. People do not *have* to go through vocational school to enter the occupation, even to become skilled members of it.

The aim of educational policy should not be to establish enough schools to see that everyone (or 75 or even 30 per cent) entering the manual trades receives training but to expand facilities only as the finances and real resources become available that will allow such schools to be operated at reasonable standards. There is a universal tendency for planners, especially those inexperienced in labor market research, to underestimate the effectiveness (and, incidentally, the low cost) of the informal processes by which most skilled workers in most societies learn their trades. There are really only two important reasons for intervening in this "natural process" and establishing formal training programs: (1) there are some occupations where there must be a certain number of persons with sufficient skill to assure the employer's ability to attain acceptable standards of product quality and where this skill depends on some theoretical understanding plus the acquisition of know-how from a master craftsman; this is the main justification for apprenticeship programs; (2) there are some occupations whose rate of expansion is so rapid that unless the natural process of skill formation is speeded up through training programs, skill shortages will constitute a serious bottleneck and wage rates will go up more than they need to. This perspective eliminates the need to offer, within the vocational schools, training in *traditional,* slow-growing occupations and in occupations *highly specialized to individual employers.*

154

The Third Plan's proposals for increasing the supply of trained manpower all centered on further development of the educational system. This is true even though a considerable amount of energy was spent trying to arrange for training programs outside the educational system, such as the introduction of apprenticeship programs, the establishment of Training-within-Industry courses, the expansion of nurse-training facilities, the establishment of vocational training within the armed forces, the encouragement of in-service courses within key government development agencies such as the Agricultural Bank and the Khuzestan Water and Power Authority, etc. But in Iran, as elsewhere, the educational system overwhelmingly dominates the supply side of trained manpower. Therefore we shall neglect these peripheral training activities and concentrate attention on the educational system.

Future Lines of Educational Development

Absence of Structural Priorities

The Third Plan for education could not be characterized by structural priorities—changing the shape of the system—since it consisted of little bits of lots of things. Originally, quantitative expansion was the least important of the Plan's educational goals. This was true even though primary and secondary enrollments were intended to rise by 50 per cent and would involve larger increments of students, buildings, teachers, equipment, and funds than in any previous five-year period. The emphasis on quality improvement was intended to be even stronger at university level than at secondary. No new university was to be established (two have been, however!) and no general attempt was to be made to increase enrollment, although numbers seemed bound to rise by 20–30 per cent at home (study abroad might not increase). There was to be no national drive to concentrate on the most rapid possible spread of primary education, or the building up of the secondary level, or the creation of tertiary institutions necessary to the production of high-level manpower, or the establishment of facilities in areas that might have been previously neglected (e.g., vocational training, teacher training, or agriculture).

The outstanding structural characteristic of the Plan was the search for improved balance—between urban and rural opportunities; between vocational and academic schools; between the capital-formation activities of teacher training, improved physical facilities, curriculum revision, and better textbooks on the one hand and the "consumption" of quantitative expansion on the other; between the traditionally favored institutions at the center (in Tehran and immediately surrounding territory) and the provincial institutions. This concern for balance would not have been possible if the system had not reached a stage where most of the major elements of a permanent system were already in existence. No country can establish secondary schools or universities until it has made reasonable progress with the lower levels on which each depends. Iran had already moved far, comparatively speaking, along the road of educational expansion and differentiation to serve modern needs. In 1960 it needed better balance and much higher quality. These were the Plan's top priorities.

The Improvement of Quality

The Third Plan contained the first comprehensive statement of the country's educational goals and how to reach them. Many besides the planners had noted that "the principal weakness in the educational structure of Iran is its educational philosophy." This philosophy had its origins in the old French system (long since abandoned in France) which was administratively highly centralized, authoritarian in its stress on rote memorization and unquestioning reliance on the teacher's word, and conceived as a single stream intended to carry all pupils toward the same goal, the university. This was a conception of education for that small portion in any society who can benefit from *university* work. Although Iranian education has in recent years developed many institutions that stand as welcome exceptions to the traditional ideal, the latter still exercises a heavy influence on educational policy, on the content of the curriculum, on the organization of university life, and on the administrative framework.

In company with most developing countries Iran today is in midprocess of adapting her educational system to serve (1) *much larger numbers* than it was originally intended to reach and (2) *the pro-*

duction of skills and attitudes required by a national development effort. These objectives are simple to state but involve a complex set of changes from the traditional scale and conception of the nation's educational effort—e.g., the attraction of much larger numbers into the teaching profession, a rapid expansion of physical facilities, far-reaching changes in the curriculum and in teaching materials, and much higher levels of financial support. Nowhere can such changes be brought about quickly, and the planners regarded the Third Plan as only the first stage in a twenty-year process of bringing Iranian education to a point where it could serve the country's needs at reasonable standards.

Access to Education, and Its Content

In the long run, it was to be national policy to make education free and compulsory for all in the 7 to 13 age group. Above this level, "the intention of the Government, to be achieved as rapidly as human and physical resources allow, is that no lack of personal means, no remoteness of location, and no physical handicap will operate to prevent any boy or girl from obtaining all the education from which he, or the nation through him, can benefit. Every young Iranian with the ability to learn and the willingness to work will be entitled to a full education as a right" *(Third Plan Frame)*. But for the next few years "there is grave doubt as to the ability of the economy to absorb a steadily increasing number of boys and girls trained under the present curriculum." Hence the de-emphasis of purely quantitative expansion until progress has been made in changing the curriculum. Two main changes were needed in the curriculum. One was the introduction of pre-vocational content into the curriculum of *general* secondary schools, altering the traditional conception of these schools as exclusively pre-university institutions. This change followed from the aim of creating a diversified system with more opportunities for branching and greater status for the majority, who should be encouraged to terminate after the first secondary cycle (ninth grade). The other major curriculum change required building up the first- and second-cycle vocational schools on more realistic expectations of what they could hope to accomplish. This means counting on the schools less, and on employers more, for the creation of vocational and supervisory skills.

157

Whether or not these educational goals would receive public and professional support was not known. To test these ideas and mobilize support for them, the Education Plan proposed early in 1961 the establishment of an ad hoc National Commission on Education to carry out "a complete re-assessment of aims and means of the entire education structure" before the Third Plan started. No such Commission was ever appointed.

Providing the Teachers

A shortage of teachers constitutes the country's largest manpower shortage and the main brake on educational expansion. Of the 137,000 skilled persons needed between 1962 and 1967 about 50,000 would be teachers of various kinds—a third of the total. Two-thirds of all teachers were needed for the primary schools: *more than one out of every four skilled persons needed was a primary school teacher.*

Iran has wrestled with the problem of recruiting and training teachers throughout the past decade of rapid educational expansion. Inevitably, standards have fallen. By 1960 some 45 per cent of the primary and 55 per cent of the secondary teachers did not meet the standards set by the Ministry and were teaching under "emergency" rules. Little wonder the Third Plan was nearly as concerned with in-service training for existing teachers as with finding more of them.

Iran already had a rudimentary structure of institutions on which to build teacher-training programs. However, normal methods of providing teachers had been unable to supply more than a quarter or a third of the numbers needed during the recent years of rapid expansion. Special measures, outside the intended channels, would be needed for several years.

The Plan did not propose any increase in the number or type of traditional teacher-training institutions. Instead it proposed much higher enrollments for existing institutions, the establishment of Departments of Education at all five provincial universities, and the expansion of emergency programs designed to produce teachers who, while not meeting the formal standards, would at least be able to fill posts.

The University System

The Institutions: Their Faculties, Enrollments, and Budgets

Iran has made a good start on a national system of universities, though the standard of education is low and research is just beginning. As Table 16 shows, the university system is dominated by the University of Tehran, opened in 1935. All five provincial universities have been started since World War II. In addition to these six institutions recognized as part of the university system there are four other important institutions of higher education, The Tehran Polytechnic, The Abadan Institute of Technology, The National Teachers College in Tehran, and The National University, a private institution established in Tehran in 1960 by a young Iranian with (originally) the Shah's backing. ✕

TABLE 16

Iran's Public Universities: Enrollments, Faculties, and Budgets, 1960

University and enrollment		Faculties	Budget		
			(million Rls.)	*(%)*	*(million $)*
University of Tehran					
13,193		Medicine, Pharmacy, Engineering, Agriculture, Science, Law, Fine Arts, Letters, Veterinary, Dentistry, and Theology	737	67	9.6
Provincial universities					
Tabriz	1,535	Medicine, Pharmacy, Letters, Agriculture, Teacher Training College, Technical College	120	11	1.6
Shiraz	1,158	Medicine, Letters, Agriculture, and Science	70	6	0.9
Meshed	929	Medicine, Theology, Letters	56	5	0.7
Esfahan	726	Medicine, Pharmacy, Letters	64	6	0.8
Ahwaz	285	Medicine, Agriculture	51	5	0.6
Total	17,826		1,098	100	14.2

Source: Adapted from the *Education Plan Frame,* August, 1961. Another 2,000 students would have been enrolled in the Tehran Polytechnic, the Abadan Institute of Technology, the National Teachers College, and the (private) National University. In addition, between ten and fifteen thousand students were enrolled in universities abroad.

Table 17 shows broadly what the 18,000 domestic students were studying in 1960. If one arbitrarily assumes that half those studying Letters, Law, and Fine Arts, and all those in Theology, were pursuing subjects not clearly related to the country's development needs, one accounts for about 25–30 per cent of the total. This means 70–75 per cent were studying subjects that, on the face of it, were directly related to high-level skills needed for development. This does not seem a bad distribution for a system that has grown up "like Topsy."

TABLE 17
Enrollment by Field in Iranian Universities, 1959–60

Faculty	Provincial universities	University of Tehran	Total	Per cent
Letters	2,146	4,554	6,700	38
Medicine	1,374	1,847	3,221	18
Science	201	1,117	1,318	7
Engineering	55	990	1,045	6
Theology	89	1,010	1,099	6
Teacher Training College		995	995	6
Law		921	921	5
Fine Arts		453	453	3
Pharmacy	193	359	552	3
Agriculture	366	368	734	4
Dentistry		329	329	2
Veterinary		202	202	1
Health	155		155	1
Nursing and midwifery	90	12	102	1
Total	4,669	13,157	17,826	100

Source: Adapted from *Education Plan Frame*, August, 1961, p. 13.
Note: It is believed that this figure excludes the 150 students enrolled at the Abadan Institute of Technology and the 500 enrolled at the Tehran Polytechnic. Inclusion of these two institutions (which lie outside the formal system of public universities) would raise the percentage studying engineering from the 6 per cent reported in the table to over 9 per cent.

Tehran was the only one of the country's six universities that offered a wide range of courses spread over many fields (see Table 16). Tehran had twelve faculties modeled after the European pattern. The largest provincial university (Tabriz) was one-tenth the size of Tehran and had only five faculties. The four others offered from two to four fields, of which medicine was invariably one. During the Plan it was intended to withhold all but minor development funds from the faculties of letters at all the universities. University expansion was to be concentrated on vocational and professional fields, spelled out in general terms. A major innovation, already noted, was the establishment of Education Departments at all the provincial universities. This step represented the Plan's major attack on the supply of secondary school teachers.

Common Criticisms of the University of Tehran

To a large extent the development of higher education depends on what happens at the University of Tehran. Unfortunately the University is imprisoned by a set of traditions that prevents it from adapting readily to the needs of the country. Tehran is organized on the lines of nineteenth-century French universities: separate, largely autonomous faculties covering each major subject-area; a notable absence of unifying administrative services giving leadership and co-ordination to the University; didactic instruction by lecture methods that emphasize rote learning; all-or-nothing testing through a single written examination at the end of the year; few contacts between faculty and students; little reading beyond lecture notes; and a pattern of part-time service from faculty members who tend to regard their posts as bases from which to engage in outside employments that often get the lion's share of their attention. Classes are scheduled in the morning, mainly to protect the faculty's freedom to engage in outside employment.

Each faculty has its own buildings, controls the use of its own classrooms, builds its own small library (there is no central library), controls its own admissions standards and procedures, provides its own service courses as needed (e.g., foreign languages, mathematics, introductory science). Effective research becomes virtually impossible where few faculty members have offices and most go to other employment after their lectures. The lack of offices encourages faculty absenteeism and makes it difficult to develop effective student-faculty relationships. The salary level is low, reflecting and forcing outside employment. The structure of salaries and the ladder for advancement in pay and rank are governed by mechanical rules that make it almost impossible to recognize talent independent of seniority and forces all hiring to be done at the bottom of the scale regardless of a man's experience.

These criticisms suggest the type and scale of reforms needed to transform the University into the kind of institution that would support Iran's emergence as a modern nation: a full-time faculty paid a respectable living and inspired by a wider conception of the

161

role of the university in the nation's life; the development of research activity supported by adequate library and laboratory facilities; the strengthening of the University's central administration to minimize the duplication of facilities and courses; the growth of closer student-faculty relationships and of university facilities and services to enrich student life; the introduction of nondegree certificate courses for evening and extension students to help fill the need for technicians of many kinds.

It is wrong to give a completely gloomy picture of the University, for there are islands of past progress and future hope. However, the scattered examples of adaptability are exceptions to a deeply rooted pattern of conservatism maintained through the tight control over University affairs exercised by a University Senate consisting of senior professors from each faculty. The possibilities of change within the University thus depend on a body which is against change. The influence of progressive individuals is restricted to the limited changes they can bring about within particular faculties, which are largely autonomous in their internal affairs.

The pattern of organization and instruction found in Tehran is duplicated at the six much smaller and weaker provincial universities. Many critics have given up all hope of doing anything worthwhile within the existing university framework. This mood partly underlay the proposal to establish in Shiraz an institution that broke completely with Iranian tradition. Pahlavi University is patterned on Western lines: a Board of Trustees independent of the existing university system and of the Ministry of Education; a single full-time faculty instead of many faculties composed of part-timers; a strong central administration; bi-lingual instruction (English and Farsi) emphasizing independent thinking instead of rote learning; and active research interests. The University started with four schools—Medicine, Engineering, Agriculture, and Arts and Sciences—and aimed at 5,000 students after six to seven years. Initial progress in bringing this proposal to life has been exceedingly slow. Its outlook is highly uncertain.

Conclusions

The foremost lesson of Iran's experience with manpower planning is the overwhelming importance of developing, among the small group of people engaged in manpower and educational planning in any country, a common way of thinking about the problems with which they are dealing. Without this, growth is at the mercy of petty administrative rivalries, personal whims and biases, and intellectual confusion. The key terms are "manpower," "education," and "training." The concepts that underlie these terms include elements that interact and overlap in the process of skill formation.

Manpower analysis is primarily concerned with labor markets, with occupational skills needed for economic growth. Its province is the analysis of the supply of and demand for skills introduced by development. Its language is technical and impersonal, the language of economics.

Educational planning is not primarily concerned with labor markets. It is concerned with people. Its vocabulary is drawn from individual and social psychology, from a culture's value system, from a nation's politics. Education is concerned with values and goals fully as important to nation-building as occupational skills. Nevertheless, educators have always had to worry about the ability of graduates to earn a living. This concern has forced them to pay some attention to what the labor market wants. Indeed the education system always provides the largest set of supply streams that are subject to government control. But no education system embraces all the supply streams of skills that deserve formal attention. There are many formal training activities that are best conducted entirely outside the educational system. Many of these activities will of course require that participants have reached a certain educational level.

Manpower and education are thus overlapping fields. Their common ground is the role of education in the formation of occupational skills. But both fields make large contributions to development independent of their common ground.

I have used the term "gearing" to express the varying degrees of relationship among manpower estimates, programming decisions in education and training, and skill formation. Unless planners understand the looseness of most of these gearing relationships they will strive for a much closer fit of supply and demand than they can possibly hope to or need to achieve. And in trying to achieve what they need not achieve inexperienced planners may spread themselves so thin that they achieve nothing that would not have happened anyway.

The reasons manpower estimates are of such limited help in educational programing are (1) the uncertainties surrounding demand estimates; (2) the lack of any close dependence of skill, in many occupations, on specific amounts and kinds of education and training; (3) the importance of essentially arbitrary policy decisions about how the various levels and branches of an educational system should be linked together; (4) the inability of quantitative skill estimates to include strategically important qualitative skills (e.g., risk-taking, organizational ability, etc.); and (5) the importance of decisions about the availability and distribution of educational and training opportunities taken on grounds of political pressures and social philosophy. Manpower planning can provide a necessary and important set of data on a more explicit basis than has been traditionally true in educational planning. But its contribution is less important and less conclusive than many discussions suggest.

In Iran, as in many countries, it is extremely difficult to get anything done, to move anything ahead, to translate a good idea into even a middling project. This may seem a paradoxical statement in view of the rapid expansion and differentiation of the educational system over the past ten to fifteen years. But when the statistics are discounted by the quality of the effort, much less has been accomplished than numbers alone suggest. Everywhere, but especially in Iran, it is easier to decide what ought to be done than it is to do things. At every turn inertia and frictions dominate the picture, so that once the general proportions of the system ten to fifteen years ahead have been fixed, somewhat arbitrarily, almost everyone's attention shifts from demand problems to the supply side: teachers, buildings, curricula, syllabi, textbooks, equipment, budgets, cash—all the detailed questions that cry for attention and get so little of it, because the greatest shortage of all is the administrative capacity for giving attention to the things that need it. Thus the subject of manpower planning takes us where so many of our other subjects have taken us, into the culture and politics of Iran, which today impose a ceiling on the country's manpower and educational effort.

It is essentially right to believe that manpower planning and, especially, more and better education are important for Iran's growth. But too many people take a mechanistic view of the contribution which these activities can make, as though an educational system were a factory capable of turning out irrigation pipe or cement blocks in just the quantities, sizes, and shapes which manpower planners could foresee would be needed. What gets too little recognition is the extent to which cultural patterns may limit the ability of a country (1) to conduct manpower and educational planning and (2) to utilize effectively the output of such activities. In the long run, education itself will be the main inspiration for throwing off the traditional culture and the traditional politics and for creating an atmosphere in which more will be possible than anyone can yet expect. In the short run, the most to hope for is the avoidance of gross mistakes in the development of education and training programs. Iran's Manpower and Education Plans provided a standard (if anyone would use it) not for doing exactly what the country needs (which no one knew) but for avoiding gross mistakes.

CHAPTER VIII

A General View of the Planning Process

The last three chapters have been concerned with sectoral planning and development. This chapter moves from the particular to the general. It presents an overview of what an economic plan tries to do, how it is put together intellectually, and how it gets written. Although rooted in the experience of planning in Iran, the chapter is intended to help practical planners in many countries. Too much of what has been written about planning comes out of economic theory, not enough out of experience. This chapter hopes to restore some of the balance. True, any practical planning operation has to be conducted with one foot in theory; but the other has to contend with the soggy realities of a particular social and political milieu. The making of a realistic and sensible plan depends on the planners' ability, individually and as a working group, to understand and reconcile the imperatives of both perspectives.

Planning is a "top down, bottom up" process. It involves a continuous interaction between general objectives and constraints and the design of the specific projects, programs, cost estimates, and government policies which constitute the flesh and blood of any plan. There is no logical priority of importance between the "top down" and "bottom up" tasks. They can start simultaneously and move forward as initially separate but converging and complementary activities. There may be political advantage in giving early expression to general objectives and magnitudes, to "top down" problems. But in terms of the justifications behind the general goals and aggregate projections—and in terms of what actually happens—the "bottom up" part of the process is fully as vital. From the point of view of time sequence, any good plan is made by simultaneously building down from the top and up from the bottom, with frequent planned interruptions so that those working on each of the two main levels are forced to examine whether or not they are going to join up successfully with the team working toward them from above, or below.

There are four main "top down" guidelines needed for drawing up a plan. These are:

1. the definition of major *objectives*
2. the definition of plan *size*
3. the making of broad *allocations* among sectors, and
4. the degree of *comprehensiveness*.

The "bottom up" process is concerned with putting together the projects and programs in each sector or subdivision of the plan. It has five main aspects:

1. the sketching of a *development "model" for each sector*
2. the setting of production *targets* in fairly specific terms for the period of the plan
3. the generation of *specific projects and programs*
4. the estimation of *costs*, and
5. the specification of a *policy framework* and the *administrative means* within which projects and programs will be carried out. Most of the chapter will be concerned with an explanation of each of these elements.

"Top Down"

Objectives

Nearly every plan contains some statement of the more important things it hopes to achieve. These goals should be capable of expression in some quantitative terms so that government officials and the public will know in advance what the plan intends to maximize and will have something to use, *ex post*, as a measure of what was accomplished. Since a plan's statement of objectives serves partly a political and educational role outside the planning machinery and partly an internal technical role in shaping the plan, formulation of objectives deserves fairly serious attention. On the other hand, every plan must respect a number of objectives any one of which, if neglected, could seriously embarrass the plan and call for emergency corrective action that would amount to a departure from the plan. A plan which maximized the rate of investment without attempting to do much about a serious unemployment situation would be unlikely to last. A plan which chose to maximize the rise in consumption would, by definition, slight capital formation and would be justified only if there were some compelling reason to do so.

Most economists would probably agree that raising the level of investment is the most important objective at which a development plan should aim. This is the course which, by definition, results in the most rapid build-up of generalized productive capacity. But the attempt to maximize investment is subject to so many technical and political qualifications that planners often find it more convenient to express a plan's primary objectives in terms of increases in national income. This is a concept everyone is assumed to understand, one that is symbolically Good and relatively free of controversy, and which allows technicians (i.e., the planners) adequate room to shift around programs and projects both during a plan's writing and later during its execution. In a sense, organizing planning around a goal of "maximizing national income" relieves both planners and politicians from having to be too specific about other goals (e.g., income distribution, employment, sectoral allocations) and avoids unproductive theological debates.

An internal memorandum circulated early in the preparation of the Third Plan stated the Third Plan's objectives in the following terms:

> We want the greatest possible increase in national income which the deployment of our initial resources permits, subject perhaps to the qualification that particularly poor regions of the country would receive extra help. The "greatest possible increase in national income" leaves too much in the air however. Since the increases in non-consumable output, in inventories and in work-in-progress are counted as increases in national income, relatively high growth rates of output may be obtained without concurrent improvements in consumption. Under present circumstances it seems best to aim at roughly equi-proportional advances in production and consumption. . . .[1]

This statement of objectives meant that if the planners aimed at a $5\frac{1}{2}$ or 6 per cent yearly rise in national income they would try to

[1] "Notes on the Third Plan," August, 1959.

distribute investment activity in such a way that the output of consumption goods and of investment goods would both rise by a similar 5½ to 6 per cent. (Such a result would be in aggregate terms; within different sectors the balance between increased output of investment and consumption goods would differ greatly.) This objective implied that the proportion of *additional* income to be saved and devoted to investment would be no higher than the society was already experiencing at the start of the plan, i.e., that the marginal propensity to save would be no higher than the average. Such an objective was much lower than most plans show. It is explained mainly by regard for a principle that ought to govern the choice of specific objectives in all plans: general objectives have to be given specific content according to the particular problems of the economy. These problems can only be identified empirically, not deductively or theologically. In Iran the Program Review of 1959 had established that too much of the Second Plan had gone into slow-yielding investment projects and not enough into the production of consumption goods. This imbalance had contributed to the inflationary pressures of the late 1950's. The Third Plan aimed at striking a better balance. In doing so, the planners were saying, in effect, that present consumers ought to enjoy somewhat more of the fruits of investment, and future consumers somewhat less, than had been true in the Second Plan. All plans have to make this choice. In theory this choice is resolved automatically by the rate of interest. In practice planners usually make it by administrative decision in the light of the behavior of price indices rather than according to results obtained with the use of a theoretical interest rate. The planners' choice then becomes a proposal to the political authorities in whose hands rest all final decisions on important general questions.

The ability to maximize the increase in national income from a given amount of investment resources depends on the allocation of these resources among sectors and projects, since these have different capacities for yielding output from a given amount of investment (i.e., they have differing capital-output ratios). We will come to the problem of sectoral allocations in a moment. First we need to look at the problem of estimating the amount of resources available for the plan. This estimate determines the size of the plan.

The Size of the Plan

The size of the increase in national income is always one of the more important aggregates in planning calculations. Some over-all marginal capital-output ratio, explicit or implicit, will be involved in the relationship between the increases in income and investment represented by the plan. Thus the growths in income and investment are usually treated as though they are uniquely linked by the capital-output ratio (in Iran, its approximate value could only be assumed).[2] Because of this relationship it is possible to build up estimates of a plan's size either *directly,* by estimating the amount of resources that can be mobilized for investment, or *indirectly,* by assuming a feasible increase in national income and deriving the investment needed through use of a capital-output ratio. In practice, if one has any reasonable notion about the recent growth in income, it is a simple matter to fix a reasonable target for future growth (say 4–6 per cent annually at constant prices), to assume a capital-output ratio (3:1 has dominated the literature) and to derive a figure for the amount of financial resources (= *ex ante* savings) necessary to reach the growth target. This figure is what we mean by "the size of the plan." Having estimated needed investment by this method, it is then necessary to check its reasonableness by the other method—i.e., by identifying and adding up all possible sources of funds for investment and seeing how close the total comes to what is needed. The two figures should not be expected to agree—the identifiable funds will always fall short of the desired level of investment. The two approaches are finally harmonized either by reducing the size of the plan, figuring out ways to raise more money (e.g., by higher borrowing abroad or greater use of deficit finance or stronger tax measures)—or some of both.

The size of the Third Plan was fixed by the process just described. Much the most difficult part of the process was estimating the volume of resources that could reasonably be expected to become available from *voluntary* domestic savings, private and

[2] The statement that increases in output are linked mechanically to increases in investment is an oversimplification. It neglects the many other factors that also constitute sources of growth, such as education, research, technological change, and other factors, all of which are less measurable and less easily controllable than investment. It is primarily the need for a convenient shorthand that explains the heavy reliance on the income-investment link in economic literature.

public. The difference between this figure and the amount of resources needed defined a "resources gap" that could only be filled by importing additional resources over and above the level assumed or by forcing the country to save more (through [1] higher taxes or [2] reducing consumption by allowing prices to rise in response to inflationary methods of financing the program).

The following framework was used in estimating financial resources. Public savings were defined as the excess of public revenues over ordinary (nondevelopment) expenditures. This amount would show how much money would be available for the development budget. The precise concept of "public savings" depended on the definitions and assumptions made.[3] Public revenues were defined to include all taxes, the oil royalties, plus the net profits of all the public enterprises supposed to be run on commercial principles. The initial estimates were made by assuming no change in tax rates, only in the size of the things being taxed (e.g., imports, consumption of taxed commodities, business and personal incomes). The results of the revenue estimates are shown in Table 18. The crucial role of the oil revenue estimate is immediately apparent.

[3] The following assumptions and definitions were used to estimate the probable flow of public savings:

a. On the revenue side it is initially assumed that existing rates of taxation will be retained during the Third Plan. Some allowance will be made however for a gradual improvement in tax collection. In addition to taxes (and customs) public revenues comprise the Government income from oil as well as the profits of public enterprises and of certain other public agencies which present more or less self-balancing accounts.

b. On the expenditure side the following public outlays will be considered as ordinary (non-development) expenditures.

i. Expenditures on the "cost of Government," i.e., on the maintenance of law and order, on defence and on the administrative machinery of Government;

ii. Interest and amortization payments on the foreign debt, and

iii. The recurring expenditures necessary to maintain and operate the economic and social services already existing at the end of the period of the Second Plan.

c. Public savings are defined as the difference between public revenues and ordinary non-development expenditures. These savings are available for financing the expansion of already existing economic and social facilities, or for the creation of new ones. They will have to cover both capital and current expenditures. Capital expenditures always carry with them recurring commitments, and it was therefore thought advisable to take these recurring expenditures on economic and social improvements straight into the development budget. The same applies to certain current expenditures on "development" (e.g., expenditure on an anti-malaria campaign). The term "saving" therefore, is given a somewhat wider connotation than is usually attached to it.

(Plan Organization, Division of Economic Affairs, Memorandum No. 16, "The Size of the Third Plan," Revised Draft, n.d.)

In Chapter III it was explained that public-sector expenditures of the Third Plan were not limited to investment alone but included an allowance for increases in those recurring costs specifically associated with development functions. Funds available for this purpose could only be estimated after allowing for increases in the government's expected ordinary expenditures *not* associated with development (for their definition see n. 3 above). The projections of these current expenditures outside the Plan came to 245.6 billion rials (IIa. in Table 19). Public saving was the difference between total revenue available to government and its estimated expenditures outside those to be financed by the Plan. Public saving plus private saving represented the total amount of *domestic*

TABLE 18
Revenue Projection for the Third Plan,
Early 1961 Estimates

	Total	Oil revenue	Customs duties	Income tax	Other direct taxes	Consumption taxes	Other revenue	Estimated surpluses of commercial public enterprises
	(1)	(2)	(3)	(4)	(5)	(6)	(7)	(8)
				(billion Rls.)				
1960	51.4	21.2	11.2	3.9	0.9	7.2	4.0	3.0
1962	57.7	23.4	11.9	5.2	1.1	8.4	4.4	3.3
1967	78.1	29.8	13.8	10.4	1.8	12.4	5.6	4.3
9/62–3/68	375.5	147.3	71.0	42.5	8.1	57.7	27.8	21.1
Per cent	(100)	39	19	11	2	15	7	6

Col. (2): Oil revenue is projected on the basis of 5 per cent annual increase over 1960 actual receipts.

Col. (3): In view of prospective foreign exchange shortages as well as the increasing importance of capital and producers goods imports, the rate of return from customs is not expected to rise more than 3 per cent per annum.

Col. (4): Based on a 15 per cent annual increase in tax yield. While this rate of increase is lower than in the preceding four years, it exceeds the assumed growth rate of the national income. This is because of the expansion of the tax base due to the increasing relative importance of the corporate sector and of income groups that are subject to direct tax. For these reasons a rise of 10 to 15 per cent in direct taxes—particularly in the income tax—is within the realm of possibility.

Col. (5): Based on 10 per cent annual increase, a rate which is in line with recent experience; it would maintain the relative position of these taxes vis-à-vis other government revenues.

Col. (6): Consumption taxes consisting of levies on sugar, tea, tobacco, alcoholic beverages, and kerosene are projected on the basis of expected increase in consumption. The actual yield of these taxes, in 1960, is expected to be about Rls. 400 million more than the estimate provided in the budget.

Col. (7): Other revenues are projected at the rate of increase of 5 per cent.

Col. (8): Based on the estimated 1958 surpluses of these agencies and 5 per cent annual growth rate; includes municipalities.

Source: "Introduction to the Third Development Plan," Division of Economic Affairs, Plan Organization, May, 1961.

resources available for the Plan, assuming no deficit financing. How much total private saving was expected? The estimate was made by building up (a) an estimate of total private investment, (b) the amount of private saving to be used by the government, and (c) the net inflow of foreign capital to the private sector. Private *domestic* saving consisted of (a) + (b) − (c). Item (b) (the amount of private saving to be used by the government) did not represent a guess as to how much of their savings people would be willing to have the government use. Such a transfer occurs as a result of decisions within the banking system without anyone in the private sector being asked if he is willing to let the government use his funds (depositors never get asked how they want their money used). In this case it was assumed that the banking system could safely increase loans to the public sector by 7.3 billion rials (i.e., deficit financing). The latter figure was simply the government's assumed share of the total increase in the money supply (24.3 billion rials) which it was felt the economy could absorb without inflationary consequences.[4] The private sector would need 17.0 billion rials of

---

[4] In the absence of any information about the velocity of circulation, the planners fell back on the simple quantity theory of money. They assumed that an economy growing at 6 per cent per annum would need 6 per cent more money just to handle the additional transactions. They also reasoned that the increasing monetization of the economy justified some additional increase in the money supply—perhaps another 1 per cent. The two factors suggested a total annual increase of 7 per cent as a safe level with little danger of pushing up prices. Using this factor for monetary growth the planners estimated that 24.3 billion rials of newly created money would be justified during the Plan. Using recent experience they then assumed that 7.3 billion rials of this 24.3 billion rials (30 per cent) should go to government.

One estimate underlying this change-in-the-money-supply estimate concerned the amount by which foreign exchange holdings of the banking system would increase (cf. Table 19, p. 174). Changes in the banking system's holdings of foreign exchange affect the money supply in the following way: when exporters or other people deposit foreign exchange receipts in a bank, the latter gives them an equivalent amount of rials in exchange, usually by crediting their deposit account. This process is called "monetization of foreign exchange." It is not automatic. Not all foreign exchange deposited in banks is inevitably matched by an equivalent increase in the domestic money supply (there would be none, for example, if the exporter took all or part of his credit in the form of notes or currency issued to him from the bank's cash-on-hand. Or government exchange receipts might be used, in whole or in part, to create a deflationary budget surplus). This process is reversible: losses of exchange can contract the money supply. In economies where foreign trade is large in relation to national income (as in Iran), changes in the system's holdings of foreign exchange exercise strong leverage on the size of the domestic money supply.

"deficit finance" to help pay for its development expenditures; what the private sector would not need—i.e., what it "saved"— would be available for the government to use.

TABLE 19
Financial Statement of the Third Plan

(billion Rls.)		
I. Development Expenditure		
Government development expenditure	190.2	
Private development expenditure	157.7	
Principal payment on foreign debt	13.0	
Increase in foreign exchange reserves	2.9	
Total		363.8
II. Available Resources		
a. Current expenditure:		
Nondevelopment expenditure	138.9	
Current cost of development agencies	100.7	
Interest on foreign debt	6.0	
Subtotal	245.6	
b. Available revenue (Table 18):	375.5	
c. Available public saving (b. — a.)	129.9	
d. Private saving:		
Available for private investment	157.7	
Available for credit expansion to the public sector	7.3	
Subtotal	165.0	
e. Public and private saving		294.9
III. Resource gap		68.9
Total: available resources + gap		363.8

The estimates of public and private savings fell short of total development expenditures by 68.9 billion rials.[5] The shortage was all in the public sector; it represented over one-third of the sector's proposed program. At this point it became clear (to the planners, at least) that tax rates would have to be increased, or more foreign borrowing would be necessary, or the size of the Plan would have to be reduced (or some combination of all these). The final Plan did not say what ought to be done. It said only that "unless finan-

[5] The oil revenues for this period were estimated at 143.1 billion rials. In other words, less than half the oil revenues was being carried through to savings. Even if it had been politically possible to earmark all the oil revenues to development, they still would have financed only about 80 per cent of the Plan.

cial resources beyond those mentioned become available, the desired growth of income cannot be obtained. Apart from further economies in non-development expenditures, there are two main sources of additional funds: foreign loans and grants, and increased public savings through higher taxation." (1961 *Plan Frame*)

The figures in Table 19 are certainly not precise, although they were the best that conscientious men could produce. The accuracy of the figures mattered very little. What mattered was that the government should understand that a development plan designed to sustain the rate of growth experienced in the late 1950's would require serious attention to raising taxes. In view of the general lack of seriousness with which the government took the Third Plan, the weakness of the Ministry of Finance, and the urgency of other political and economic problems, it is not surprising that this tax problem never got any attention. Instead, the size of the Plan was cut by one-third during the week it began!

One other important set of calculations was made in fixing the size of the Third Plan. This was an estimate of the "external balance," or what the balance of payments would look like under various assumptions. The upshot of these calculations was to show that despite Iran's large foreign exchange earnings the government would have to take deliberate steps to limit the import of consumer goods. Such steps would have to go beyond the higher levels of taxation needed to finance the Plan. If such limitations were not imposed, the needed volume of capital-goods imports could not be financed.

The review of the plan-size calculations should make clear how infirm and elastic were the key figures which finally emerged. This weakness did not matter much, since the important requirement (so far as writing a plan was concerned) was that reasonable boundaries of the plan should get established fairly early. Increased accuracy could be left for later, when and if better figures became available.

Sectoral Allocations

The division of the economy into a number of "sectors" is a necessary convenience. It helps in thinking and talking about planning and in allocating specific planning responsibilities among different administrative units. But the definition of sectors is an arbitrary process in the sense that it does not make much difference where the divisions fall. What matters is that there must be a close relationship between the categories used and the organizational structure of the planning agency, so that the people who do the planning know in advance what they will be responsible for and whom they must talk to. In framing the Third Plan, only five sectors were initially used. Soon after the sectors were defined each one was given a trial allocation and told, in effect, to propose how the sector would use it.

There are no formal principles which can provide objective guidance for sectoral allocations. The common sense of men who are knowledgeable about the economy and its major problems is the best guide to rational allocations. In theory, of course, funds should be allocated to sectors which present projects capable of yielding the highest returns. This is easy to say but almost impossible to measure. The practical problems of measuring relative yields among projects competing for funds are so great in a country like Iran that the judgment of knowledgeable and disinterested individuals is the best guide to broad allocations. Indeed, it is the only one available. Initial allocations have to be made long before most projects and programs are well developed. In Iran, the three most important *qualitative* considerations in making initial allocations were:

1. The need to give all sectors fair consideration, so that a wide range of possibilities was taken into account.

2. The need to achieve balance between slow-yielding and quick-yielding sectors to avoid building up inflationary pressures without providing any means for relieving them. This decision involved choices between the infrastructure and social overhead sectors on the one hand (which tend to be slow-yielding) and the directly productive or commodity-producing sectors on the other.

3. The absorptive capacity of the sectors. Within limits, sectors that could spend money effectively got more funds than others which could not, even though the latter might have been desirable "on paper." But it would have produced great distortions to make allocations solely on the basis of relative ability-to-spend; special efforts had to be made to find ways of doing things in sectors where

certain objectives seemed important. These judgments were not reflected as fully in the initial allocations as in the later revisions.

The most important *quantitative* guide to the plan's sectoral allocations—in the sense of a base from which adjustments were made upwards or downwards—was the current level of expenditure in each sector.

The notion that sectoral allocations could be roughly adjusted so that the marginal social product per rial would be equal in each sector was implicit in the following explanation from an internal PlanOrg memorandum:

> It should be clearly understood that our hypothetical allocations are merely a device which should help *determine* the final or actual allocations. This is the way it works, in brief: in each Sector there will be investments which are just sub-marginal at the level of the present allocation; they would be undertaken if the Sector had more money. The question which we have to decide when these provisional programs are in is whether the sub-marginal investments in Sector B contribute more, rial for rial, than the supra-marginal investment in Sector A, and so on. Should we therefore shift some resources? This is a *precise* issue which can be settled. By this we do not mean that there are always precise *answers* to such questions, i.e., answers that can be proved to be right in the way a logical proposition can be proved. We only mean that sensible decisions can be reached once the questions are set out in this way. This presupposes that care is taken to identify the projects, or blocks of investment, which are on the margin between acceptance and rejection. What we shall be doing here is the same work which a rate of interest could perform under "ideal" conditions: that is, we ration investment by drawing a line of roughly equal advantage across the Sectors. The point is that this rate of interest—or its equivalent—is uniquely determined as long as aggregate investable resources are assumed to be fixed.... As the amount of funds changes, so does the rate of interest, and what some people are interested in is to find an optimal rate of interest for planning purposes, i.e., an optimal rate of *saving*. To this question there is no objective answer.[6]

This is a pedagogically useful explanation of what the planners tried to do. However, despite its pragmatism the quotation still suggests an unrealizable degree of precision and formalism in the allocation process. Where the number of prepared projects falls so far short of tentative allocations in each sector, as was true in Iran,

[6] General Economics Group Memorandum No. 3, October 29, 1959.

comparisons among sectors could be made only in terms of the size of a line of credit people wanted to establish for certain general programs and projects to be worked out in future. This did not mean that no comparisons could be made; it meant only that they were extremely rough and subjective. Since there was no other way to proceed, there is little profit in wishing for anything more than the situation could have yielded.

Sectoral allocations represent the planners' positive response to the necessity of saying what ought to happen in the economy. They can do this only in fairly general terms, until ministries and consulting engineers come forward with project proposals that would use plan funds. The real contribution which quantitative economics has to make to the problem of *sectoral* allocations is not in refined calculations of marginal adjustments but in appraising the probable benefits and costs of the relatively small number of *big projects* that get proposed for every plan. It is, after all, the big projects where big (and lasting) mistakes can be made. And in many sectors a few big projects often dominate the sectoral allocations.

Comprehensiveness

Iran's First and Second Plans were partial plans in the sense that they pushed forward with government development expenditures but made no attempt to control all government investment and little attempt to influence the volume or direction of private investment. As noted, a major conclusion of the 1959 *Program Review* was that the economy was headed for trouble because the development plan had not been comprehensive. To prevent such trouble from recurring it was decided that the Third Plan should be a comprehensive one, embracing all sectors of the economy, public and private. This decision was accepted, verbally, by the political authorities, and instructions were issued to this effect.

"Comprehensive planning" does not mean that a plan needs to mastermind the whole economy. It does mean that all the major targets for the economy should be stated in the plan, with nothing of major importance left outside that might either upset the plan or contribute to its fulfillment.

Comprehensiveness in Iranian planning meant much more than calculating the amount of investment going on in the government and private sector outside Plan Organization, establishing output targets, and identifying the increases in ordinary expenditures required by the government's investment activities. A comprehensive frame of reference implied taking account of *all* the major variables in the economic system and trying to control them so as to produce the results for which planning had been undertaken. It is these implications of "comprehensiveness" that impose such difficult problems of co-ordination among the many government agencies responsible for the factors that need to be considered, controlled, and harmonized. The difficulties are great enough in any country. In Iran the culture and political tradition put the probability of success very low indeed. The main hope was that a minimum level of effective co-ordination among key agencies (especially PlanOrg, the Central Bank, and the Ministry of Finance) could be achieved so as to prevent the Third Plan from being wrecked by inattention to the major variables (such as the money supply, the balance of payments, and the government's annual budget).

"Bottom Up"

The "bottom up" part of planning consists of the five elements listed on page 167. These are the responsibility of people working in the sectoral departments of the planning organization and, hopefully, in the ministries. Although work at the bottom can begin before the general marching orders come down from the top, the final size, shape, and content of the sectoral plans can never be considered fixed until the entire plan is orchestrated into a harmonious whole. But even at this stage, which occurs late, a plan still contains many more questions and unspecified details than may be imagined by those who have not participated in such an exercise. The orchestration problem is discussed in the next section. This one is concerned with the five elements of the "bottom up" process.

The Necessity of a Long-Run Sectoral Model

Any section of a planning agency concerned with education, health, agriculture, industry, fuel and power, transport, communications, housing, or any other subject must begin by roughing out a general conception of what ought to happen in the sector over the fairly long run (i.e., for the next 15 to 25 years). This is a process of examining alternative expansion paths, alternative means to achieve ends, alternative policy frameworks, alternative priorities in tackling major tasks, and an identification of the key problems likely to be met as the sector moves forward. This delineation of alternatives is an exercise in scanning the future with imagination. Some of the big-project possibilities will become visible during this preliminary stage, revealing what must be studied intensively so that final decisions, cost estimates, and administrative arrangements can be made. At this stage sectoral planners must have a good appreciation of the ideological framework within which their sector will develop (e.g., private-public ownership decisions depend mainly on this). Knowledge of the government's present and future administrative capability is also vital to the construction of a realistic model. So, too, is a good understanding of the present state of the sector, in terms of its size, its inputs and outputs, its investment and operating costs, its administrative arrangements and ownership pattern (i.e., its institutional structure), and its major problems. It is more important that sectoral planners be familiar with the empirical realities of their sectors than with the theoretical subtleties of planning.

Establishment of Specific Sectoral Targets

Target-setting is a process of translating generalities into specifics. Apart from the hortatory, political role of targets, they provide data for testing internal consistency among the various parts of a plan—e.g., industry's target for vegetable oil output has to be tested against agriculture's target for oilseed production and expected yields. Thus target-setting involves establishing how many secondary school teachers should be trained during the plan; how many meters of cotton or wool cloth should be produced during the last year of the plan period; how many additional hectares of irrigated land should be brought under cultivation; how many additional bushels of wheat, barley, cotton, or tobacco should be produced; how many additional sheep should be in flocks by the plan's end; how many tons of bauxite or iron ore or chromite can be produced (and sold); how many agricultural extension agents and mobile health teams will be needed; how many additional kilometers of hard-surfaced and secondary roads should be built; and so on down a long, long list, sector by sector.

The process of building up targets is one of continuing refinement involving the interplay of demand estimates, estimates of investment costs, appraisals of administrative capabilities, the weighting of priorities within the sector, the judgment of capital-output relationships, the identification of input bottlenecks and the chances of overcoming them, and so on. The task could easily become hopelessly complex and detailed if it were not approached selectively and with a proper disrespect for exact values. In practice, any sector will break down into perhaps three to fifteen subsectors. These will identify themselves quickly to planners with good knowledge of their sectors. The main difficulties usually arise out of the absence of reliable statistics regarding (1) present capacity of each subsector and (2) the growth of demand. However, the importance of statistical shortcomings is often overrated; there are adequate ways of "making do" with unofficial statistics gathered on an ad hoc basis.

The gradual clarification of sectoral targets depends on gathering a large amount of quantitative and qualitative information. This data is available only outside the planning offices—in ministries, in the central bank, from consultants, from education officials, from bankers, industrialists, foreign embassy commercial attachés, private merchants, foreign technical experts, the plans and experience of other countries, and from other offices within the planning agency itself. The need to rely on the information and judgment of people outside the planning agency constitutes the technical rationale for establishing a great many interagency planning and advisory committees. (There is, of course, an important political and psychological reason for establishing such committees—to mobilize understanding and support for the plan and to educate officials in economic thinking.) In Iran, these committees were a mixed blessing—partly because many of them did not contain the technical expertise they ought to have had and partly because in Iran few committees operate so as to produce the results a Westerner expects of well-run committees (no agendas, no preliminary staff work, no notes taken or minutes recorded, undue deference to the senior official present, no follow-up). Despite the occasional

181

usefulness of certain committees, a majority of them existed mainly "on paper" and rarely if ever met more than once or twice. This meant that the expertise which committees were supposed to contribute had to be gathered on a highly personal and often unofficial basis, by seeking out those individuals who were most knowledgeable about each subsector. The importance of seeking out such people and of writing down what they have to contribute and gradually building up a file of notes and statistics back in the planning offices sounds elementary and routine. It was not so in Iran.

It is useful to recognize the distinction between "real" and "financial" planning. All plans eventually find summary expression in financial terms, as the only language giving common meaning to the diverse physical quantities of tons of cement, kilowatts of installed generating capacity, etc.—the "real" dimensions of output and capital. But the essence of the "bottom up" aspect of planning is "real," not financial. Sectoral planning is relatively meaningless unless it is expressed in real terms—the number, location, and size of production units, the quantities of outputs aimed at, and so on. The "real" nature of the "bottom up" process stands in contrast to the essentially "financial" nature of the "top down" process, which is concerned with aggregates that can be handled only by the common measure of money.

This perspective suggests it is false to speak of a "choice" between real and financial planning: a plan constructed only in financial terms cannot be anything more than a summary guide to future expenditures, lacking in the depth and detail which any plan ought to have and which can be given only by real planning. Any respectable plan is therefore a marriage of real and financial planning.

The Generation of Specific Projects and Programs

The textbook picture of planning is one where a central planning agency issues a call to the operating units of government for the submission of spending proposals to be financed with plan funds. The function of the planning agency is to assess the soundness of these proposals and to measure their relative contribution to the objectives set for the plan. One pictures long lists of projects and programs flowing to the planners, who proceed to rank them in a priority list. Schematically, the plan is made up by going down this priority list until a package of projects is accumulated whose cost equals the resources available for the plan.

This model is analytically valid but tells us little about reality, at least in Iran. One of the most difficult and discouraging aspects of Iranian planning was the lack of interest shown by most ministries in working up project proposals for consideration by the planning agency. The role of Plan Organization was precisely the reverse of that suggested above: instead of screening proposals made by "applicants" Plan Organization spent much of its time trying to generate specific project proposals for inclusion in the Third Plan. This situation was a measure both of the government's lack of interest in planning and of the sheer inability of many government departments to think up and prepare project proposals. Consequently such proposals as were available for the Third Plan right up to its start were mainly those (1) which Plan Organization had been able to prepare on its own initiative (securing *pro forma* ministry approval in some cases) and (2) those which had been contracted out to foreign consulting firms, such as the future road program, the Khuzestan regional program and a few others.

In one sense the process of giving specific content to the sectoral plan was not as gloomy and unpromising as I have suggested. In two key areas (industry and agriculture) the main programs consisted of credit allocations to banks for relending to private borrowers. Here the main problem was to work out the details of credit programs, not the design of individual investments. The latter would appear spontaneously in the form of loan applications as the plan proceeded. Also, the inability of most ministries to plan left PlanOrg's sectoral planners free to do their own programing. which could then be presented to the executing ministry for approval and adoption as its program. Needless to say, this is not a way of educating government officials to the problems of their ministries, or of securing the participation and support needed for vigorous execution of the plan. But during the relatively brief periods when many plans are actually written the main pressure is to get them written. In Iran, if the planners had waited for the government to show some interest in the process, they might have had to wait for years.

A high proportion of any plan's expenditures consists of public construction projects. No projects, and particularly none of the large ones that usually account for such a high proportion of expenditures, can be approved and started until they have been justified by careful study; until engineering designs have been completed, until specifications have been prepared, tenders have been let, and bids adjudicated. For a large project, and many small ones, this process takes one, two, or three years; it is not something that can be arranged at the last minute in a few weeks or months. Consequently, the successful beginning of a plan requires a backlog of approved projects ready to start—exactly the same problem that arises in using public works for countercyclical effects in developed economies. Unless people involved in the planning process can appreciate the lead-time involved in getting projects ready and can make available the funds and contract authorizations needed for economic surveys and engineering studies, effective planning is impossible. A plan with projects not supported by this kind of studies will remain nothing more than a catalogue of suggestions and hopes; the essential "bottom up" job will remain undone. Or a plan may be unbalanced, in the sense that some sectors have well-supported proposals while others do not, since planners should commit more money to sectors with absorptive capacity than to those without it.

In Chapter II we noted that the First Seven Year Plan was preceded by two general surveys by two foreign engineering companies, Morrison-Knudsen and Overseas Consultants, Inc. It was these firms which largely developed the "candidate projects" out of which the First Plan and much of the Second was made. During the vigorous administration of Plan Organization by Mr. Ebtehaj, "tooling-up" money was made available and the necessary administrative decisions were made to translate the Second Plan's financial allocations into specific projects. After his resignation in August, 1959 (three years before the Third Plan was to begin) Plan Organization lost most of its capacity for preparing surveys and studies. It was not difficult to secure verbal assent that studies were needed. It was not difficult to secure budgetary appropriations for them. But it was next to impossible to get anyone to propose specific surveys and studies and to carry survey proposals forward to the point where they resulted in definite decisions and survey contracts. Why? Most of the studies would have to be conducted by foreign consultants, and foreign consultants were under political attack during much of the period. Equally important, sectoral planners (within Plan Organization and outside) proved incapable of devising good study proposals. Finally, Plan Organization's top administrators were unwilling to push ahead vigorously on a piecemeal and somewhat disorderly basis, preferring to delay any study proposals until all of them could be considered together and priorities determined. The best became the enemy of the good. In view of the painful slowness with which survey proposals took shape, there was no danger of exhausting budgeted funds. Under such conditions a nice concern for "priorities" made no sense.

Estimating Costs

Only part of a sector's program takes the form of projects that are quite definite at the time the plan begins. It is only these quite definite projects that represent objectively costed elements in the program. Yet the total cost of the sector's complete program has somehow to be calculated so it can be put down in tables and so that people can argue whether the sector's program is too big or too small. It is here that a great deal can be done with "back-of-the-envelope" arithmetic, using rough approximations for certain types of "modal" investments (e.g., a 15,000-ton sugar mill, a 500-student elementary school, a 25,000-spindle textile mill, a 45,000-kilowatt thermal generating station, etc.). Here is another area where the aggressive pursuit of the practical is more important than theoretical refinement. Sufficiently good figures can be picked up from earlier plans or the plan of other countries or from engineers or manufacturers' representatives. The costing of subsector programs must be regarded mainly as a scaling process, not as something requiring a high degree of accuracy, which in most cases would only be illusory. I would not emphasize the unimportance of the accurate initial costing of program elements if printed plans and the literature of planning did not give the illusion that costs were something definite and precise. There was a time when I labored under the illusion that a five-year plan which contained a table allocating, say, 3.42 million rupees to credit for citrus fruits really meant that the authorities wanted to spend this amount because someone had calculated that this was just the amount needed to get the job done. I now realize that most of the apparent precision in plan tables results from working backwards from very rough total and subtotal allocations, which remain more or less constant while detailed proposals become elaborated and assigned some place in the table. As the planners adjust their tables to accommodate their emerging projects and programs they adjust previous tentative allocations to provide money for newcomers. As soon as one introduces a few decimals into the table (perhaps because he decides that "a third of the textile allocation ought to go to woolens") the groundwork is laid for the "precision illusion." If the table has a few component columns (e.g., showing how much of the chemical industry allocation will go into the private sector, how much public, and how much foreign exchange each will need), the illusion spreads. A point may be reached where the labor involved in adjusting every preceding figure as any new element is introduced becomes so frightening that the program itself tends toward stability. And so it is that in the financial tables of plans we often find the obverse of the usual statistical footnote about totals not adding to 100 "because of rounding": exact subtotals are devised to preserve the rounding of the totals.

It does not follow from this account of how planners achieve precision in their tables that cost estimates are unimportant or fictitious. (The place where accurate estimates become vitally important is in *project* budgeting and financing.) My point is simply that the financial tables in development plans should be read with a "knowing eye" and not the eye of innocence.

Framing of Suitable Policies

In non-Communist plans private investment is often as large as or larger than public investment. But the amount and composition of private investment is highly sensitive to the structure of government policies, incentives, and controls. Clearly, government policies may make it possible or impossible, easy or difficult, profitable or unprofitable for private investors to use their funds in certain ways, or even to use them at all.

The number of policy issues that might require consideration by comprehensive planners is legion. They range over such topics as whether or not education or irrigation water shall be free, the subsidization of food prices in the cities or of export commodities,

the support of farm prices, the degree of protection for infant industries, rates of taxation, the licensing of new investment, and so on.
The existing structure of policies forms the starting point for whatever policy recommendations the planners think will be helpful.
The planners' task, within each sector, is to identify the important
policy issues, to try to define and evaluate existing policy, and then
to take whatever steps they think appropriate and feasible to move
government policy in the directions they think it should go.

Meshing "Top" and "Bottom"

Neither the "top down" nor "bottom up" tasks can be completed
until the two sets of data are brought together and harmonized
into a single interlocking system. The process by which this har-
monization is achieved illustrates once again the great gap between
theory and practice in writing an actual plan.

In theory a plan constitutes a tightly locked system of interrela-
tionships such that if any one magnitude is changed every other
magnitude also has to be changed. In reality it is impossible to
handle a plan in this fashion. Any realistic plan has to contain a
large amount of elasticity so that as the defects of the plan become
clear or circumstances dictate changes, some parts of the plan can
be adjusted without having to adjust all other parts. Nearly every
plan contains more built-in elasticity than may appear on the
surface. Not only is the total size of any plan itself open-ended in
some degree (represented, let us say, by contingent estimates of
foreign or deficit financing) but most sectors will have "residual"
programs that can easily be adjusted upwards or downwards. Credit
programs are one of the most obvious of these residual accounts.
Alternatively, each sector may have been able to identify marginal
projects and programs, i.e., things it can add or omit depending
on the availability of resources and the absorptive capacity of the
sector. This was tried in constructing the Third Plan by designating
certain programs as "core" programs which were considered top
priority. However, the "core" accounted for only about one-sixth
of the Plan! It was not meaningful to regard five-sixths of the
Plan as a set of proposals that could be discussed in conventional
terms of marginalism. The non-core program doubtless contained

the marginal projects but no one had any idea which ones they were.

Paradoxically it is the tentativeness and imprecision implicit in a plan's elasticity that make it possible to "put a plan to bed," to say the work is done and to present it to the political authorities as a finished document. There are four main tests that must be satisfied before this stage is reached. All four are consistency tests:

1. *Over-all balance of financial resources and expenditures.* The proposed volume of total expenditures must be matched by an equal volume of resources to finance it or (as in the case of the Third Plan) by measurement of the resources gap and proposals for closing it. This test cannot be applied until both the "top down" and "bottom up" processes are substantially completed, since neither the resource nor expenditure positions will be known with confidence until this stage is reached.

This test also has one extremely important subsidiary aspect:

a. *Balance between foreign exchange resources and expenditures.* There are many countries able to generate sufficient savings to finance an investment program but unable to generate (from trade, borrowings, or grants) the amount of foreign exchange the program will require. In such cases the availability of foreign exchange, not saving, determines the maximum size of the plan. Although Iran periodically runs short of foreign exchange, this results from inability to manage a very generous supply, not from any shortage of the latter. From the standpoint of finance, the maximum size of Iran's development program is set by the amount of domestic saving, not the availability of foreign exchange.[7]

---

[7] This is an area of analysis where it is easy to confuse savings and finance. Over a plan period the amount of actual or *ex post* saving will exactly equal the amount of investment. When the plan is being made, *ex ante*, there is often a gap between savings and investment (as there was in Iran). Some people make the mistake of saying, "Well, if we cannot generate the savings at home we will make up the difference by getting foreign loans or grants—we will use the savings of foreigners." The gap that is closed by such foreign funds is, at the time the funds are acquired, a financial gap, not a savings gap. When the foreign funds are spent they will then generate *domestic* savings (in the sense that after the funds have been spent they will have been used for nonconsumption purposes).

On the strength of the preceding paragraph some readers may wonder why a development plan should not be expanded to whatever limit the planners believe they can finance, using foreign loans and grants to the utmost, or deficit

2. *Consistency of sectoral and over-all objectives.* The sectoral programs, in aggregate, must serve the general objectives of the plan. If the plan is intended to maximize short-run employment opportunities or the increase in national income the sectors must be able to show that their programs serve this end. If the saving of foreign exchange is an important objective, each much be able to defend its program in the light of that objective. If a plan aims to drown out inflation by concentrating on quick increases in output, the sectors must demonstrate how they have done this. And so on. Individual sectors may have programs whose objectives do not further the over-all objective of the plan. Such sectors must be able to defend their alternative orientation, which has the effect of forcing other sectors to carry the burden of achieving the plan's over-all objectives.

3. *Sectoral balance of inputs and outputs.* Each sector must show that its output targets are reasonable in the light of required inputs, including both fixed capital inputs and operating inputs (e.g., raw materials, power, transport, labor, and financial working capital). Statistical estimates of capital-output ratios, raw material availabilities, foreign exchange requirements, power requirements, etc., are important here. Even more important is first-hand familiarity with each subsector so that planners have a realistic judgment on probable outputs from new investments and on the realistic requirements for and availabilities of operating inputs. This judgment also requires that people working on any subsector keep in close touch with those in other parts of the planning agency who are working on the expansion of their key inputs.

---

finance, or a mixture of both. This is a perfectly sound approach, *within limits*. The limit is reached when this rising volume of spending begins to produce inflation, i.e., when the often-flexible limits of financial resources begin to strain the much less flexible limits of real resources. This "inflation threshold" defines the optimum size of a development plan. This concept explains why it may be necessary to scale down a plan before exhausting all the financial resources one can collect at home and abroad. This was Iran's situation during the boom years of 1958–61. It explains why the two or three best Iranian economists were then arguing for scaling down the investment program to a level that could be financed without foreign borrowing. They wanted to see the financial limits set by voluntary savings plus taxation. If saving were subordinated to finance, and ministers were free to go abroad hunting for credit, then some saving would take the involuntary form of inflation.

4. *Balance of supply and demand at project and sector levels.*
Each sector and each project must be able to show that its output
targets are consistent with some measure of the economy's need for
these outputs. This target-demand test involves subtle questions as
to how far ahead of demand certain sectors should be built, to what
extent national self-sufficiency should be sought in certain lines
(i.e., the practical working out of the theory of comparative advantage), the probable elasticity of demands for different goods, the
government's ability to expand key services, opportunities for shifting demand from imported to domestic goods, possibilities for
improving the quality of output, and so on.

The application of these tests is not a "point" process that occurs
at some unique moment in time. It is a continuing process that
works by a series of successive approximations spread out over a
long period. There are inevitably many gaps, many unsure but
necessary judgments. That is why it is important for planners, when
they begin, to understand what they will be doing—so they can
start doing it early.

There is something else to say concerning the means of applying
the four consistency tests: every planning agency should build into
itself, structurally, some sort of confrontation process. This can be
done by arranging occasions when each distinct working group has
to come before some higher authority and defend what they are
proposing. Iran's planners had a confrontation process that involved
a testing of sectoral proposals by the general group responsible for
doing the "top down" work. The arrangement worked quite well.
The testing of the "top down" work was done in meetings where
vigorous discussion was encouraged. Where Iranian planning was
weak was in securing criticisms of proposals by public and private
groups outside the planning office. This was not just a matter of
oversight; there were many good reasons why in the Iranian situation planners were unable to do what they would like to have done.

There is one important but pedestrian force that exerts a rising
influence on the planning process as it proceeds. This is the "production imperative," the simple necessity of producing a finished
product by a given date. This time-constraint plays a more important role in determining plan preparation than is usually acknowledged. The final deadline against which a planning agency works
breaks down into a series of earlier deadlines for various parts of

the document and for the submission of various drafts to different authorities within the planning and political machinery—e.g., drafts for higher levels in the planning machinery, consultations with the Cabinet, the King, the World Bank, etc. Without such deadlines most plans would never get finished. It is they that force the planners to "place their bets," lay down their pencils, and let the race begin. Without them, the unanswerable questions involved in every plan would never be given answers, the missing data would always be used to avoid judgments, the discipline of confrontations would be put off, and the hard tasks of writing and editing would never get done. The imperative to produce a plan by a given date puts an end to needless and unreal refinement, justifiably throws many of the detailed tasks of continuing planning into the plan period itself, and forces the over-all integration that makes a plan out of possibilities and proposals.

Epilogue: Do Planners Need Economics?

In this chapter I have attempted a general overview of the planning process. In identifying the main elements and processes involved in making a plan I have time and again emphasized the roughness of the numerical magnitudes used, the controlling role that judgment plays in determining allocations, and how important it is that planners should have good factual knowledge of a country's economic structure and of its administrative strengths and weaknesses. There is one other factor to which I would also give great weight, particularly because so little note of it is taken in discussions of economic planning. This factor concerns the internal processes of agencies responsible for making plans. I am not referring to questions of organization and management, of a planning agency's internal efficiency. I refer instead to the importance of assuring that there are enough checks and balances in the planning process so that all important numbers, proposals, and judgments are exposed to criticism before decisions are made. Other authors, writing of other countries, have frequently emphasized the importance of making plans that take account of legitimate political considerations and of information and advice contributed by experts and groups outside the planning machinery. In Iran, these more common external influences were exceedingly weak and could not be given much recognition. Thus the task of planning was confined to a relatively small group of economists and engineers. Since there were so few external checks and balances it became doubly important to seek them within the internal administration of the planning machinery. Indeed, this "process" consideration—the requirement that plans and projects go through certain steps that assure opportunities for criticism of data, proposals, values, and opinions—is at least as important as most of the purely technical points that are given so much more attention in the literature of planning and project appraisal. If there are two words which summarize what these processes should assure, they are "discussion" and "confrontation." I am not speaking in any general political terms. I am speaking of the utility of classic democratic safeguards within the relatively small group of professional people who do the planning.

Has my emphasis on judgment, on empirical knowledge, and on process relegated formal economics to a secondary role in economic planning? Are we to take quite literally the following statement by Professor W. Arthur Lewis? "I [deny] that economic science has produced criteria which enable us to decide whether a plan is good or not . . . one decides whether a plan is good in the light of common sense and experience and not by applying any tests which economic science has devised."[8]

Here Professor Lewis is in danger of letting himself say too much. Everything depends, I suspect, on what we mean by "economic science" and the kinds of claims we make for it.

The literature of planning overflows with economic terms. Some are familiar from introductory courses, some only from advanced graduate courses, and beyond. A sampler of terms might include: shadow prices, commodity balances, comparative advantage, cost-benefit ratios, capital-output ratios, input-output matrices, income-elasticity, price-elasticity, capital-employment ratios, accelerator effects, the multiplier, linear programing, cash-flow projections, value added, marginal costs and revenues, the rate of return, private and social profitability, opportunity costs, average savings ratio, marginal savings ratio, the investment rate, welfare functions, production-possibility curves, and so on down a long list of technical terms that make up the tools and building-blocks of economics. Presumably Professor Lewis is not saying that these concepts are of no use. But he does seem to say that formal laws built up with the use of such

[8] W. Arthur Lewis, "On Assessing a Development Plan," *The Economic Bulletin of the Economic Society of Ghana,* June–July, 1959.

terms are of distinctly secondary use in making decisions about what to include in a plan and what to leave out, about the size of a plan and the sensibleness of its allocations.

What Professor Lewis may have wanted to emphasize is the inability of economics to say what progress consists of (i.e., what a plan's allocations should be) and the importance of confining economics to the analysis of the technical relationships among economic forces that must be respected if a desired result is to be achieved. There must be savings. Savings must be converted into capital. There are so many things to be done that not everything can be done at once. Choices must be made, distributing investments through time and space. Investment A will not yield its potential output unless there is an adequate input of B, which depends on more investment in B-producing facilities, etc. If people have too much money they will drive up the prices of available goods and services and this will introduce abnormal relationships and expectations and behavior, which will affect the economy's ability to achieve progress. And so on, through an almost infinite list of economic relationships. It is the business of planning to analyze and to influence the more important of these relationships. The job certainly cannot be done without thinking and talking economics.

The clash between science and common sense in putting economics in the service of planning arises mainly from the irrelevance of *advanced* economic techniques for most planning situations in developing countries. A large proportion of the professional journals are preoccupied with techniques and problems on the frontier of economics. These often deal with problems in such unreal and abstract terms, expressed in terms of mathematical models, that they are incapable of being translated into practical terms even by the few people who can understand them. *In time,* many of these explorations will yield useful, relevant results. Many will prove sterile and empty and will fade away. By that time, the surviving truths will have found their way into the introductory courses. It is mainly at this level of the science that we find the techniques and concepts of greatest use in practical planning situations in most developing countries.

There is one more aspect of the never-ending tension between "the theoretical" and "the practical" that deserves comment. It is a comment that brings the two perspectives somewhat closer together. The point is this: when practical planners think they are relying mainly on common sense, judgment, and experience to the neglect of the formal techniques of their profession they may be unduly apologetic. In many cases a quick, summary, "common sense judgment" about investment choices reflects implicitly the results of systematic economic calculations which it would be a waste of time to make. "Experience" means that a planner can assign some decisive value to a crucial variable (such as administrative incompetence or the unavailability of a market or a raw material) which amounts to a direct reading of what could be carried through as a formal cost-benefit or rate-of-return analysis. One may also find oneself in an exactly opposite position, i.e., where the calculation of costs and (especially) benefits is so arbitrary and hypothetical that it would be naïve or dishonest to pretend that a numerical result meant anything more than a simple judgment could yield. Some investments in transport and communications, for example, which typically account for 20–35 per cent of any development plan, are little more than acts of faith and common sense and cannot be defended *ex ante* with convincing objective calculations. The same is true of programs and projects in other sectors, e.g., education and health. The point I am making is that the margin of error in figures is often as great as the margin of error in judgments. This is not an argument against striving for better measurements. It is a warning against the pseudo-science of number worship.

I come back to my central point—that simple economic tools are more useful in framing a development plan than the quotation from Professor Lewis suggested. Iran's experience with planning offers countless examples of how planning was helped because people trained in economic science participated in the process. Professor Lewis would surely agree that economics is not only helpful but essential in passing judgment on the content of a development plan. But the economists's professional tools are only part of the total equipment needed for realistic planning, which is, as Lewis suggests, an art and not a science. Within the contribution economics can make common sense and judgment are more needed than elegant analytics. The question of when common sense and judgment must be tested by more formal analysis is itself a matter of common sense and judgment.

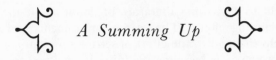

CHAPTER IX

A Summing Up

There can be no doubt that over the past generation Iran has made substantial economic progress. It has been a jerky, uneven, much-interrupted progress; but in this Iran is hardly unique. If we compare the country's growth under Reza Shah with its growth since World War II, the earlier period probably carries off the honors—a higher rate of investment, better management of the budget deficits and the balance of payments, probably less unemployment, and a larger number of important institutional innovations. The chief measure on which Reza Shah's performance compares badly with postwar levels is consumption. The faster growth in postwar consumption is attributable mainly to the growth in imports financed by a much higher level of oil revenues and the postwar boom in private industrial investment, which had no prewar parallel.

Viewing the past thirty to forty years as a whole, five factors stand out as prime causes of the country's growth: (1) the existence and growth of the oil revenues; (2) the emergence of a surprisingly vigorous class of industrial entrepreneurs, mainly since World War II; (3) the development of a modern banking system; (4) the interaction of Iranians with Westerners and Western civilization; (5) the initiatives launched by government, which, for all its historical weaknesses, have nevertheless contributed some powerful stimuli. More needs to be said about this last point, since the Iranian Government so rarely has anything put down to its credit.

All through this book I have dwelt upon the failings of government and the great handicaps this imposes on economic planning and effective administration. In view of the chronic weakness of governments in many less-developed countries the special facts of Iran's case may not put that country in a class by itself; they may simply add to a growing literature of doubt about the efficacy of formal planning efforts. The reason governments and those who would help them go to the effort of setting up planning and development programs is because "planning is supposed to make a difference." But in the economic evolution of Iran the big "differences" have come not so much from *planning* as from *nationalism*, or rather from the by-products of nationalism. I have in mind such events as the establishment of a national bank in 1928, the regaining of control over the note issue from the Imperial Bank in 1930, the ending of the tariff treaties with Russia and Britain that had tied Iran's hands in setting and using customs duties, the upward revision of oil royalties in 1932, and, most recently, the nationalization of the foreign-owned oil industry in 1951. Each of these events captured for domestic use strategic resources originally created and owned by foreigners. If these events had not occurred, Iran would be a considerably less developed country than it now is and would have much poorer prospects. The fact that British interests happened to be the chief target of these nationalistic moves only indicates the large role which Britain has played in carrying the foreigners' contribution into Iran. If history moved by personal laws, there would be much ingratitude in Iran's treatment of Great Britain.

It is a paradox that the oil industry is so important in Iran's economy that people come to take it for granted. The bounty of oil relieves Iran of many of the classic budgetary and balance of payments problems that constitute the chief constraints on growth in many countries. Or rather it should have largely removed these constraints. In fact Iran has often wandered to the brink. But the existence and growth of the oil income has often allowed Iran to ride out financial crises without having to summon up the discipline and reforms and sacrifices that alone could have rescued her if oil did not smooth the troubled waters.

We can generalize the point just made: if we think of *natural* and *human* resources (skills, attitudes, and institutions) as two great sets of resources out of which economic development is built, Iran is an example of the substitutability of natural for human resources. In effect, oil makes up for many of the weaknesses in the structure of Iran's man-made resources and yields the country a far higher standard of living, and much better prospects, than it could have if this natural resource did not exist and had not been made into an asset—originally by the foreigner, subsequently by the operation of nationalistic pressures. There are other countries of the world where precisely the opposite relationship exists, i.e., where human resources make up for relatively thin natural resources, e.g., Britain, the Low Countries, and Japan. In the long run economic development goes fastest and farthest, of course, in countries where these two sets of resources stand in a relationship of complementarity instead of substitutability. At the other end of the scale stand societies which have neither natural nor human resources working in their favor.

In recent years it has become fashionable to limit the role of capital formation in explaining economic growth and to point to the role of certain other factors (such as education, research, and technological change) as important sources of growth. These "other factors" (commonly lumped together as an undifferentiated "residual") include most of what is meant by a broad interpretation of "human resources," e.g., a society's population, with its education, skills, and cultural values; its institutional development; and its politics and administrative capacities. Iranian experience reminds us that the "residual" can work against investment, lowering efficiency as well as raising it. The domination of the government's economic role by this "negative residual" has a number of implications.

Organization of the Development Effort

A decade's experience has shown that Iran is not as ready for planning and programing as people hoped when they tried to lead Plan Organization into these functions from its more limited original role as a project-executing authority. Iranian politics is *anti*-planning, *anti*-programing. This statement means that planning, programing, and financial control cannot be fitted into the normal apparatus of government without having them fall apart and come to nothing. A classic planning effort simply will not work in Iranian society as presently organized. The 1949 decision to establish Plan Organization as an unorthodox planning-and-executing agency outside the regular machinery of government was therefore a sensible and necessary structural accommodation to Iran's political situation. The fact that Plan Organization carried its independence farther than anyone originally foresaw is partly explained by the imperatives for getting things done in Iran, by the tendency of any power-center to expand its activities, and by the strong personality of PlanOrg's Managing Director during the years of its greatest success (1955–59). But long after the resignation of this controversial leader it still appeared that Plan Organization would have to remain a "government within a government" if Iran wanted to have a development effort even in the limited sense of a set of major public investment projects, reasonably well selected, well prepared, and well executed. Unless the key functions involved in this limited form of development effort were separated out so that they would not be "captured by the dominant forces of the political system," there was little hope that the functions would ever get performed at all.

The specialized structure represented by Plan Organization in the 1950's is thus a "necessary" condition for an Iranian development program. But it is not a "sufficient" condition. Three other conditions also seem necessary: (1) PlanOrg must have a Managing Director capable of minimizing and managing the inevitable tensions between Plan Organization and the ministries; (2) PlanOrg must employ a certain number of foreigners—because PlanOrg itself exhibits, in lesser degree, many of the cultural characteristics that dominate Iranian politics and administration (foreigners help progressive nationals overcome "anti-planning" forces in their own culture); and (3) PlanOrg and the government should be under the discipline of periodic accountability to external financing institutions, mainly the World Bank and the Monetary Fund (bilateral aid is too political to exercise an effective discipline). "Accountability" is a loose and limited concept that refers mainly to the constructive role that "confrontations" can make to good behavior —confrontations backed by the power of the purse.

In the mid-1960's it did not seem likely that the Iranian development effort would move in the direction just described as necessary. Instead the government was trying, without much success, to hold to the larger conception which had inspired the Third Plan, i.e., comprehensive planning. In the present condition of Iranian politics it is impossible to define the ideal structure and functions of Plan Organization in anything more than general and therefore vague terms. The actual functions will depend greatly on the relative strength and compatibility of top officials in PlanOrg and the ministries. When strong leadership is lacking, PlanOrg will simply be incapable of assuring the high volume of public investment the economy needs and which should be among its primary functions.

Few readers will be satisfied with such a loose and indeterminate resolution of the problems of structure and function of Iran's development agency. I can only say that tidier solutions will be false and unrealistic. The quest for certainty and order falls before the inherent ambiguities and indeterminacies of Iranian politics and culture. Given this fact, it is not Iran but her friends who must change their thinking.

One point that seems beyond question is the need to have some kind of special institution, other than the Ministry of Finance, to act as a trustee for the oil revenues. Without such an institution there could be no pretense of a development effort, since one source of PlanOrg's power, such as it is, rests on its control of funds. If the Ministry of Finance controlled the entire oil revenues the nourishing stream of oil income would continue to irrigate the economy. But some fields would get little or nothing and others would get much more than they needed. There would undoubtedly be growth and development, because at Iran's stage of institutional development it would be well-nigh impossible not to have heavy spending produce growth of some sort. Two conditions might frustrate this progress-in-spite-of-itself outcome. One is the administrative and technical incapacity of the ministries to come forward with enough projects to sustain a high level of investment. The other depressant might be the frightening of private investors by political events. This happened in 1962–64. The slow-down in private investment for three years was not offset by a vigorous public investment program.

Absorptive Capacity

The government's limited economic capabilities—its limited absorptive capacity to spend funds rationally—has an important lesson for how public funds can best be spent. In general, any broadly conceived Iranian development plan that depends for its success on the establishment of a number of new or greatly improved administrative agencies is bound to fail. The more sensible strategy is to concentrate on a few large public projects that lie outside the private sector and, for the rest, to look hard for ways of getting money spent through existing institutions. The most important of these will be the banks, since banks, as a rule, tend to be run better than ministries. This conclusion implies that a large share of development resources will be used as earmarked funds to finance private investment. This can work, of course, only to the extent that private investors want to borrow funds for investment purposes. Since in Iran the prospects for private investment depend so heavily on the volume of public spending, it will be important, for many years to come, that the development agency concentrate on maintaining a large volume of expenditure. This objective focuses attention on the problem of project preparation, a field in which Iran (in company with many less-developed countries) will remain weak unless it invests heavily in this function through the employment of consulting engineers and the commissioning of technical studies.

The policy of minimizing dependence on inefficient government agencies and resisting the temptation to create new ones does not mean that *no* attempts should be made to create new agencies or develop new programs in existing agencies. All one can do is to plead for tough-mindedness and realism in starting programs dependent on institution-building, since each project requires almost impossible amounts of time, energy, and patience in the face of high risks of failure. In particular, foreigners must avoid the mistake of overestimating the role which technical assistance can make in raising the society's absorptive capacity.

The Role of Technical Assistance

During the past fifteen years Iran has received huge amounts of economic aid, including technical assistance. More aid has gone to Iran than to any country in the Western hemisphere, to any country in Africa, or to any other country in the Middle East except Turkey. The combination of American economic and military aid from the United States alone between 1950 and 1964 was well over a billion dollars. The value of U.S. Point IV aid (technical assistance) is included in this figure. The significant point about the

Point IV program in Iran is not its cost (which is small) but its size in comparison with Point IV programs in other countries. Up to 1961 India was the only country in the world which had received more Point IV assistance than Iran. This statement was true not only of the American TA program but also of the U.N.'s. Each year, from 1952 to 1962, the U.S. had between 200 and 300 technicians at work in Iran, with the U.N. accounting for another 100–150. Other bilateral projects brought the total number of foreign experts to 400–600. There is scarcely any area of institution-building that has not had the benefit, or at least the presence, of one or more foreign experts.

Any large program of technical assistance presents a mixed record: there have been some notable successes, some conspicuous failures, some overlapping and confusion and institutional rivalries and jealousies. Perhaps the most lasting effect of these TA programs will prove to have been their involvement and support of many of the younger generation of trained Iranians in nation-building tasks. Many failures and shortcomings on the side of those supplying technical assistance and other forms of aid must be acknowledged. But in appraising the absorptive capacity of the Iranian Government, the most serious difficulty was the lack of top-level administrative support for and interest in either the projects for which foreign experts were recruited or in making use of the experts. It would be wrong to suggest that no members of the Iranian Government ever showed any interest in making effective use of technical assistance. But a lack of sincere interest was encountered so often by American, U.N., and other aid officials that it is fair to say that Iran's propensity to request technical assistance substantially outran the government's inclination to make use of it. This fact is one reason the U.S. closed out Point IV assistance to Iran in 1965. Iran's frequent inability to profit from technical assistance is symptomatic of the lack of commitment to economic development in Iranian politics and administration that has bedeviled not only technical assistance but most other forms of aid as well.

The pervasive unwillingness of most senior government officials to face up to the responsibilities of development—to take development seriously—has showed itself in countless ways: in the ignoring of foreign experts whose services had been requested; in doing little to sell off selected government plants which it had long been agreed should be sold to private buyers; in doing nothing, from 1958 to 1960, about the rapidly declining foreign exchange reserves until only emergency measures could help; in the appointment of unqualified persons to key leadership positions; in the frequent and repeated failure to do things after giving assurances that they would be done; in the unduly tolerant and protective attitude taken towards the system of corruption that determined who got government business and which sometimes affected the standards of contractors' performance. The most telling symptom of all, however, was the unwillingness of many ministers to conduct their ministries with reasonable regard for the government's need for fiscal responsibility. This lack of cohesiveness and discipline meant the government was unable to hold down the level of nondevelopment expenditures, to enforce reasonable standards of financial management so that budgetary commitments could be honored and administrators would have the money to do what they were supposed to do, and to raise taxes to cover the inevitable increases in the cost of government that are part of development. Not only did the government do nothing to add new taxes during the years of rapidly rising budgets; the Ministry of Finance did not even put anyone to work studying the problem. The inevitable result of this lack of seriousness about raising public revenues and limiting public expenditures was a chronic budget deficit—the unintended kind that frustrates development.

The source of Iran's recent budgetary problems lay not in bad luck nor (as some have complained) in the failure of Iran's friends to give it as much aid as they said they would give. The source lay in the political values and mores that have ruled in Tehran for many years now and which cannot rule much longer if the country is to qualify for external assistance by any reasonable performance tests. Unless Iran can bring its ordinary budget under control—something that cannot be done without a firmer commitment to development than has so far been demonstrated—the governments of the day are bound to repeat in the future what they have frequently done in the past, namely, they will divert more and more of the country's oil revenues away from the development plan to finance an ordinary budget that is not under effective control.

There are many able, well-intentioned men scattered through public and private life in Iran who understand better than I the sickness of their country. But there are not enough; not, at least, where it counts, at the center of political and social power. The combination of instability, corruption, and a highly personal style of public administration make it extraordinarily difficult for any foreign government, no matter how well-intentioned, to enter into effective long-term working relationships with individuals and offices of the Iranian government. It would not be surprising if more than half the technical assistance projects which the American government has launched in Iran over the past decade have fallen so far short of their original intentions that they count as failures. Even the few successes may only be awaiting their hour of defeat. I am speaking in terms of the explicit purposes of the projects that make up the technical assistance program, a program designed to "set Iran on the road to economic development." There may be side-effects or by-products of the aid program whose long-run benefits will be considerable. The greatest of these indirect benefits may be simply the "foreign presence" in the country, a presence which has the effect of exposing many more Iranians to alternative political and social values than they would otherwise encounter. This exposure occurs both through the personal associations involved in direct employment and working together on aid projects, and through the massive expansion in education, both at home and abroad, which foreign aid has helped generate and support. This hopeful view of technical assistance rests on faith. Any such positive judgment of technical assistance, however, must depend on viewing it primarily as an investment in cultural change, not as technical assistance. The first generation of technical assistance should probably be regarded as a "shot-gun" program of generalized investment in human beings necessary as a precondition to the rifle-aimed transfer of specific know-how which technical assistance was originally meant to provide.

The U.S. military assistance program and the large amount of general budgetary support that has accompanied it have to be judged on other grounds: they have played a major role in strengthening internal security, in keeping the Communists out, and in providing the power-base which the regime needed to remain in power *in the short run.* The successful prevention of a Communist take-over was a major success, although a purely negative one: unfortunately the time bought with security has not seen the positive achievements which technical assistance was intended to help provide. More important, political changes needed to give the regime *long-run* security have been resisted because they involved risks—the inevitable risks of freedom. The past decade strongly suggests that the growth of constructive social values and new institutions will be disappointing until there are fundamental changes in the distribution of political power in Iran. Nearly everyone in Tehran, including the Shah himself, lives in expectation of such changes. No one knows when, where, or how they will originate or what directions they will take beyond the obvious point that in any organized coup the military will play an important role.

Perspective on Corruption

There is no doubt that better economic decisions would be made, investment costs would be somewhat reduced, and the tone of society would be raised if corruption were reduced. However, there is frequently a tendency to make more of this issue than it deserves, to underestimate the difficulty of eliminating it, and to overestimate the improvement in administration to be expected from its decline.

One may forget that in the eighteenth and early nineteenth centuries Britain was probably as corrupt as any country in the world today. An explanation of Britain's gradual evolution from abysmal corruption to exemplary leadership in the conduct of public affairs has been given in a provocative book by Ronald Wraith and Edgar Simpkins, *Corruption in Developing Countries*.[1] This study makes clear that Britain was reformed by the gradual, cumulative effect of many forces which made corrupt practices more and more difficult to pursue and more and more unacceptable to social mores. The process took more than a century. Legislative reforms and controls tended to follow more basic influences, such as the growth of political parties and a popular press, the extension of education, and the puritanical yeast of nineteenth-century Methodism. But these "most easily identifiable" influences operated with the help of "other influences operating further in the background—the reform of the legal system, a well-trained and incorruptible civil service, more efficient methods of accounting in Parliament and business, the development of the trade union movement and of professional

[1] Ronald Wraith and Edgar Simpkins, *Corruption in Developing Countries* (London, 1963).

bodies with high standards, and at the deepest level a religious
influence which probed not only into private but into public mor-
ality."[2] In applying the lessons of British history to modern Africa
(their main area of concern), Wraith and Simpkins conclude that
"it is the new middle classes, if anyone, who will effectively tackle
bribery and corruption in the developing world."[3] But what these
classes can do will be determined largely by the spread of education below them—not because education itself is a panacea but
because it is a precondition for so many of the institutional reforms
that gradually create an atmosphere in which legal controls can be
effective.

The unhappy condition of Iranian politics and administration
would set a much lower ceiling on the economic outlook if the oil
revenues did not exist. But they do exist and there is no reason to
doubt that these revenues will continue at a high level over the
next generation. Iran's other natural resources are reasonably good.
There is no foreseeable danger of oppressive population increases.
The economy is already highly monetized and market-oriented.
There are even considerable human resources in being, notably a
sizable entrepreneurial class, a large number of contracting firms,
a network of modern banks, a rapidly-growing number of technically trained university graduates, and a growing supply of urban
labor with skills readily adaptable to factory work. Thus the ingre-
dients exist for a vigorous growth in the important industrial sector.
But industrial growth is not enough and it is not assured. Now that
a vigorous foreign trade sector and technical education have created an entrepreneurial class, the two most important things the
government can do to release this energy are (1) to assure a large
program of public expenditures (even if mildly inflationary) and
(2) to fuel entrepreneurial activity with cheap credit. Except in
efficient dictatorships and democracies with a highly developed
social contract, this process of "inflating for growth" can never be
an orderly affair. It will inevitably involve waste and inefficiency.
It will always threaten to get out of hand by generating too much
inflation and too many of the wrong kinds of projects. It will always
alarm the citadels of orthodoxy. It will almost inevitably run the
risk of a crisis, large or small, in the balance of payments. In Iran,

[2] *Ibid.*, p. 76.
[3] *Ibid.*, p. 194.

the main hope that these risks can be contained within tolerable limits lies with the Central Bank and with the country's need for continuing relationships with the World Bank and the International Monetary Fund.

Over the next decade or two the government's performance in the following five areas is likely to influence heavily the economy's growth: (1) land reform, which will involve the destruction of one social order in the countryside and the construction of a new one, with unpredictable effects on production; (2) the reform of fiscal administration, on both the revenue and expenditure sides, but particularly the former; (3) the improvement of educational quality at the same time as the system continues its rapid expansion; (4) the building up of governmental capacities in the cities and towns, now so weakly governed and so inadequately financed; and finally (5) the transformation of the political basis of Iranian society, so that a greater sense of social contract, of civic pride and civic virtues, of constructive nationalism is established in men's hearts. De Tocqueville had much to say on the relevance of this factor in pre-Revolutionary France; indeed, it is difficult to find a more suggestive book for present-day Iran than *The Old Regime and the French Revolution*.

Almost all foreigners leave Iran with the memory of frustrations and inefficiencies and instabilities uppermost in their minds. These impressions dominate even those who have lost their hearts to the land and made many friendships. It is difficult to avoid cynicism and a feeling that Iran is unlikely to go much of anywhere very fast. It may not. But on any larger reckoning, it is doubtful that Iran's economic and political systems work any less satisfactorily than those of a great many other countries. If the weight of negative forces seems heavier in Iran than in many countries this may be because Iranians are a sophisticated, cosmopolitan, and gracious people, wise in the ways of the world and of their own country. They are, in short, a people from whom one comes to expect more than their society yields. What matters is not that many foreigners feel this way but that a rapidly growing number of Iranians do. Where this elemental force will carry the country no one knows. Indeed, as the London *Economist* once observed about Iranian politics, "Anyone who really knows what is going on in Iran must be grossly misinformed."

Index

Abadan Institute of Technology, 146, 159–60
Absolute advantage, 123
Absorptive capacity, 26, 85, 108, 176, 199–201
Administrative capacity. *See* Absorptive capacity
Agricultural Bank, 85, 90, 91, 155
Agricultural Extension Service, 90, 91, 92
Agriculture: role in development, 71; productivity in, 71–72; debt, 72; distribution of income from, 72, 76, 77; subsistence, 72; output in, 73ff.; and foreign trade, 74ff.; production in, 77, 81; terms of trade, 77; research and experimentation in, 82, 84; rate of return in, 84–85; credit, 85, 90; animal feedstuffs, 87ff.; land, 91, 155; Grown Lands, 93; fertilizer project, 112–13, 115. *See also* Food
Agriculture Plan (Third): goals, 76ff.; production targets, 79ff.; project benefits, 84ff.; key programs, 86ff.; tactics and agencies, 89–92
Aid: bilateral, 198; foreign, 200. *See also* Point IV; Technical assistance

Almond, Gabriel A., 20n
American Embassy, vii, 24, 25
Amin, Dr. Ali, 94, 95, 96
Anglo-Persian Treaty of 1919, 7–8
Animal feedstuffs, 87ff.
Apprenticeship, 154
Army, 9
Arsanjani, Dr. Hassan, 94, 96, 97
Ataturk, Kemal, 9, 12

Balance of payments: role of oil, 12, 69, 196; trade deficit, 12, 13, 53ff.; typical development pressures, 53, 205; Third Plan projections, 60–62; effects of Third Plan, 131–32
Balance of trade. *See* Balance of payments
Banani, Dr. Amin, 10n., 144n
Banking: Imperial Bank of Persia, 6, 13; Bank Melli, 13, 24, 25, 115, 129; Industrial and Mining Development Bank of Iran, 114, 117–20; Industrial Credit Bank, 117, 120, 121, 127, 129
Battle Act (U.S.), 67n
Benedick, Richard E., 114n
Benefits, indirect economic, 83n
Binder, Leonard, 20n
Blackmer, Donald L. M., 20n

207

Planning and Development in Iran
by George B. Baldwin

designer: Gerard A. Valerio
typesetter: Monotype Composition Company, Inc.
typeface: Linotype Baskerville
printer: Universal Lithographers, Inc.
paper: 60 lb. offset
binder: Moore and Company, Inc.
cover material: G.S.B. S/535

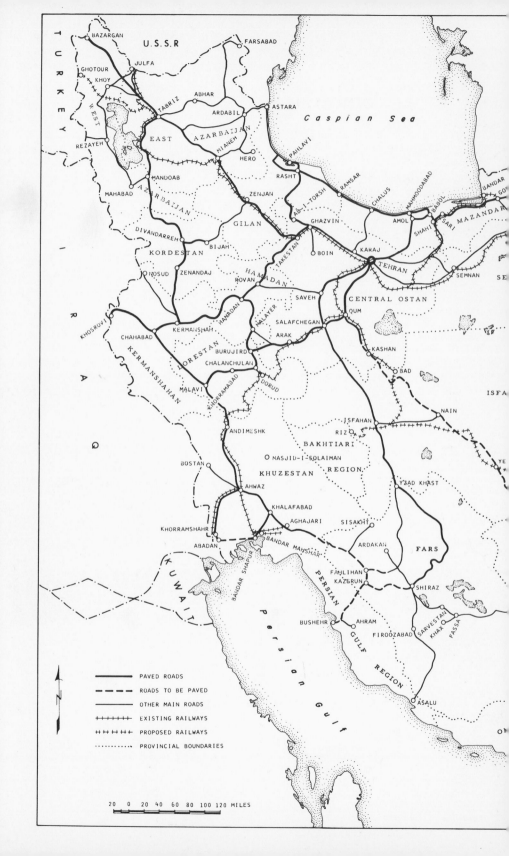